Susan Brownmiller is the author of *Against Our Will*, the classic study of rape, which was extremely influential in both Britain and the United States. *Femininity* is her second book. A network newswriter for the American Broadcasting Company and a staff reporter for the *Village Voice*, she has been a journalist for more than twenty years. She lives in New York.

FEMININITY

'She is amusing, very honest, and at times downright confused by it all . . . a lively, intelligent account of the current state of play'
Irish Times

'A wonderful book on the romantic, historical and biological jumble called femininity. Witty, provocative, energetic, iconoclastic – a positive joy to read'
Chicago Tribune Book World

'A lively, erudite and thoughtful treatment of one of life's great questions'
Washington Times

SUSAN BROWNMILLER

Femininity

PALADIN
GRAFTON BOOKS
A Division of the Collins Publishing Group

LONDON GLASGOW
TORONTO SYDNEY AUCKLAND

Paladin
Grafton Books
A Division of the Collins Publishing Group
8 Grafton Street, London W1X 3LA

Published by Paladin Books 1986

First published in Great Britain by
Hamish Hamilton Ltd 1984

First published in America by Simon & Schuster

ISBN 0-586-08534-3

Printed and bound in Great Britain by
Collins, Glasgow

Set in Baskerville

Contents

Prologue

We had a game in our house called 'setting the table' and I was Mother's helper. Forks to the left of the plate, knives and spoons to the right. Placing the cutlery neatly, as I recall, was one of my first duties, and the event was alive with meaning. When a knife or a fork dropped to the floor, that meant a man was unexpectedly coming to dinner. A falling spoon announced the surprise arrival of a female guest. No matter that these visitors never arrived on cue, I had learned a rule of gender identification. Men were straight-edged, sharply pronged and formidable, women were softly curved and held the food in a rounded well. It made perfect sense, like the division of pink and blue that I saw in babies, an orderly way of viewing the world. Daddy, who was gone all day at work and who loved to putter at home with his pipe, tobacco and tool chest, was knife and fork. Mommy and Grandma, with their ample proportions and pots and pans, were grownup soup spoons, large and capacious. And I was a teaspoon, small and slender, easy to hold and just right for pudding, my favourite dessert.

Being good at what was expected of me was one of my earliest projects, for not only was I rewarded, as most children are, for doing things right, but excellence gave pride and stability to my childhood existence. Girls were different from boys, and the expression of that difference seemed mine to make clear. Did my loving, anxious mother, who dressed me in white organdy pinafores and Mary Janes and who cried hot tears when I got them dirty, give me my first instruction? Of course. Did my doting aunts and uncles with their gifts of pretty dolls and miniature tea sets add to my education? Of course. But even without the appropriate toys and clothes, lessons in the art of being feminine lay all around me and I absorbed them all: the fairy tales that were read to me at night, the brightly coloured advertisements I pored over in magazines before I learned to decipher the words, the movies I saw, the comic books I hoarded, the radio soap operas I happily followed whenever I had to stay in bed with a cold. I loved being a little girl, or rather I loved being a fairy princess, for that was who I thought I was.

As I passed through a stormy adolescence to a stormy maturity, femininity increasingly became an exasperation, a brilliant, subtle aesthetic that was bafflingly inconsistent at the same time that it was minutely, demandingly concrete, a rigid code of appearance and behaviour defined by do's and don't-do's that went against my rebellious grain. Femininity was a challenge thrown down to the female sex, a challenge no proud, self-respecting young woman could afford to ignore, particularly one with enormous ambition that she nursed in secret, alternately feeding or starving its inchoate life in tremendous confusion.

'Don't lose your femininity' and 'Isn't it remarkable how she manages to retain her femininity?' had terrifying implications. They spoke of a bottom-line failure so irreversible that nothing else mattered. The pinball machine had registered 'tilt,' the game had been called. Disqualification was marked on the forehead of a woman whose femininity was lost. No records would be entered in her name, for she had destroyed her birthright in her wretched, ungainly effort to imitate a man. She walked in limbo, this hapless creature, and it occurred to me that one day I might see her when I looked in the mirror. If the danger was so palpable that warning notices were freely posted, wasn't it possible that the small bundle of resentments I carried around in secret might spill out and place the mark on my own forehead? Whatever quarrels with femininity I had I kept to myself; whatever handicaps femininity imposed, they were mine to deal with alone, for there was no women's movement to ask the tough questions, or to brazenly disregard the rules.

Femininity, in essence, is a romantic sentiment, a nostalgic tradition of imposed limitations. Even as it hurries forward in the 1980s, putting on lipstick and high heels to appear well dressed, it trips on the ruffled petticoats and hoopskirts of an era gone by. Invariably and necessarily, femininity is something that women had more of in the past, not only in the historic past of prior generations, but in each woman's personal past as well – in the virginal innocence that is replaced by knowledge, in the dewy cheek that is coarsened by age, in the 'inherent nature' that a woman seems to misplace so forgetfully whenever she steps out of bounds. Why should this be so? The XX chromosomal message has not been scrambled, the oestrogen-dominated hormonal balance is generally as biology intended, the reproductive organs, whatever use one has made of them, are usually in place, the breasts of whatever size are most often where they should be. But clearly, biological femaleness is not enough.

Femininity always demands more. It must constantly reassure its audience by a willing demonstration of difference, even when one does not exist in nature, or it must seize and embrace a natural variation and compose a rhapsodic symphony upon the notes. Suppose one doesn't care to, has other things on her mind, is clumsy or tone-deaf despite the best instruction and training? To fail at the feminine difference is to appear not to care about men, and to risk the loss of their attention and approval. To be insufficiently feminine is viewed as a failure in core sexual identity, or as a failure to care sufficiently about oneself, for a woman found wanting will be appraised (and will appraise herself) as mannish or neutered or simply unattractive, as men have defined these terms.

We are talking, admittedly, about an exquisite aesthetic. Enormous pleasure can be extracted from feminine pursuits as a creative outlet or purely as relaxation; indeed, indulgence for the sake of fun, or art, or attention, is among femininity's great joys. But the chief attraction (and the central paradox, as well) is the competitive edge that femininity seems to promise in the unending struggle to survive, and perhaps to triumph. The world smiles favourably on the feminine woman: it extends little courtesies and minor privilege. Yet the nature of this competitive edge is ironic, at best, for one works at femininity by accepting restrictions, by limiting one's sights, by choosing an indirect route, by scattering concentration and not giving one's all as a man would to his own, certifiably masculine, interests. It does not require a great leap of imagination for a woman to understand the feminine principle as a grand collection of compromises, large and small, that she simply must make in order to render herself a successful woman. If she has difficulty in satisfying femininity's demands, if its illusions go against her grain, or if she is criticized for her shortcomings and imperfections, the more she will see femininity as a desperate strategy of appeasement, a strategy she may not have the wish or the courage to abandon, for failure looms in either direction.

It is fashionable in some quarters to describe the feminine and masculine principles as polar ends of the human continuum, and to sagely profess that both polarities exist in all people. Sun and moon, yin and yang, soft and hard, active and passive, etcetera, may indeed be opposites, but a linear continuum does not illuminate the problem. (Femininity, in all its contrivances, is a very active endeavour.) What, then, is the basic distinction? The masculine principle is better understood as a driving ethos of superiority designed to inspire straighforward, confident success, while the feminine principle is composed of vulnerability, the need for protection, the formalities of compliance and the avoidance of conflict – in short, an appeal of dependence and good will that gives the masculine principle its romantic validity and its admiring applause.

Femininity pleases men because it makes them appear more masculine by contrast; and, in truth, conferring an extra portion of unearned gender distinction on men, an unchallenged space in which to breathe freely and feel stronger, wiser, more competent, is femininity's special gift. One could say that masculinity is often an effort to please women, but masculinity is known to please by displays of mastery and competence while femininity pleases by suggesting that these concerns, except in small matters, are beyond its intent. Whimsy, unpredictability and patterns of thinking and behaviour that are dominated by emotion, such as tearful expressions of sentiment and fear, are thought to be feminine precisely because they lie outside the established route to success.

If in the beginnings of history the feminine woman was defined by her physical dependency, her inability for reasons of reproductive biology to triumph over the forces of nature that were the tests of masculine strength and power, today she reflects both an economic and emotional dependency that is still considered 'natural,' romantic and attractive. After an unsettling fifteen years in which many basic assumptions about the sexes were challenged, the economic disparity did not disappear. Large numbers of women – those with small children, those left high and dry after a mid-life divorce – need financial support. But even those who earn their own living share a universal need for connectedness (call it love, if you wish). As unprecedented numbers of men abandon their sexual interest in women, others, sensing opportunity, choose to demonstrate their interest through variety and a change in partners. A sociological fact of the 1980s is that female competition for two scarce resources – men and jobs – is especially fierce.

So it is not surprising that we are currently witnessing a renewed interest in femininity and an unabashed indulgence in feminine pursuits. Femininity serves to reassure men that women need them and care about them enormously. By incorporating the decorative and the frivolous into its definition of style, femininity functions as an effective antidote to the unrelieved seriousness, the pressure of making one's way in a harsh, difficult world. In its mandate to avoid direct confrontation and to smooth over the fissures of conflict, femininity operates as a value system of niceness, a code of thoughtfulness and sensitivity that in modern society is sadly in short supply.

There is no reason to deny that indulgence in the art of feminine illusion can be reassuring to a woman, if she happens to be good at it. As sexuality undergoes some dizzying revisions, evidence that one is a woman 'at heart' (the inquisitor's question) is not without worth. Since an answer of sorts may be furnished by piling on additional documentations, affirmation can arise from such identifiable but trivial feminine activities as buying a new eyeliner, experimenting with the latest shade of nail colour, or bursting into tears at the outcome of a popular romance novel. Is there anything destructive in this? Time and cost factors, a deflection of energy and an absorption in fakery spring quickly to mind, and they need to be balanced, as in a ledger book, against the affirming advantage.

Throughout this book I have attempted to trace significant feminine principles to basic biology, for feminine expression is conventionally praised as an enhancement of femaleness, or the raw materials of femaleness shaped and coloured to perfection. Sometimes I found that a biological connection did exist, and sometimes not, and sometimes I had to admit that many scientific assumptions about the nature of females were unresolved and hotly debated, and that no sound conclusion was possible before all the evidence was in. It was more enlightening to explore the origins of femininity in borrowed affectations of upper-class status, and in the historic subjugation of women through sexual violence, religion and law, where certain myths about the nature of women were put forward as biological fact. It was also instructive to approach femininity from the angle of seductive glamour, which usually does not fit smoothly with aristocratic refinement, accounting for some contradictory feminine messages that often appear as an unfathomable puzzle.

The competitive aspect of femininity, the female-against-female competition produced by the effort to attract and secure men, is one of the major themes I have tried to explore. Male-against-male competition for high rank and access to females is a popular subject in anthropology, in the study of animals as well as humans, but few scholars have thought to examine the pitched battle of females for ranking and access to males. Yet the struggle to approach the feminine ideal, to match the femininity of other women, and especially to outdo them, is the chief competitive arena (surely it is the only sanctioned arena) in which the American woman is wholeheartedly encouraged to contend. Whether or not this absorbing form of competition is a healthy or useful survival strategy is a critical question.

Hymns to femininity, combined with instruction, have never been lacking. Several generations of us are acquainted with sugar and spice, can recite the job description for 'The Girl That I Marry' (doll-size, soft and pink, wears lace and nail polish, gardenia in the hair), or wail the payoff to 'Just Like a Woman' ('She breaks like a little girl'). My contribution may be decidedly unmusical, but it is not a manual of how-not-to, nor a wholesale damnation. Femininity deserves some hard reckoning, and this is what I have tried to do.

A powerful aesthetic that is built upon a recognition of powerlessness is a slippery subject to grapple with, for its contradictions are elusive, ephemeral and ultimately impressive. A manner that combines a deferential attitude with ornaments of the upper class and an etiquette composed in equal parts of modesty and exhibition are paradoxes that require thoughtful interpretation. A strategy of survival that is based on overt concession and imposed restrictions deserves close study, for what is lost and what is gained is not always apparent. By organizing my chapters along pragmatic lines – body, hair, clothes, voice, etcetera – I have attempted a rational analysis that is free of mystification. Coming down hard on certain familiar aspects while admitting a fond tolerance for some others has been unavoidable in my attempt to give an honest appraisal of the feminine strategies as I have myself practised or discarded them. I do not mean to project my particular compromises and choices as the better way, or the final word, nor do I mean to condemn those women who practise the craft in ways that are different from mine. I offer this book as a step towards awareness, in the hope that one day the feminine ideal will no longer be used to perpetuate inequality between the sexes, and that exaggeration will not be required to rest secure in biological gender.

SUSAN BROWNMILLER
New York City
September 1983

Body

The nude, said Kenneth Clark in his study of the ideal figure, was an art form invented by the Greeks in the fifth century B.C., 'just as opera was an art form invented in seventeenth-century Italy.' In the masculine urge to celebrate erotic perfection, the sculpted naked body was a harmonious design that illustrated divinity and strength. Wrinkles and other imperfections were never permitted. Geometric proportion was a mystical religion. The first great nudes were beautiful young men. Somewhat later they were joined by beautiful young women.

According to the classical Greeks, in the perfect female torso the distance between the nipples of the breasts, the distance from the lower edge of the breast to the navel, and the distance from the navel to the crotch were units of equal length. Centuries later, the Gothic ideal was strikingly different. With the breasts reduced to oval spheres that Clark finds 'distressingly small,' and with the stomach expanded to a long ovoid curve that suggests an advanced state of pregnancy, at least to the modern eye, Clark finds that 'the navel is exactly twice as far down the body as it is in the classical scheme.' The Greek, the Gothic and the Renaissance ideals do share some similarities. In all three forms the feet and toes are wide, strong and sturdy, and the fingernails, when they show, are trimmed short and blunt by modern standards.

Ectomorph, mesomorph, endomorph, whatever natural variations the human form can take, the idealization of the feminine form in a given age is usually one form only, and ideas of perfection can change with lightning speed. Not surprisingly, the ideal feminine shape most often goes under the name of Venus, for Venus is the goddess of love, and as the poet Byron expressed it for his sex, 'Man's love is of man's life a thing apart; 'Tis woman's whole existence.' The first discovered example of a famous paleolithic figurine, all breasts, belly and buttocks, which defied any accepted standard of feminine beauty, was sarcastically named the *Venus of Willendorf*, as a joke among men.

The tyranny of Venus is felt whenever a woman thinks – or

whenever a man thinks and tells a woman – that her hips are too wide, her thighs are too large, her breasts are too small, her waist is too high, her legs are too short to meet the current erotic standard. In London society on the eve of World War I, a Venus painted by the seventeenth-century Spaniard Velásquez was thought to be the most perfect Venus of them all (she still has her champions today). Known as the *Rokeby Venus*, she reclines odalisque-style with her back to the viewer while she regards her face in a mirror (oh, feminine vanity; oh, feminine wiles). The most memorable aspect of the *Rokeby Venus*, indeed the focal point of the painterly composition, is – to put it straightforwardly – the voluptuous expanse of her naked behind.

In 1914 when the militant suffrage campaign in England had reached the stage of guerrilla warfare and Mrs Pankhurst was on hunger strike in Holloway prison, a movement activist named Mary Richardson, alias Polly Dick, decided on an audacious act. Making a stunning connection between the public celebration of the erotic feminine nude and the refusal of Britain's male Parliament to grant women the vote, Mary Richardson walked into the National Gallery with a small axe tucked into the sleeve of her jacket and broke the glass that protected the *Rokeby Venus* before she was dragged off by the guards.

With a symmetry that may be as common in politics as it is in art, the new wave of feminism that began fifteen years ago in the United States coincidentally chose to attack a symbol of Venus in its first dramatic act. In 1968 the Women's Liberation Movement announced itself to a startled public by staging a demonstration at the Miss America contest in Atlantic City, protesting, among other points, 'Women in our society are forced daily to compete for male approval, enslaved by ludicrous beauty standards that we ourselves are conditioned to take seriously and to accept.'

At what age does a girl child begin to review her assets and count her deficient parts? When does she close the bedroom door and begin to gaze privately into the mirror at contortionist angles to get a view from the rear, the left profile, the right, to check the curve of her calf muscle, the shape of her thighs, to ponder her shoulder blades and wonder if she is going to have a waistline? And pull in her stomach, throw out her chest and pose again in a search for the most flattering angle, making a mental note of what needs to be worked on, what had better develop, stay contained, or else?

At what age does the process begin, this obsessive concentration on the minutiae of her physical being that will occupy some portion of her waking hours quite possibly for the rest of her life? When is she allowed to forget that her anatomy is being monitored by others, that there is a standard of desirable beauty, of individual parts, that she is measured against by boy-friends, loved ones, acquaintances at work, competitors, enemies and strangers? How can she be immune to the national celebration of this season's movie star sporting this season's body, to the calendar art in the neighbourhood filling station, to the glamorous model in the high-fashion photograph, to the chance remark of a lover, the wistful preference of a husband, the whistle or the unexpected hostile comment heard on the street?

As I remember, a thin, fragile wrist easily encircled by the fingers of my other hand was the first demonstration of femininity I demanded of my growing body; the second was a small and tightly belted waist. Staying shorter than the boys, or at least not vying for the place in line of tallest girl, became the next consuming worry. 'My, she's growing up,' and 'Isn't she getting big?' were warning rumbles. By the fifth grade I knew that bigness was not what I was after. Slight and slender were my grownup ambitions. Too often for comfort my mother, statuesque and on the heavy side, had teased (in front of my father!) that I was going to inherit her ample bosom. No I *won't*, I'd mutter, in awe of what I'd seen when we shared a bath. Even worse was the fear that I might not develop at all, that I'd be stuck wearing undershirts for the rest of my life.

She had communicated to me, without really meaning to, I think, that breasts were a problem. Hers had been ruined, she believed, when she had bound them tightly to achieve the flat, boyish, flapper look of the 1920s. 'Don't ever bind your breasts,' my full-figured mother would say as she poured her flesh into a long-line brassiere-and-girdle combination. As it turned out, this was advice I never needed. At college in the Fifties, the Jane Russell/Marilyn Monroe inflated mammary era, I agonized that I was miserably flatchested and wore my small breasts unnaturally high and pointed in a push-up bra with foam-rubber padding.

At least I wasn't broad-shouldered and I didn't have thick ankles. As for dimpled knees, I found that concept puzzling, for mine were bone-hard and knobbly, but even more unsettling was their failure to touch when I stood up straight with my feet pressed together. I had to admit I was hopelessly bowlegged. In truth, I didn't form an opinion about my rear end until the middle of the Sixties, for I had grown up in the era of the panty girdle and the two-way stretch, when all young ladies were said to require some abdominal support and containment of our shaking buttocks, not to mention a secure means of holding up our stockings. By the mid-1960s when I put away my bra and girdle in response to a newer model of the feminine body, I found that without one iota of change in my physical dimensions, my breasts were suddenly not too small, and my thighs, hips and buttocks had passed the supreme test – they could fit without chafing into a pair of men's jeans.

In recent years my stomach has been showing signs of spread, implacably female instead of teenage flat, and I cannot pass a group of construction workers on a New York City street without involuntarily sucking in my gut. I do my yoga every morning, eat less than I used to and try not to think about chocolate. Staying thin has replaced staying shorter than the boys and 'We must, we must, we must increase our bust' as my bodily desire, and I expect I will continue to be obsessed with weight until, like Léa in *The Last of Chéri*, I am past the age of sexual judgement and no longer concerned with what a man might think.

At the moment of birth, gender difference in anatomy is a fairly simple prospect. *It's a girl . . . It's a boy.* Those age-old cries of relief arise from one fast look at the baby's genitalia. Patterned by the chromosomal message – XX for a female, XY for a male – a tiny vulva or a little penis is what we see. Beyond the genitals, sexual dimorphism in size and shape does not occur until puberty, when according to a hormonal mechanism that is usually in working order, the boys shoot up and the girls fill out to complete their maturation.

Triggered by her oestrogens, the adolescent girl's genitals increase in size and sensitivity, her mammary ducts enlarge, her uterus expands and her pelvis widens. Her ovaries and Fallopian tubes ready themselves for their reproductive function and menstruation begins. Coming of age is marked externally by the appearance of fatty tissue that cushions the pelvic area and mammary glands – the distinctly female soft flesh, the ideally feminine rounded curves of the breasts, hips, buttocks and thighs. Reproductive maturation gives a young woman her figure, the somatic emblem of her sexual essence. Exalted by poets, painters and sculptors, the female body, often reduced to its isolated parts, has been mankind's most popular subject for adoration and myth, and also for judgement, ridicule, aesthetic alteration and violent abuse.

When the human male comes of age his genitals also enlarge and become reproductively functional, and he is the proud recipient of increased muscle mass in his arms, chest, back, shoulders and legs. This swift jump in musculature and strength may be enhanced by exercise and sports, but the basic cause is genetic and hormonal. The oestrogenic property that adds soft fat to the female body has been used with great success by poultry breeders who want to fatten and tenderize their products for the market, but testosterone would make for a mighty tough chicken. At adolescence a male's skeletal frame grows larger than a female's in all directions except for hip width, and his bones become more dense. Broad shoulders, big bones and rippling muscles characterize the ideal masculine form; they separate the men from the boys, and the man from the woman.

A girl's serious growing is usually over by the age of thirteen or so, shortly after first menstruation, and she has reached her adult height by the time she is eighteen. Just when she despairs that she will never find a boy tall enough, the boys begin their big spurt. Males, who enter puberty two years later than females, may continue to gain inches until they are twenty. When the sex hormones act in concert with the growth hormones, testosterone is a powerful additive, but a longer growing season for males because of their later maturation is the basic reason why they end up 5 to 10 per cent taller.

An explanation for why girls mature more rapidly than boys, and why they stop growing in skeletal size after menstruation begins, may be rooted in our primitive past when life expectancy was low and a female needed to get on with the important job of reproduction as quickly as possible. Obviously, the sooner she reached puberty the better – no such biological urgency would attend the male rate of maturation. Once she started to bear offspring it would be biologically unsound if a mother herself were growing. A developing foetus and a suckling infant require enormous amounts of protein, calcium and other essential minerals, and these life-or-death demands would create a double strain and a severe nutritional hardship on a body hellbent on its own enlargement. A mother whose skeletal growth had stopped would stand a better chance of survival, and so would her baby. In a phenomenon stressed by Ashley Montagu, for the first few years after the start of menstruation a girl usually is not fertile despite outward signs. These are her years of minor but continued growth, and infertility seems to be nature's way of cutting down on infant and maternal deaths.

Anthropologists view superior size as a reproductive advantage for the male in terms of competition for access to females. In the popular imagination masculinity always includes the concepts of powerful and large, while slight and weak are feminine descriptions. A man-size portion puts more food on the plate and the Man-Size Kleenex packs more tissues in the box. The average American male measures in at a shade over five feet nine inches, and the average American female stands at five feet four and a half inches. If a woman fits neatly into the averages, a few inches shorter than a member of the opposite sex, she is probably going to feel comfortable about size, sweetly in harmony with the proportional aesthetics of male-female relations. However, 10 per cent of all American women stand above five feet seven and a half inches, and they hover over that 10 per cent of all American men who are under five foot six inches. (Ten per cent of the population defy the averages for their gender in other signs of dimorphism such as hip girth and width of the shoulders.) Five per cent of the female population, the really tall women, upset the order of conventional proportion by standing above the mean height of men.

Most of the gestures of etiquette and the rules of good manners were designed for a conventional disparity in size and strength. A small man protectively holding an umbrella for a taller woman looks faintly awkward, and a conventional difference in size is considered the norm in romantic expectations. The world's tallest woman has said she could never fall in love with a shorter man – at seven feet seven inches, alas, she remains unmarried. Cher is taller than Sonny, but was not in their television promotions. Only a half-inch shorter than Prince Charles when she wore her flat heels, Lady Di was reduced in stature by a full head for the postage stamp that commemorated their royal wedding. 'She looked up into his eyes' is more than a breathless phrase from a Gothic novel; it is an expression of the heterosexual relationship as we expect to find it. When a woman stands taller than a man she has broken a cardinal feminine rule, for her physical stature reminds him that he may be too short – inadequate, insufficient – for the competitive

13

world of men. She has dealt a blow to his masculine image, undermined his footing as aggressor-protector. To show a man that he may not be needed is a terribly unfeminine stance, and she knows she will pay for it unless she can compensate in some other manner.

Even though I'm not quite five feet six inches, a lucky size for feminine appearance, I usually feel lumbering in relation to a smaller man. The familiar ratios are out of kilter; the level of eye contact is oddly reversed. Perhaps with an unwitting, forceful gesture I might accidentally tip him over. I suffer for his shortness and I feel guilty for the unalterable fact of my height. I slouch, I twist, I tilt my head. I reach into my little bag of feminine tricks, anything to diffuse my apparent solidity, my relative strength. Once on a crowded subway car in Tokyo I felt at the outer limits of appropriate size, in peril of being a rude affront to all Japanese men and a gross insult to their country's sense of exquisite proportion. It was hardly my fault that Americans in general are a taller people, but I did not want to seem unfeminine – outsize, overbearing, impolite.

America produces some of the tallest women in the world, outranked only by the Swiss, the Swedish, the Germans and the Norwegians. We're the same size as many men in southern Europe, Asia and Latin America. We're taller than most Vietnamese, Thai and Laotian soldiers. We're bigger than the Yanomamo warriors of Brazil, the fierce tribesmen of New Guinea, the Javanese, the Lapps and the Maya and Quechua Indians. We're indisputably larger than Kalahari bushmen, the Pygmies and a few other African tribes. American women can tower over Yemenite Jews, Siberian natives and entire village populations in Sardinia and parts of Spain. We're appreciably taller than most French, Italian and Spanish women and we're almost the same height as Polish men. Genetics and nutrition have given us the edge. More than our supposed independence, brashness or sexual liberation, sheer size may give us our unshakable reputation for a certain lack of femininity in comparison to women in other parts of the globe.

The equating of maleness with bigness persists as a dearly loved concept. I've heard 'Look at the big males' while viewing an elephant matriarch and her offspring in Kenya, and 'Look at the big male' while sighting a female musk ox and her young in Alaska, and I've gnashed my teeth on both occasions. Authoritative women who correct false impressions are unfeminine and bossy but it is equally true that amateur observers of wildlife tend to assume that the largest animal in any grouping must be a male, and furthermore, that he must be in charge.

Early sexual maturation puts a fast brake on growth in baboon and gorilla females while males of these species continue to gain in size for several more years. Whiskers, shaggy manes, long canines and other dimorphic signs that distinguish a male usually make their appearance during these additional years of growth. Male and female gibbons, on the other hand, mature at approximately the same age and can barely be distinguished by size and external appearance. (A lack of dimorphism is found in 18 per cent of all primate species, and interestingly, these are the species where monogamy prevails.) The poor reputation suffered by hyenas has much to do with their homeliness and jarring chortles, but it does not help the hyena's case that the female is larger than the male (she reaches reproductive maturity a year later than he does), is dominant to him and has a huge, long clitoris and a sham scrotal sac. Hyenas were thought to be hermaphroditic, homosexual, orgiastic and lewd when Horace Walpole called Mary Wollstonecraft 'a hyena in petticoats,' slandering her femininity and the movement for women's rights in one wicked phrase.

Contemplation of a big female mating with a smaller male is so at odds with our human perspective and the sort of anthropomorphizing that is found in books for children that many intelligent people are surprised to hear that in a majority of species, females do happen to be the larger sex. This is an evolutionary adaptation with probable reproductive advantage for the American bald eagle, the king crab, the snowy owl, the gypsy moth, the chinchilla, the garter snake, the python, the right whale, the humpback whale, the grey whale, the blue whale (thus the largest creature in the world is female), all families of rabbits and hares, the hawks and the falcons, toads, sharks, salmon, flounder, most hummingbirds and turtles, and other fish, birds, reptiles, amphibians and insects too numerous to mention. Admittedly most of these species with big reproducing females are clustered on the lower rungs of the evolutionary ladder, suggesting that Mother Nature had an eventual change of mind or found a more efficient style of motherhood for her later models, but nevertheless, a correction of the total picture is an excellent antidote to some common assumptions about bigness and maleness in all creatures great and small.

But when we return to humans and most other primates, we confront a disparity of size and strength with serious implications. As expressed by the anthropologist Sarah Hardy, 'Males are bigger than females and are able to bully them.' Bullying is generally called 'dominance' in primate studies, and for gorillas and baboons it usually boils down to who gets to sit on a favourite branch or who gets the available fig. Among humans, quite obviously the stakes are higher. Possibly one day a scientist will prove that initiative and assertion are not given a boost by the confidence that comes from superior physical strength, but somehow I doubt it. Competition among men has a very long history that is marked by physical aggression, and the ability of most women to compete successfully with men in feats of strength is based on a biological difference. We can ponder the exceptional ring-tailed lemur who is smaller than the male yet dominant to him – she remains oblivious to his posturing displays and cuffs him around when she wants to – yet when push comes to shove, we are not ring-tailed lemurs.

Yet neither are women as weak, slight or insubstantial as the current aesthetic ideal suggests. Sexual dimorphism may distinguish the male by muscle strength and height, but femaleness is not the opposite side of the coin. Soft fatty tissue deposited in sizable masses identifies the female dimorphic state, a biological adaptation to the pressures of motherhood and survival. A woman's body typically has a fat content of 25 per cent, while 15 per cent is normal for males, a difference that is not caused primarily by exercise or strenuous labour. Millions of years ago when our evolutionary attributes were established, food resources were probably uncertain and the female body most likely developed its cushion of subcutaneous fat as a reserve supply of nutrition. A mighty 80,000 calories sustains a pregnancy to term, and body fat is utilized in the production of milk. Dr Rose Frisch of Harvard has theorized that a critical level of adipose flesh is needed to kick off and maintain the cycle of ovulation. Anorectics usually cease to menstruate because they have fallen below the critical level. Professional athletes, too, may temporarily lose their menstrual cycle in the course of converting their ratio of fat to lean muscle.

Fleshiness, as we know, is problematic to the present-day feminine illusion, for while fat creates the celebrated dimorphic curves of womanhood, it is also the agent of massiveness and bulk, properties more readily associated with masculine solidity and power. What seems to be a natural tendency of the female body to acquire substantial, if wobbly, mass runs counter to the preferred ideal of delicate shapeliness. Furthermore, breasts, hips, stomach and thighs, the familiar places where fat cells collect, do not necessarily expand in uniform proportion; genetic differences among women are rife. Yet nearly every civilization has sought to impose a uniform shape upon the female body, a feminine aesthetic that usually denies solidity by rearranging, accentuating or drastically reducing some portion of the female anatomy or some natural expression of flesh.

In past centuries a woman of status was required to endure some painful device of immobilization that shortened her breath or shortened her step by tightly constricting some specific part of her body – waist, abdomen, rib cage, breast, neck or foot – in the belief that she was improving, supporting or enhancing an aesthetically imperfect, grossly shapeless natural figure. In the East she was subject to the Japanese obi, the Burmese neck ring and the Chinese bound foot; in the West she wore the steel-ribbed corset and whalebone stays. Each device of beautification restricted her freedom and weakened her strength; each provided a feminine obstacle course through which she endeavoured to move with artificial grace. Each instrument of discomfort was believed by her to be a superior emblem of her privileged position and a moral requisite for correct behaviour, and each ingenious constriction was sentimentalized by men as erotic in its own right, apart from the woman it was designed to improve.

Bernard Rudofsky, a provocative social critic, has theorized that men find deep sexual excitement in the hobbling of women. Such a statement is darkly inflammatory but impossible to dismiss. To envision a Chinese nobleman's wife or courtesan with daintily slippered three-inch stubs in place of normal feet is to understand much about man's violent subjugation of women; what is less clear is the concept of exquisite feminine beauty contained within the deforming violence: the sensuous incapacitation and useless, ornamental charm perceived in the fused, misshapen bones. A lotus blossom with a willow walk: romantic imagery for man's improvement over nature. Pruned from childhood, her tiny foot was said to resemble the lotus, a most revered flower, and with the support of a long staff or leaning against a husband or servant, she walked like a whisper of wind through the willows, swaying tremulously with each timid step. Making love to the lotus foot, an elaborate art of manipulation, postures and poses, was a dominant theme in Chinese pornography for eight hundred years while the custom of foot-binding flourished.

Distasteful though it may be, the bound foot illustrates several aspects of the feminine aesthetic. It originated in the rarefied atmosphere of a decadent upper class where the physical labour of women was not required, and it became an enviable symbol of luxury, leisure and refinement. It isolated a specific part of the female body which differed from the male body in some respect, in this case a slightly smaller foot, and cruelly exaggerated the natural difference in the cause of artistic perfection. It imposed an ingenious handicap upon a routine, functional act and reduced the female's competence to deal with the world around her, rendering that world a more perilous place and the imbalanced woman a more dependent, fearful creature. It rendered a man more competent and steady – in other words, more masculine – by simple contrast. It romanticized, and thereby justified, the woman's tottering gait by turning it into a sexual attraction, and it elevated her 'perfected' part, her tiny, useless foot, to the realm of ornamental beauty. It instilled in every woman a deep sense of insecurity born of the conviction that some natural part of her was profoundly ugly (in China the common term was 'goosefoot') and required some extreme corrective measure. And finally, it demanded the shared complicity of mother and daughter in the desperate work of beautification and the passing on of compliant, submissive feminine values, for the anxious mother was the agent of will who crushed her suffering daughter's foot as she calmed her rebellion by holding up the promise of the dainty shoe, teaching her child at an early age that the feminine mission in life, at the cost of tears and pain, was to alter her body and amend her ways in the supreme effort to attract and please a man.

A different approach to the feminine aesthetic prevailed in the West, where the entire torso from breast to hips was believed to require artistic improvement, and the ingenious device that hampered a woman's motions as it moulded her figure to a romantic ideal was the imprisoning corset with its inflexible stays of whale-bone or steel. We know from the art and documents of the sixteenth century that two powerful queens, Catherine de Medici of France and Elizabeth of England, were among the first to wear the compressing cage, taking on, as it were, the armour of their noble knights to push the soft flesh and rib cage inward. How fascinating that history's first tight-lacers should have been the Medici and the Virgin Queen, two bold, ambitious women who were called 'unnatural' in their thirst for power. Why did they do it? What made them want to subject their chest and stomach to such discomfort, they who negotiated treaties and plotted murder with such competent skill? Could it be that the singular quality their enemies whispered they did not have – a womanly weakness, a soft, yielding nature – might best be proved and ceremoniously displayed by that excessively small and breathlessly feminine bodice? The slender waist was not exclusively a feminine vanity. Elizabeth's father, Henry the Eighth, compressed his middle in order to give his chest that extra-burly look – but King Henry and other men stopped short of physical pain.

Two points must be stressed right here. The first is that no discussion of the feminine body in the Western world can make much sense without getting a grip on the corset, no matter how familiar the material may seem, for the corset has played not a supporting but a starring role in the body's history. The second is that whatever sartorial devices men have put on to bolster their bold image – codpieces, elevated shoes, padded shoulders, a boxy jacket – these did not constrict or cause pain. The truth is, men have barely tampered with their bodies at all, historically, to make themselves more appealing to women. The development of biceps and pectorals is an honourable by-product of hard physical labour and an aid to competitive feats of sport and strength. Muscle-bound body builders, the man in the elevated shoe or the baldy who wears a toupee have been grist for the jokester's mill, under the masculine theory that real men do not trick themselves out to be pleasing. (They have better ways to prove their worth.) A woman, on the other hand, is expected to depend on tricks and suffering to prove her feminine nature, for beauty, as men have defined it for women, is an end in itself.

Not only did the corset induce a regal posture and smaller, feminized motions – a lady could barely bend at the waist or take a deep breath, but her bosom heaved and her fan fluttered in her agitated efforts to get enough air – it became a necessary under-structure for anyone who cared about fashion. The quest for the perfect body in the perfect dress was contained in the quest for the perfect corset, which could uplift, augment or flatten the breasts, widen or narrow the hips, pinch or elongate the waist, sway the back, slope the shoulders and push in the stomach, in accordance with the fashion ideal of the times. An estimated twenty to eighty pounds of pressure might be exerted by the corset's squeeze, depending on the season's style and the determination of the wearer. Corseting up was a challenge that taxed her stamina and the strength of her maidservant, or a convenient bedpost, the laces pulled tighter as evening drew near. But oh, the admiring glances that fell upon the fragile waist which could be spanned and lifted by a pair of strong hands. And oh, the delightful charms of the fainting, swooning lady who so exquisitely needed masculine protection. Or so she has been romantically presented. Realistically, the typical corseted woman was no wasp-waisted Scarlett O'Hara flirting at a glittering ball. She was a solidly built matron who loosened her stays in private as often as she could, and who was annoyed to find her maid servant 'putting on airs' by corseting up on the sly.

Among its persuasions, the corset encouraged the idea that the female body was structurally unsound and needed to be supported by artificial contraptions at strategic points. A woman of the nineteenth century believed she was born with a clumsy waist, and that a stiff foundation would compensate for the inability of her spine and musculature to support the weight of her breasts and stomach. Since her muscles were miserably atrophied from disuse and binding, she had authentic reason to be grateful to her supporting stays, and without them she feared she might collapse into a degenerative heap, both physically and spiritually. Her erect, formal posture was identified with moral rectitude and social propriety (the term 'straitlaced' owes its origin to the corset), and loosening the stays or leaving the house without them was interpreted as a sign of loose, licentious behaviour. Training the body to accept the corset was a discipline that began in childhood, for it was never too early for an anxious mother to correct the slovenly posture with which her daughter was born. Initiation into the mysteries of the hooks and laces was a rite of passage into the mysteries and responsibilities of becoming a young lady; the confines of the corset signified the submissive, self-conscious values of the feminine sphere.

Art historian Anne Hollander observes in *Seeing Through Clothes* that much of the world's great painting celebrates the nude female body not in its natural configurations but in conformance to the dress and corset styles of the period, with pushed-up breasts or widely separated breasts, with a high waist or a low waist, with a rounded or a flat abdomen, etcetera. Apparently the corset could shape not only the woman but the artist's erotic preference. Corset fetishism in the history of pornography is astonishing and shows no sign of phasing out in today's freer more natural age. A comical, dated interest in girdles, brassieres and criss-cross of garters (I have yet to see a pornographic picture of a woman in pantyhose) seems to say that a network of feminine impediments is a more potent sexual tonic for many men than the direct reality of an unencumbered body.

Of course, women's underwear is imbued with erotic value at least partially because it lies close to the forbidden female mysteries. In the step-by-step procedure of the old-fashioned seduction the formidable girdle must be breached, the brassiere unhooked, the soft flesh released and the moral inhibitions overcome by the determined lover. Given this standard scenario based on the double standards, decorative lingerie with its contradictory message of harness, display and frivolous trim takes on a sexual life of its own. During the Gay Nineties a frilly lace garter thrown from the stage by a music-hall performer was a titillating gesture of naughty, provocative promise. In our own day there seems to be popular agreement that black lace is charged with sexual current, since it bespeaks narcissism that is wickedly assertive although the wearer herself may remain conventionally passive. Black lace has been certified as sexy for so many generations that for some women it represents the ultimate in feminine lingerie while others believe it is vulgar and cheap. On the reverse side of the picture, white cotton underpants have a feminine reputation for chastity and refinement in some quarters and are too plain, dowdy and childish for the taste of others.

I campaigned hard for my first brassiere, for my mother was of the opinion that I didn't really need one. Need one? The need was in my head, not in my bosom. Half the girls in my class were proudly showing off their bra lines under their Sloppy Joe sweaters

– how could I look sophisticated and get a boy with nothing to show but the scoop of a kiddy undershirt? Despite my mother's unsettling reassurance that all too soon I would fill out and begin to resemble her side of the family, the only enlarging I did was from 34-A to 34-A padded. This was rotten luck in an era where the boys said they could tell a C-cup from a D-cup, and Howard Hughes publicized *The Outlaw* by revealing how he applied his engineering technology to design a special uplift for Jane Russell. Watching Jane Russell on television last year doing brassiere commercials for the full-figured woman, I had to admit that Mother was right. I didn't really need one. By the late 1950s I had discarded the padding and by the mid 1960s I had discarded the bra.

Brassieres had no reason to exist before the 1920s since the upper portion of the corset was designed to keep the breasts supported and contained. In the tumultuous years of female emancipation that began during World War I, the corset was cast aside in a delirious rush towards freedom and modernity that included job opportunities, bobbed hair, bright lipstick, short skirts, disposable sanitary pads and the right to vote. Dress-reform movements that were partly feminist and partly hygienic in tone had paved the way for the corset's demise. For generations female doctors had spoken at public meetings of crushed ribs and atrophied internal organs, and concern for a sound, healthy body inspired women's participation in the physical-culture movements that sprouted in American soil – the fresh air advocates, the bicycle enthusiasts, the back-to-nature cultists, and the artistic dancers in their Grecian tunics who were followers of Isadora Duncan. Even the government got into the act when the War Industries Board announced that if American women were released from their armour, 28,000 tons of steel would be freed to build and furnish two battleships.

Women could do anything, or so it seemed, and a collective sigh of relief was heard when the corset was taken off and the flesh was allowed to spread in the name of the loose, unstructured Paris fashions. But what about the unfamiliar, loose shape of the body? The dancing flapper who epitomized the postwar generation was ideally thin and small-breasted in her waistless shift. Her unlucky sisters who also wanted to be New Women resorted to binding in order to suppress the superfluity of their bosoms. By the 1930s, however, breasts and the belted waistline had made a comeback, and corsetry had become a two-part solution. A lighter, rubber-ized girdle was introduced to contain the stomach and hips, and the bandeau that suppressed the breasts was redesigned to pull them up by means of adjustable straps. For those who wanted more support, the upper and lower contraptions could be hooked together.

Only at brief, vivid moments in the Western world have breasts been unencumbered by a restraining device worn under the clothes: Madame Récamier reclining on her sofa in a Grecian gown, Jean Harlow slithering to a dinner party in white satin, feminists in T-shirts marching on Fifth Avenue – but the rare privilege of this freedom has been seized happily and exemplified in fashion almost exclusively by small-breasted women. Historically, breasts of every shape and size have been crammed tightly into a V-shaped bodice, pushed upwards and presented like two oranges on a platter, flattened downwards into obscurity, projected forwards into a singular front-porch effect known as the monobosom, underpinned and braced like a shelf to maximize rising cleavage, forcibly separated by wire frames and pointed straight ahead like missiles, or persuaded by a combination of straps, clasps, elastic and stretchy fabric to stay put at some designated place mid-chest without jiggling.

The containerizing of breasts is a significant question, and not one that can be written off strictly as a matter of decoration. Whatever configuration the corset took in a given period, and however much attention was devoted in the fashion journals, and later in the costume history books, to the dazzling waistline, the slope of the torso or the flare of the hips, the unvarying function of any corset (and obviously, of the brassiere) was always to secure the breasts in some manner that reduced their independent motion. In fact, I suspect that the true reason women put up with the tribulations of the corset for so many centuries, abandoning it finally when the bra made its appearance, was that the majority of them felt more at ease physically – better armoured, so to speak – when their breasts were immobile and firmly contained. It is no accident, I think, that the use of breasts for nursing as a routine public act, as it still is today in Africa and other parts of the globe, fell into disfavour in the Western world, especially among the upper classes, at approximately the same time that the corset took hold as a necessary undergarment of fortitude and fashion. What to do with the breasts, if one is not actually using them, has preoccupied the feminine mind for a very long time.

Breasts are the most pronounced and variable aspect of the female anatomy, and although their function is fundamentally reproductive, to nourish the young with milk (placing 'Man' among the mammalian species), it is their emblematic prominence and intrinsic vulnerability that makes them the chief badge of gender. Breasts command attention, yet they are pliable and soft, offering warmth and succour close to the heart. Breasts seem possessed by an independent momentum, an autonomous bob and sway that forever reminds and surprises. Breasts may be large or small, droopy or firm, excitable or impassive, and variably sensitive to hormonal change, swelling in pleasure or in discomfort or pain. Breasts are an element of human beauty. Breasts are subject to cancerous lumps. Breasts are a source of female pride and sexual identification but they are also a source of competition, confusion, insecurity and shame.

Although they are housed on her person, from the moment they begin to show, a female discovers that her breasts are claimed by others. Parents and relatives mark their appearance as a landmark event, schoolmates take notice, girlfriends compare, boys zero in; later a husband, a lover, a baby expect a proprietary share. No other part of the human anatomy has such semi-public, intensely private status, and no other part of the body has such vaguely defined custodial rights. One learns to be selectively generous with breasts – this is the girl child's lesson – and through the breast iconography she sees all around her, she comes to understand that breasts belong to everybody, but especially to men. It is they who invent and refine the myths, who discuss breasts publicly, who criticize their failings as they extol their wonders, and who claim to have more need and intimate knowledge of them than a woman herself.

Without doubt it was men who created the fetish of size and shape, for the ability to breast-feed has nothing to do with external dimensions, and pleasurable sensation resides in the erectile tissue of the nipples, not in the bulk. But the otherness of breasts, their service in the scheme of male erotic satisfaction, long ago promoted the myth that a flat-chested woman is non-sexual or ungiving. At the other extreme, a woman with large breasts is usually assumed to be flaunting her sex or inviting attention. 'Gay deceivers,' the charming turn-of-the-century euphemism for what later generations referred to pragmatically as falsies, implied that a faked bosomy opulence was more appealing in its deceitful flirtatiousness than the honest reality of an unspectacular chest. The assumption of a ready-to-go sexual nature in big-breasted women is reminiscent of the time when generous sensuality was assigned to large, meaty thighs, and the phrase, 'She has no thighs,' implied an erotic stinginess or a sensual failure that bore no relationship to a woman's own orgasmic response.

An uptilted cup shape is idealized in Western art, for high, round breasts are associated with youth. Yet an uplifted sphere is invariably smallish in nature, since a large mass cannot defy the laws of gravity except when securely trussed in a bra or shot up with silicone, and 'the larger the breast, the lower the pull' is a reliable rule. The essential contradiction between a large breast and one that tilts upward is generally resolved by a fantasy that combines both desirable traits. Clothes are never designed for low-slung pendulous breasts, and rarely do we see this shape extolled in the nude. A strikingly different tradition, however, is evident in African art. Wood carvings from Mali celebrate a figure whose breasts point downwards sharply. A sharp downward thrust also typifies New Guinea and Kwakiutl carvings.

Obviously there is no such thing as an average breast, but the amazing variety is something that Western civilization chooses to deny, for it is the containerized breast that greets the world and imposes a uniform shape that is considered most highly erotic and fashionable in a given era. Most women cannot help but think that the shape of their breasts and the line of their clothes can be improved by a standardized bra. Blouses with side darts used to leave no doubt where the nipples should point. Sweaters look snug and chic only when the breasts curve upwards, or so our eye is trained to believe. Arguments in favour of the bra, however, go well beyond the concerns of fashion, or rather, they combine the aesthetic with other considerations, echoing the protests once articulated by fervent tight-lacers: Without a secure foundation the chest muscles will hurt from the strain, the breast will flop shamelessly; the jiggle is a source of discomfort; when the nipples point down they look droopy and sad; a sagging breast is the sign of an old lady; one breast is bigger, or lower, or different from the other; going braless is brazen and sloppy.

In this melange of concerns the one with serious implications is that a large-breasted woman needs artificial support to carry the weight of her breasts. Anthropological theories generally attribute the origin of upright walking to the male, who found it advantageous to see across the tall grass of the savanna, throw a spear, carry home the meat, or whatever else a man of importance might have done when he raised himself up from a four-legged trot. And females, of course, were brought along by this evolutionary development, but alas, less perfectly. Rarely do we read that the initial advantage might have accrued to the female who needed one arm to carry her child while she gathered and carried the fruits and leaves.

Is there something unsound in the female's anatomy when she walks on two legs? Did the evolution of bipedalism tax the female in a special way? There is no medical evidence that going braless can hurt a small-breasted woman, but large, full breasts do present a burdensome strain on the chest, spine and back. A body does move less efficiently, less graceful, more slowly and with greater caution when its balance is affected by the hanging weight of two inert, semi-autonomous masses. In sudden or vigorous moves, jumps and twists, there is a fractional delay in coordinated timing; the motion of the breasts falls slightly behind. Heavy, large breasts that slap repeatedly against the chest wall during strenuous action can strain the supporting tissue. A prominent frontal load pulls the shoulders forward and can affect the trajectory or get in the way of a swinging arm. For these physiological reasons, small-breasted women usually predominate among professional female athletes and dancers. To the pleasure of manufacturers, the fitness and jogging craze that began in the Seventies created a new demand for a firm, sturdy sports bra, the equivalent of a jockstrap, that would minimize bobbing.

A woman who is larger than a C-cup will never race like the swift Atalanta no matter what brassiere she puts on, and a woman who needs a D or larger may never be free of minor discomfort in her everyday life. The cantilever principle of the brassiere that projects the breasts forward by suspending the weight from the shoulders causes its own considerable problems. Women who are Ds or double Ds typically suffer from nagging lower backaches and painful grooves where the bra straps have cut into the flesh.

Big breasts are one of many factors that have slowed women

down in the competitive race of life. Symbolically, in the conservative Fifties, when American women were encouraged to stay at home, the heavily inflated bosom was celebrated and fetishized as the feminine ideal. In decades of spirited feminist activity such as the Twenties and the present when women advance into untraditional jobs, small, streamlined breasts are glorified in fashion. Styles in breasts even seem to differ across the country. On the fast-tempoed, businesslike East Coast, plastic surgeons report that the current trend is towards reductions for physical comfort, while California starlets and housewives on the Hollywood fringe still go in for augmentations, as did many Asian prostitutes during the Vietnam war in order to appeal to American GIs.

A famous speciality act on the strip show and topless bar circuit features a performer in Day-Glo pasties or fringed tassels who twirls her long breasts this way and that until there is only a blur of motion. Patrons find this amusing. I am reminded of Desmond Morris (did he once watch a tassel twirler semaphoring in the dark?), who proposed in *The Naked Ape* that the full female breast evolved 'to make the frontal region more stimulating' to men. Teleological arguments aside, the cultural belief that breasts are primarily decorative and intrinsically provocative seems related historically in Western civilization to the elimination of the routine sight of breasts as a means of nourishing the young.

The American male's breast fixation dates from the war years of the Forties and remains unmatched throughout the world for obsessional fervour. Perhaps it can be partially understood as symptomatic of a new imperialist nation's desire to overcome or transform the childhood experience of nestling in dependence against the mother's bosom, or perhaps in the theory that Americans were fighting a Puritan heritage that believed all displays of sex and sexuality to be shameful. But we must admit that the national breast obsession is often less than amicable and frequently is downright unfriendly. The phantasmagorical spectre of the engulfing super-breast that has appeared in the work of Philip Roth and Woody Allen is more alarming than sexual, and slangy familiarities such as boobs, jugs and titties are basically hostile appraisals, despite attempts by some women to incorporate these contemptuous descriptions into their own vocabulary as hip terms of demystified endearment.

Who can blame women for being confused about their breasts?

And what good does it do to point to our bare-breasted sisters in other cultures, for we have seen too many pictures in *National Geographic* of wizened old females with sagging, shrivelled teats or with udderlike breasts that hang forlornly to the waist. No, not sexy. Not pretty and attractive. Entirely too remindful of the she-animal function, of milking the cow until she runs dry. Who wants to dwell on the thought that breasts can look like udders, that breasts *are* udders, dry, full, swollen, dripping with milk, squeezed, sucked on, raw, tender, in pain – and ultimately used up and withered. No, we're Marilyn Monroe in her calendar pose. We're Friday-night entries in a college town wet-T-shirt contest. We float down the avenue in a Maidenform bra and the nipples don't show.

How ironic that the sight of a mother breast-feeding her baby is unnerving to many of the same people who like to see – or to show – some cleavage in a dinner dress. In a curious reversal the suckling infant becomes the embarrassing stand-in for the adult male lover. The nipple tease is the historic basis for décolletage in fashion: a certain amount of exposure is sexy but an accidental display of the areola is crudely beyond the pale. It is still considered rather risqué in some quarters to go braless, not necessarily because of the jiggle and bounce but because nipples have a spunky way of asserting themselves according to their own agenda. Nipples and lactation appear to be a problem – yet nipples and milk ducts are really what breasts are all about. Not surprisingly, although the erectile tissue is present, masculine sexuality has rarely featured or even admitted its own nipple responsiveness as a source of erogenous pleasure. (When and if it does, will men grow shy about going shirtless?) The little boy who draws two dark, angry circles on the poster of a fully clothed woman has already absorbed society's lesson: the nipples on his chest are invulnerable and sexless but a girl's are shameful and dirty. And the nursing mother suffused with sensual feelings when the child is at her breast may wonder if her response is wrong or indecent.

After decades of frantic obsession, breasts evidently were such a thoroughly colonized province of masculine sexuality that the sight of a braless woman on the street in the late 1960s could inspire a strong negative reaction. The hoots and catcalls eventually sub-sided, but the initial emotion was something akin to rage. It was as if men had come to believe that taking off a brassiere somehow was their right and privilege. Understandably, many women also shared the point of view that a braless woman was deliberately provoking dangerous attention. In discussions of rape one heard, 'Well, what do those young girls expect when they go around braless?'

No one in the women's movement ever burned a bra in public protest, yet as soon as feminists began to march, the myth of bra burners spread like wildfire in the nation's media, and the flames were fanned by journalists who should have known better. As near as I can figure out, the legend may have started innocently enough by some feature writer searching for a clever phrase. Militant war resisters had burned their draft cards at public bonfires, so it was laughably imaginative to apply the metaphor to militant feminists, some of whom indeed were braless. Bra burning suggested a wanton, fiery destruction of safe, familiar values. The imagery symbolized the feared feminist assault on all established traditions that kept women and their sexual nature confined and contained in an orderly fashion. A bra burner might be a bomb thrower, if she weren't so silly and self-destructive. And so the myth caught on, for it struck at the heart of feminine insecurity – the fear of not being supported and protected, not only socially and economically but in a vulnerable aspect of bodily shape.

The ideal feminine shape has always been subject to change, not only structurally by means of foundation garments, but by the amount of flesh that has been considered desirable in a given age. Botticelli's Venus is slender enough for the 1980s but Tintoretto's Susannah might disappoint today's Elders with her gargantuan buttocks and thighs. Alas, the twenty-five plump lovelies who loll about *The Turkish Bath* by Ingres look as though they might have a trial membership in a reducing salon. To conform to a fashionable body, today's woman wants smaller breasts and hips than she did at the turn of the century when the billowy Gibson Girl with the sway-backed figure represented a voluptuous ideal, or when Florenz Ziegfeld glorified the Lillian Russell-type showgirl in his *Follies* and declared that feminine perfection was 36–26–38, with a decided accent on the hips.

Statuesque Lillian was much larger than that. Although she was mum about her lower proportions, her bosom and waistline measured 42 inches and 27 inches respectively with the help of tight lacing. Her friendly rival Anna Held, Ziegfeld's headliner and wife, was under five feet tall and plump, but her vital statistics were 36–20–36 when she put on her Parisian corsets. When Held died of a bone disease at the age of forty-five, stories circulated that she had had two ribs surgically removed to narrow her spectacular waist, but these were ghoulish rumours and nothing more. The important point is that at the time of Held's death in 1918, the hourglass body she exemplified had already been replaced by a thinner, less exaggerated shape, the bosomless look of the uncorseted flapper.

In the 1950s the bathing beauty who hoped to get a Hollywood contract displayed her pulchitrude at 35–25–35 – an inch thinner in the bust and waist and three inches thinner in the hips than Ziegfeld's ideal, but her breasts could hit the tape to male applause at forty inches or more in the manner of Jayne Mansfield without being considered top-heavy. For street wear she usually wore a waist-cincher to nip in her middle. However, within a decade the typical starlet with the busty chest and the wiggly rear had become a fashion liability, too much of a muchness, even for the beach. She didn't look good in a bikin – there was too much overhang in all directions – and that was the start of her downfall.

Of all the fashion changes that revolutionized the female body in the 1960s, the French bikini deserves special credit, for when this import hit the American shoreline the reverberations were shocking. Named for an obscure Pacific atoll that was used for atomic testing, the bikini was considered wildly daring in the Fifties. A decade later it had become *the* bathing suit of choice. Although European women of all shapes and sizes felt free to sun themselves in the tiny, unstructured bandannas, a Puritanical American sensibility viewed the body inside the bikini with a more critical eye. Fleshy curves that spilled out of the Band-Aid top and postage-stamp bottom looked gross. A less endowed figure looked more aesthetically pleasing. Overall slenderness, not just at the waistline, became crucial at the beach.

The Sixties also marked a revolution in street wear, made possible by new artificial fibres. In the designs of Courrèges, Saint Laurent and others, the belted waistline summarily vanished, and a doll-like thinness replaced the cinched waist with fullness above and below that characterized the Fifties figure. Pucci's clingy silk jerseys looked best with a bra-slip and panty-hose, not with a girdle, and Jacqueline Kennedy in the White House, a determined dieter and a conscientious follower of fashion, looked adorable in A-lines (and later in minis). American fashion in the restless, youth-oriented

Sixties was reaching for a radical ideal, and in 1967 a teenage British model named Twiggy, ninety-two pounds on a five-foot-seven-inch frame, with no breasts and hips to speak of, was promoted as the body type of mature women's desire.

With the passing of the girdle, in part because it spoiled the line as clothes grew clingier but also because its regimentation was out of keeping with the turbulent times, the average woman was forced to assume direct responsibility for the shape of her body. Not since the Twenties had a woman's figure been expected to stand on its own without a foundation garment, and the Twenties vogue was not only shortlived, it had made allowances for hips. Florenz Ziegfeld happened to be right in his ideal proportions. It is a fact of genetics that most women are built wider below the waist than above. The war of attrition against hips and thighs began in the Forties when women were still in the thrall of the two-way stretch. In the full-scale battle that developed, a campaign of diet and exercise that causes more frustration and tears of self-hatred than loss of real inches, there is a poignant illustration of the feminine aesthetic at odds with femaleness in its natural state. Bottom-heavy has been out of style for forty years.

Once it was conventional to think of models as tall young women with good bone structure who were forced to lose one-third of their normal weight because, poor creatures sipping their bouillon, the body photographed heavier than it looked in real life. But model thinness is no longer considered extreme. The Seventies popularized the sylphlike vision of the ballerina on pointe, and she herself is thinner and more exquisitely ethereal than ever before in the history of dance, competing for weight loss with other members of the company and subsisting on Tab and coffee with Sweet'n' Low between arduous classes. After her White House years, Jacqueline Kennedy got even skinnier to stay in fashion, Pat Nixon and Rosalynn Carter matched each other ounce for vanished ounce, and Nancy Reagan nibbles little more than grapes and lettuce to keep the right shape for her Galanos gowns. Presidents' wives who pose several times a day for photographs seem no less determined to stay thin than models and ballerinas, or the 'new' Diana Ross, or the 'new' Gilda Radner, and they are hardly alone in this intense form of feminine competition that takes the form of denial of food.

A higher basal metabolism enables men to burn up calories and expend physical energy at a faster rate than women. Not only can they eat more cake and ice cream to fill out a larger frame, but because of their dimorphic muscle mass they can eat more cake and ice cream without its turning to fat. A man may consume 50 per cent more calories than a woman in the course of a day without gaining weight, or at least without worry that he might be getting hippy. If one likes to eat well and would like to keep thin, one has to concede that here is an arena in which the male has a decided advantage. Men and women do not approach the dinner table from a position of equality until they reach old age, when the metabolic differences taper off. Even when men do decide to watch their consumption, it is usually fear of cholesterol and heart attack that provides the impetus – important, life-threatening stuff, not the lack of attractiveness in a spreading belly. (Gay men worry about keeping their figures 'just like a woman'. In a sexual marketplace controlled by male values, those who are trying to please had better look good.)

The American feminine obsession with weight goes beyond sexual differences in caloric conversion, beyond the issue of sex appeal, and beyond the intriguing question of how to cope with a female reproductive tendency towards fleshiness in a fast-moving, self-conscious, much-photographed era. In *Competing with the Sylph*, Dr L. M. Vincent makes the sage observation that slenderness and refinement have become synonymous to striving women. Indeed, the saying attributed to socialites, 'You can never be too thin or too rich,' seems to illustrate this theme. Dieting is an act of choice confined to privileged people who have access to a surplus of good food. When there is not enough food to go around, emaciation is a sign of poverty, not of will-power or chic. The typical adolescent anorectic usually comes from a privileged background and she is often described as an over-achieving perfectionist whose obsessive pursuit of thinness has crossed the line into self-destruction. In a characteristically feminine way, ambition in women frequently expresses itself in meaningless or destructive exaggerations of the cultural ideal: the smallest foot, the narrowest waist, the biggest breast, etcetera. Granted that the anorectic suffers from a deep psychological disturbance, but if she lived in another age, perhaps the one that Zola brought to life in *Nana*, she might stuff herself with cream-filled cakes and hope the poundage would settle gracefully on her thighs, or chest, or arms or wherever it might win approval.

Most women do not carry the desire for slenderness to anorectic extremes, but fad diets and wonder plans usually are not unknown to us, and we maintain an eternal vigilance against the slice of bread, the potato chip, the plate of fettuccine or the extra mouthfuls of steak that we know would make us happy, at least while we were chewing. I rarely consume as much food as I would like to. An excellent dinner in good company is one of the rewards of life that never fails, but I am too competitive to stand by and watch my middle thicken while other women parade their thinness like an Olympic medal. Dieting is the chief form of competition among women today, at least among upwardly mobile women who strive to perfect the feminine illusion as they strive in other ways to achieve success.

Despite genetic variation, rarely is more than one type of female physique given sexual adulation in a given age, and the imposition of a single ideal pits woman against woman in a peculiar form of physical struggle. A popular chorus in traditional blues music goes like this: 'I'm a big fat mama with plenty of meat shaking on my bones, and when I shake, a skinny woman loses her home.' The skinny woman and the big mama are competitors in song because with each change in the standards of attractiveness they are competitors in life, vying for attention as a means of survival.

Hippy or scrawny, busty or flat, the general principle governing the feminine body is not subject to change. How one looks is the chief physical weapon in female-against-female competition. Appearance, not accomplishment, is the feminine demonstration of desirability and worth. In striving to approach a physical ideal, by corsetry in the old days or by a cottage-cheese-and-celery diet that begins tomorrow, one arms oneself to fight the competitive wars. Feminine armour is never metal or muscle but, paradoxically, an exaggeration of physical vulnerability that is reassuring (unthreatening) to men. Because she is forced to concentrate on the minutiae of her bodily parts, a woman is never free of self-consciousness. She is never quite satisfied, and never secure, for desperate, unending absorption in the drive for a perfect appearance – call it feminine vanity – is the ultimate restriction on freedom of mind.

Hair

I have been at odds with the hair on my head for most of my life. Neither straight nor curly, it is merely wayward. Left on its own it is messy, unkempt. People have said nice things about many parts of me but no one, not even my hairdresser, has ever said that my hair was my crowning glory.

I harbour a deep desire to wear my hair long because, like all the women I know, I grew up believing that long hair is irrefutably feminine. I could certainly use the advantage that long hair confers, but I happen to look terrible when my hair is long. I know what some people think about short hair – they say short hair is mannish, dykey. I could risk wearing my hair quite short if I wore makeup and dresses, or put on some earrings, or if I weren't a feminist and an ambitious careerist, or if I were married and had two children, but close-cropped hair on someone like me adds to an image I do not mean to project. I am aware of the conflict. I need to go my own way, yet I also need to stand on the safe side of femininity. So I keep my hair at a middling length and fret about its daily betrayal.

My hair and I have been struggling towards a feminine accommodation since I first discovered boys and bought a white angora sweater. I was clever in school but I did not excel at pin curls. When technology advanced, my girlfriends became adept at big rollers but I could not learn to sleep eight hours without moving my head. There was a time that stretched over many years when I placed myself in permanent bondage to Elizabeth Arden. There, two lunch hours a week, I was shampooed and curled with setting lotion, winding papers, plastic rollers and metal clips, gently cushioned around the ears and forehead with cotton wool, tied in a pink hairnet and placed under a hot dryer for thirty-five minutes. Mercifully released, I was unpinned, unwound, brushed out, teased and fluffed into a fair approximation of the season's latest fashion. After a blast of noxious spray I was sent out the door in a forged state of feminine chic that lasted for the rest of the day – that is, if it didn't rain. I always felt like a poser at Arden's. Not once did I let them shape and polish my nails, not once did I submit to the ritual of the pedicure, the waxing of the legs, or the mysterious rites of the Full Day Treatment. They must have sensed my lack of commitment. But they had a powerful hold on my hair. They tugged at the roots of my deepest insecurity.

At Arden's my feminine insecurities changed with each new style. When the look was sleek my problem was too much volume, which required thinning. When I wore the pixie cut my problem was a low, untidy hairline at the nape of my neck which required shaving. When the style turned bouffant I was informed that back-combing disguised a certain flatness at the back of my skull but the scraggly wisps on my forehead were hopeless. When the blunt cut became the rage my hairdresser threw up his scissors in disgust. My wayward waves would not be blunted. I crept out of his presence defeated, for my worst nightmare had been realized. Despite the best professional help my hair was a failure.

In the 1960s the balance of power between client and hairdresser subtly shifted. When the hippies let their hair grow long, nobody was more surprised than I that some of the young men had beautiful tresses while some just looked messy like me. Black women were letting their hair go natural, creating a more permissive attitude for all women, and the hand-held dryer offered liberation from the beauty parlour wash and set. Finally, the feminist movement made the entire matter of bandbox neatness, the 'set' look, seem ridiculously old-fashioned. In principle, a good cut and a blow-dryer were all one needed.

But just when the winds of change were finally blowing in my direction, my hair was struck by a cruel new problem. It is called premature greying – is greying ever not premature to its victims? – and it requires the application of a colour solution that comes in a bottle. I did not come easily to the decision to colour my hair despite those persuasive Clairol commercials. I thought, and still think, that artifical colour is a shameful concession to all the wrong values. Wasn't it high time, I argued to my mirror and my friends, to put up a fight against the unfair double standard that says some grey at the temples makes a man look wise but makes a woman look like she doesn't care about her appearance? But it wasn't pleasant to bear living witness day after day in all sorts of social encounters to the sorry fact that grey hair does not look youthful, dazzling, feminine, with-it. I hated my martyrdom. I needed to look as good as I could. I wanted to look pretty. Vanity (or was it competitive pragmatism?) won out, with a big assist from a determined friend who came over to the house one Christmas and with lots of teenage giggling poured a bottle of Loving Care on my head. My ambivalence vanished with the first simple one-step application.

From time immemorial, hair has been used to make a visual statement, for the body's most versatile raw material can be cut, plucked, shaved, curled, straightened, braided, greased, bleached, tinted, dyed and decorated with precious ornaments and totemic fancies. A change in the way one wears one's hair can affect the look of the face and alter a mood. A uniform hair style can set a group of people apart from others and signify conformity or rebellion, devotion to God or indulgence in sensual pleasures. Hair worn in a polarized manner has served to indicate the masculine and the feminine, the slave and the ruler, the young, the old, the virgin, the married, the widowed, the mourning.

In the Western world, parental concern that the sex of an infant not be mistaken led to the social convention of the pink blanket or the blue. The second convention of social importance is the haircut. Shorn of ringlets a toddler is certifiably a boy, and woe unto the mother who delays for too long this critical event, for she will be accused of trying to sissify her son. Yet the rock-bound belief that short hair makes a boy and long hair makes a girl is as arbitrary as blanket colour. Given a sample lock for analysis, an expert would not be able to say if it came from the head of a man or a woman. There are known racial differences in the way hair grows on the human scalp, but the only true sexual difference is the phenomenon of balding.

Unhappily for white men, baldness is an inherited characteristic that afflicts Caucasian males more frequently than other racial and sexual groups. Genes for baldness are carried without regard to sex on the autosomal chromosomes of males and females, but they are less frequent in the genetic pools of blacks and Orientals. Even though white men and women both carry the baldness genes, it takes the androgens, the hormones that induce male sexual development, to make the characteristic express itself. About 60 per cent of all white men show some degree of hair loss by the time they reach the age of fifty, and a receding hairline or a bald spot at the back of the head may begin to show when a man is in his early twenties. A similar pattern of thinning hair occurs later and less extensively in white women.

Like the big nose on the male proboscis monkey, baldness is troubling to the neo-Darwinians. They can't figure out what possible advantage it might give to the male sex, and to white males in particular. Using their favourite line of argument, one could propose that baldness serves an important function in sexual selection by warning a young Caucasian female that here is a fellow who would not make a desirable mate because he is past his prime and too old to provide for her and the children. But I don't like this sort of argument. I prefer to see baldness, like many other natural differences between men and women, as merely accidental, a hormonal happening that has no larger evolutionary meaning whatsoever.

But however irrelevant baldness might be to reproduction and evolution, it appears to be the key to one of the more tenacious beliefs about masculine men and feminine women, for the idea that long hair is feminine and that men by contrast should wear their hair short took hold and flourished in white European civilization, while in the East and in Africa, where men seldom go bald, this artifical polarity was either reversed or met with great resistance, or was never taken up at all.

Egyptian pharaohs and their royal families had their heads plucked clean of natural hair and covered with wigs that were sexually distinct, while their slaves wore their own hair by law. Among the Masai and other African and Indian tribes that still hold to their traditional customs, an imposing mass of long hair ornamented with shells, feathers or beads remains a proud masculine emblem, inspired perhaps by the lion's mane or the colourful plumage of exotic birds, while the heads of tribal women go unadorned, covered or shaved. A long tangle of braids that seems to frighten the white folk is a common sight on the island of Jamaica, where male Rastafarians made the dreadlocks a part of their religion. The great classic periods in Japanese art show that long, elaborate hair styles were a vogue for men and women, although an expert can detect a sexual difference in a decorative comb. During the tenth-century Heian civilization Japanese noblemen wore their long hair in a topknot while court ladies wore theirs loose and flowing. Oriental hair is usually suited to luxuriant growth, so it is not surprising that both sexes in Japan and China treasured long hair until Western influence established a new concept of masculine appearance. It may be recalled from the lessons of American history how the pigtail on the Chinese railroad worker became an object of racist scorn.

Belief in the intrinsic femininity of long hair took centuries to establish even in the West, for an older tradition identified long hair with physical strength, holiness and other masculine values. Luxuriant tresses are not significantly associated with feminine beauty in the Old Testament, but references to long hair as a sign of beauty and strength in men abound. Samson's uncut hair was the secret source of his fabled power, as the wicked Delilah discovered. The beautiful Absalom had long, heavy hair but it got entangled in an oak tree, where King David's soldiers finished him off.

Etruscan warriors prided themselves on their noble tresses and the soldiers of Sparta spent hours combing and preening their manes before they went into battle. But Caesar's legionnaires who set out to conquer long-haired Gaul were close-cropped and clean-shaven, and the apostle Paul, who lived under Roman rule, made the grand mistake of assuming that the customs of Roman warfare were a natural rule of God. Christianity owes to Saint Paul the erroneous belief that the length of male and female hair is a gender characteristic.

It was Paul who told the Corinthians that a woman's long hair is 'a glory to her,' but the saint did not mean his words as a compliment to feminine beauty. He was laying down the creed that Christian men should offer up prayer with their heads uncovered because they were created as the image and glory of God, but women should cover their heads in church because they were created as the glory of man. 'Judge in yourselves,' he wrote in his epistle, 'Is it comely that a woman pray unto God uncovered? Does not even nature itself teach you that if a man have long hair it is a shame unto him? But if a woman have long hair it is a glory to her: for her hair is given her for covering.'

Paul's thoughts about hair come after his famous creed that 'the head of every man is Christ; and the head of the woman is the man.' 'It follows,' wrote Saint Chrysostom, 'that being covered is a mark of subjection and authority. For it induces her to look down and be ashamed and preserve entire her proper virtue.'

Puritan moralists in sixteenth- and seventeenth-century England hammered away at this theme. The feminine woman, the virtuous woman, the woman who knew her place, was the female who wore her hair long, neatly arranged, with a concealing cap on her head. A wife's long hair, railed the pamphleteer Philip Stubbes, was her God-given 'signe of subjection' before her husband and master, 'as the Apostle proveth.' Pamphleteer William Prynne also called up the apostle's proof. Women's long hair, he echoed, was something that 'God and nature have given them for a covering, a token of subjection, and a natural badge to distinguish them from men.' Denouncing the worldly fashions of his day – 'our shorn English viragoes' – Prynne blasted off, 'A woman with cut hair is a filthy spectacle and much like a monster.'

So the male moralists protested, but always with the understanding that although a woman's long hair might be sacred it was also profane. Since it was given her by God to cover her nakedness, it was also a distressing symbol of her sexual nature. Out of control – unpinned, dishevelled or free of a concealing cap – it was invested with dangerous powers. In myth the beautiful Lorelei, who sang while she combed her long blonde hair, lured sailors to wreck their boats on treacherous rocks. Sight of Medusa's hair of living snakes turned men into stone. The long, loose tresses that covered the nakedness of Lady Godiva as she rode her horse through town to honour her husband's oath seem less a 'sign of subjection' than a very sexy image, and although it was hardly Saint Luke's intention, the unnamed sinner of his Gospel (often confused with Mary Magdalene) who penitently wiped the feet of Jesus with her hair became a paradigm of sensuality to Renaissance artists who delighted in painting this Biblical scene.

In *Paradise Lost*, Milton crystallizes the theme of subjection and feminine sexuality when he describes the hair of Eve as seen by Satan:

> She, as a veil down to the slender waist,
> Her unadorned golden tresses wore
> Dishevelled, but in wanton ringlets waved,
> As the vine curls her tendrils – which implied
> Subjection, but required with gentle sway,
> And by her yielded, by him best received,
> Yielded with coy submission, modest pride
> And sweet, reluctant, amorous delay.

A woman's act of unpinning and letting down a cascade of long hair is interpreted as a highly erotic gesture, a release of inhibiting restraints, a sign of sexual readiness which may be an enticement or a snare, a frightening danger or, in some cases, a possible salvation. According to psychologist Bruno Bettelheim, the prince who called to Rapunzel to let down her hair was pleading for rescue from an impotent condition. The erotic appeal of a full mass of hair was recognized in the extreme by the denial of a natural head of hair to the Catholic nun and the orthodox Jewish wife, an attempt to desexualize them in the eyes of strangers. After the liberation of France in 1944, the common form of retribution inflicted upon a woman accused of consorting with Germans was to forcibly shave her head and parade her in shame through the village, a far cry from the ride of Godiva.

In addition to the erotic value attached to sheer length, elaborately arranged coiffures requiring the work, and often the hair, of others were regarded historically as imposing signs of aristocratic grandeur. Marie Antoinette and Lady Pompadour are the enduring examples, but the wigs of British barristers still derive from this conception of the noble head. Under the laws of supply and demand, impoverished women were encouraged to view their own hair as peasant women in Europe and Asia were expected, as wet nurses, to view the milk from their breasts. Hair and milk were exploitable commodities that could serve the upper classes, an exploitation less stigmatized (and less financially rewarding) than the selling of sex. Liane de Pougy, the great courtesan of France during the Belle Epoque and herself of middle-class origins, remarked with some surprise in her diary that daughters of the poor quite often had glorious heads of hair. Of sociological note, the elaborate coif lost its usefulness as a status symbol in America during the 1950s when the beehive hairdo became identified with tackiness and the lower classes.

We remember the Roaring Twenties as a time when women demonstrated their newfound emancipation by bobbing their hair, though the trend actually began during the First World War. The flapper experience has been trivialized as just so many flat-bosomed, short-skirted, short-haired debs drinking gin and dancing on tables, but the decision to bob, like the decision to go without a corset, was for many women an anguished act of rebellion.

Two classic American short stories published less than fifteen years apart illustrate the deep sense of loss from a romantic male perspective when a woman cuts off her hair. In O. Henry's 'The

Gift of the Magi' (1906) Jim and Della sacrifice their proudest treasures to buy Christmas gifts for each other. Jim sells a gold watch that belonged to his father and grandfather to purchase a set of jewelled tortoise-shell combs for Della, whose hair ripples and shines 'like a cascade of brown waters.' But Della has sold her brown cascade to buy a watch fob for Jim. O. Henry's tale is an exquisite parable of good intentions and crossed purpose and it deserves its place as the ranking Christmas story in American literature, but the notion of a hank of hair as a woman's greatest treasure is sad and, frankly, demeaning.

When F. Scott Fitzgerald published 'Bernice Bobs Her Hair' in the *Saturday Evening Post* in 1920, the majority of young women were cutting their hair not for the price it could bring or because they were copycats but because they wanted to be free of a tiresome bother, yet that is not what Fitzgerald chose to see. Bernice is a simple girl from Eau Claire who visits her city cousin Marjorie, a modern, popular flirt. To get attention from Marjorie's fast crowd, Bernice announces that she is going to have her hair bobbed at the Sevier Hotel barber shop. Forced to put up or shut up by Marjorie, Bernice marches in dread to the barber – even he is aghast – and has her 'dark brown glory' chopped off. Fitzgerald mourns the results: 'Her face's chief charm had been a Madonna-like simplicity. Now that was gone and she was – well, frightfully mediocre – not stagey; only ridiculous, like a Greenwich Villager who had left her spectacles at home.' Bernice had been had. She goes home to Eau Claire, but not before she performs her act of revenge. While Marjorie is asleep Bernice takes a pair of scissors and snips off her cousin's blonde braids.

Female competition and flapper confusion are Fitzgerald's themes, but he and O. Henry turn their tales on a deeper message: the tragedy of a young woman who foolishly discards her greatest asset. Romantic sentiment over the nature of feminine beauty is the heart of the matter. If one doesn't feel that short hair is a tragic feminine loss, the stories lose much of the poignant drama.

Decades before O. Henry and Fitzgerald put their words to paper, Louisa May Alcott used the drama of shorn female tresses in *Little Women* (1868). Her heroine and alter ego, Jo March, sells her long thick hair so her mother can travel to her sick father's bedside. Meg, Beth, Amy and Marmee are full of tender compassion, for coltish, plain Jo has sacrificed her 'one beauty.' Jo has her arguments marshalled. Her head feels 'deliciously light' and cool and soon she will have 'a curly crop which will be boyish, becoming, and easy to keep in order.' But even sturdy Jo is not immune to the sense of feminine loss, and we know that 'boyish' is a loaded word. Late that night Meg hears her sister stifle a sob.

'Jo, dear, what is it? Are you crying about Father?'

'No, not now.'

'What then?'

'My – my hair!'

Meg comforts, Jo rallies, but privately Meg holds to her opinion that Jo's cropped head 'looked comically small on her tall sister's shoulders.' Meg's reservations illustrate the unwritten rule of compensatory femininity and the aesthetic ideal. If Jo had been shorter, prettier and more graceful, the boyish trim might not have been such a disaster. It might even have looked adorable on someone like Meg, whose 'lady' credentials were in order.

Bernice cuts her hair to be modern and popular with boys, Della performs the sacrificial act to buy her husband a present, Jo March cuts and sells her 'one beauty' to help her father and the family's finances, but Alcott at least allows her heroine to argue that short hair is a real advantage – it is 'deliciously light' and 'easy to keep in order.'

When women with braided coils that had not been cut since childhood arrived at the emotional decision to get rid of and be done with them, they needed to supply the men in their lives with an explanation for what was taken as a rash, destructive gesture. Practicality and manageability, they argued. Health and cleanliness, they protested. Sticky pomades and greasy dressings made long hair a hospitable nest for dirt, soot and head lice, and thorough washings were frequent and troublesome, particularly for the urban poor who lived in infested tenements and shared a communal tub and sink. But even beyond the problems of hygiene there were other vexations a bob might cure. Freedom from hairpins, freedom from holding combs, freedom from rats (the irksome rolls of wire mesh that supported the upsweep), freedom from switches (the store-bought pieces that filled out a thin coiffure), freedom from fear of a strong gust of wind, freedom from boring, repetitive hours spent washing and drying and brushing and combing and dressing and braiding and pinning and winding and curling on damnable rags, and freedom, simply, from a heavy, burdensome load.

But the men, so proprietary about women's hair, were not easily won over. They howled in rage. And although the issue was cast by feminists in practical terms – Charlotte Perkins Gilman took to the lecture ciruit to champion short hair as sensible and sanitary – it was glamour in the person of Irene Castle that probably caused a national change of mind. When America's favourite dancing partner cut her hair and wrapped a string of pearls around her forehead, the daring act became the Castle Clip, and suddenly short hair was romantic, chic and very classy.

Irene Castle claimed full credit for the short-hair craze. 'I believe I am largely blamed for the homes wrecked and engagements broken because of clipped tresses,' she gaily wrote in the *Ladies Home Journal*, taking care to warn her readers that the new style was not for every head – an older, greying woman might look 'a bit kittenish and not quite dignified' – and she cautioned that 'rather small features also help.' Castle was rich and famous, a glamorous star for whom the ordinary rules did not apply, but for women who could not dance their way to economic independence the bob still was fraught with role rebellion.

Charlotte Perkins Gilman, who had rescued herself from a life of neurasthenic invalidism, was among the first to understand. *Herland*, her feminist utopian novel of 1915, told of an athletic, happy, all-female society where everyone wore her hair short, 'some few inches at most . . . all light and clean and fresh looking.' A male visitor to Herland complains, 'If only their hair were long, they would look so much more feminine,' but in the wonderful manner of utopian fiction he is quickly converted.

In March of 1916 Gilman addressed the Working Women's Protective Union in New York City with these words: 'It was not the Lord who gave men short hair while women's is long,' she told her audience. 'It was the scissors. I am not asking you to go home and cut your hair, though I think we would all be much cleaner and happier and more comfortable with it short. You wouldn't do it anyway. But I do ask you if this isn't a joke: If a woman – who has no more natural reason for wearing her hair long than a man – goes and cuts it off, people say, "Oh, shame: she wants to be a man!" But what do they say when the case is reversed? Whiskers are a man's natural prerogative, but now when he shaves off his whiskers and goes with a smooth face, why don't they say to him, "You want to look like a woman!"'

Charlotte Gilman had taken on convention, and the following day *The New York Times* took on Mrs Gilman. 'City Sends Up Mighty Protest Against the Fiat That Beauty Should Be Cropped,' the *Times* headlined, continuing, 'Sounds End of Romance/History, Literature, and Poetry Must Be Made Over to Meet Mrs Gilman's Proposal.' The satirical piece, run as straight news, pretended to quote the man in the street: 'Women's beauty is in her hair, and it's her first duty to be good-looking.' There was also a waggish response from a barber: 'If a woman needs a haircut she may need a shave.' Citing 'great opposition among milliners,' the *Times* deadpanned, 'Makers of combs and hairpins, horse growers who furnish false hair, manufacturers of mirrors as well as publishers of style books are expected to organize a crusade against Mrs Gilman's idea.' From 'among the literati at Columbia' came the dire prediction that poets 'will talk no more of tresses but rather of pompadours and shaves.'

Funny stuff, but a mockery of the question. And beneath the mockery, the real concerns of men.

A woman's right to wear her hair short, and the social implications of her action, garnered as much newspaper space in the 1920s as the question of long hair on men received some forty years later, and for similar reasons. Well-meaning people were affronted by what they considered to be a frightening challenge to the conventions of the masculine-feminine polarity. They responded with an anger that they themselves poorly understood, and they covered their confusion with ringing laughter and pious sentiments over decency, dignity and moral codes.

Five years after Gilman's lecture the issue of bobbed hair could no longer be treated as a joke. Chicago's largest department store, Marshall Field, publicly dismissed a salesgirl, Miss Helen Armstrong, on the grounds that her bob was not 'dignified.' Other Marshall Field employees who dared to cut were told to report to work in hairnets until their bobs grew out. The liberal conscience was finally pricked. That repository of social concern *The Nation* rose to the defence of short-haired women in a stirring editorial. Marshall Field, the magazine charged, 'was guilty of an unwarrantable infringement of personal liberty.' *The New York Times* weighed the issue on its editorial page and conceded that 'Some women find that bobbed hair is convenient and sensible.'

As late as 1927 the women's magazines were still doing features on both sides of the hair-length question. Opera diva Mary Garden was called upon to tell the world why she made the decision to cut – 'I consider getting rid of our long hair one of the many little shackles that women have cast aside in their passage to freedom,' she wrote with conviction – and America's Sweetheart, Mary Pickford, defended her waist-length curls by pleading that if she took up the shears, her mother, her husband, her maid and, above all, her fans would never forgive her. 'Can you imagine a fairy princess with short, bobbed locks?' asked the silver screen's own princess. 'It is unthinkable and almost shocking.'

She was right. Who can imagine a fairy princess with hair that is anything but long and blonde, with eyes that are anything but blue, in clothes that are anything but a filmy drape of gossamer and gauze? The fairy princess remains one of the most powerful symbols of femininity the Western world has ever devised, and falling short of her role model, women are all feminine failures to some degree.

A shrewd businesswoman who was one of the founders of United Artists, Pickford hesitated to tamper with her personal trademark. She was the Girl with the Curl, and her fans wrote letters pleading with her not to cut her hair. 'I haven't the courage to fly in the face of their disapproval, nor have I the wish,' she admitted. 'For their love and affection and loyalty I owe them everything, and if curls are the price I shall pay it.' According to her biography the price was steep. When she was shooting a movie, it took Mary Pickford three hours each morning to wash, set and dry her naturally straight hair on rags and rollers. In humid weather she needed another hour in midday, while shooting came to a halt, to revive the drooping curls. But big, fat, sausage-shaped ringlets were a fantasy about what little girls should look like, and Mary Pickford was thirty-six years old at the time she made her public promise not to cut her golden curls. One year later, however, she did just that. A photograph of Pickford under the scissors was published in newspapers around the world with captions that mourned the end of an age of innocence. 'You would have thought I murdered someone,' she later said, 'and perhaps I had.'

Pickford wanted to play grownup parts in a grownup hairdo. 'It was a very sad business indeed to be made to feel that my success depended solely, or at least in large part, on a head of hair,' she wrote. But the public wanted the Girl with the Curl, and a few years after her publicized haircut, Mary Pickford retired from the screen.

Of all the wonders Hollywood has created, nothing can match the pantheon of celebrated blondes who have fed the fantasies of men and fuelled the aspirations of women ever since the flickering image began to move across the giant screen. Did Hollywood create the American cult of blondeness, or did it merely magnify the collective dreams of a melting pot that despite democratic intentions placed the highest value in feminine beauty on Nordic fairness and flaxen hair? Surely the dark-haired immigrant entrepeneurs from Eastern Europe and their first-generation sons who abandoned the steamy garment centre of New York to pioneer a motion picture empire in the sunshine of the West were fully aware that the visions of blonde loveliness they projected on to their screens bore no resemblance to their mothers and sisters, or to the women they might have been expected to marry. Those who hand-cranked the dream machine spun their own fantasies of California gold, angel-haired virgins and peroxide sirens who had never seen the inside of a ghetto.

In *Popcorn Venus*, her history of women in film, Marjorie Rosen suggests that from the beginning of the talking motion picture, hair style and hair colour eclipsed voice and talent in the making of a movie goddess. When it came to the machinery of sex appeal and hype, magnificent hair had an advantage over magnificent breasts and legs on the person of a manufactured star. With the help of artful studio hairdressers who could alter a hairline as easily as they could change a colour, and with studio publicists who could stretch a fact to make a story, a mass of healthy hair could be turned into a phenomenon of such magical unreality that mortal women flocked to the beauty parlour to achieve the effect for themselves. The blonde was enshrined for her blondeness, and it didn't matter if the inspiration began in a bottle. Brassy, wisecracking Jean Harlow skyrocketed to fame as the Platinum Bombshell in the 1930s and started a national craze for peroxide bleach. A decade later the sultry dip worn over one eye by diminutive, blonde Veronica Lake catapulted her to stardom as a siren of the screen. The Veronica Lake dip was copied in hair salons across the country and the Veronica Lake hairbrush was hawked by Fuller salesmen from door to door.

From 1941 to 1943 *Life* magazine ran five pictorial features on

Veronica Lake, and in retrospect they tell the brief story of her sudden rise and fall, a casualty of an unexpected collision between Hollywood hype and wartime propaganda. Two weeks before Pearl Harbor *Life* celebrated Veronica's hair as a national treasure, divulging the approximate number of hairs on her head (150,000), and reporting that the length was seventeen inches in front and twenty-four inches in back, falling eight inches below her shoulders. The silken cascade, *Life*'s readers learned, was shampooed twice, treated with oil and rinsed in vinegar each morning. Because the long blonde strands were so fine (.0024 inches in cross section) they tended to snag on buttons and bracelets, and more than once Veronica had singed her golden treasure while smoking a cigarette.

In 1943, alas, the peekaboo blonde was a war menace. Defence-plant workers with the Veronica Lake dip were getting their hair caught in the machines, and the War Production Board, promoting its own image of Rosie the Riveter, asked the star to give up her famous trademark 'for the duration.' On the advice of Paramount she posed again for *Life* with her golden tresses braided and pinned to her scalp and announced, 'Any woman who wears her hair over one eye is silly.' Veronica Lake had done her part for the war effort, but without her sultry, languid dip her movie career sputtered into oblivion. Other blondes soon rose to take her place, and each has had her season in the sun, and sometimes her own signature hairdo, like Veronica's or Farrah Fawcett's, that briefly becomes the national look of the glamorous American girl.

It is hard not to be influenced by the popular judgement that blondes are to the manner born, that whatever their individual features, they are prettier and luckier than dark-haired women, blessed by the Gods with a halo of good fortune. To be sure, I make my obeisance only before natural blondes, but this is a stubborn quirk that does not seem to be shared by the legions of men who are unabashed adorers of blondes, who will date only blondes, or who throw up their hands charmingly and confess that they have 'a thing' for blondes whether or not they are dark at the roots.

Blonde hair has been associated with the goodness of sunshine, the preciousness of spun gold, the purity of the Madonna, the excitement of paid-for love, and the innocent, pastoral vision in literature, myth and art – quite an impressive, if contradictory, set of values. Golden hair was definitely an attribute of feminine beauty in Imperial Rome, where it became the fashion for prostitutes and wealthy matrons to wear blonde wigs made of hair brought back from conquered Gaul. In fifteenth-century Florentine art, reddish gold and flaxen were the colours of choice to grace the heads of Botticelli's pagans as well as his Madonnas, and for the Annunciations, Adorations and Virgins with Child of Fra Angelico and Filippo Lippi.

When the farmland of the American Midwest was settled by fair-haired Protestants from Germany and Scandinavia while the Eastern industrial cities were filled with teeming masses of dark-haired Catholics and Jews from middle Europe, the dark-light, urban-rural dichotomy was given a firm geographical basis. The farmer's daughter was a living symbol of wheat and corn, of fresh milk and sweet creamery butter. When she ventured outside her ethnic circle, she became a rare exotic flower. Her pale hair and skin looked particularly feminine next to those of dark-haired, dark-skinned women: less aggressive and dynamic, more pleasing and mellow in their muted tones. Her pastel coloration seemed particularly effective in the city, where clamour, contrast and soot were symbols of masculine progress. The Nordic blonde might be tall and imposing, but her placid fairness served to neutralize the effect of her height.

America's cult of blondeness reached its zenith in the Forties and Fifties, ironically at the moment in history when Nazi Germany and the cult of Aryan supremacy went down to defeat. The differences between the two sets of values are important to examine. Aryan supremacy had equated pale hair in both sexes with strength, intelligence and superior racial stock, whereas blondeness American style is a glittering prize that men seek in women but don't give two hoots about for themselves, except for a small group within the homosexual community who trade on blond hair as a way of appealing to other men. In the American tradition, blondeness is not associated with strength or intelligence. On the contrary, 'dumb blonde' is practically one word on the lips of some people, and her innocent vapidity and daffy humour is counterposed to the loud, emotional intensity of know-it-all dark-haired women. (Even if the blonde is obviously smart and knowledgeable, she is perceived as less threatening or overbearing, and therefore more acceptably feminine, than her brunette sisters. There is no other way to explain the disproportionate number of blondes who hold coveted jobs as correspondents and newscasters on network television.)

Not surprisingly, America's most slavish blonde-lovers come from those obstreperous dark ethnic groupings that the Nazis despised, for on this the Aryan supremacist and the American blonde-fancier agree: the blonde looks coolly unflawed by a grubby, compromised past. In American democracy the son of an ethnic minority shows he is reaching high by having a blonde on his arm, or the picture of a blonde taped to his locker – and of course a woman can take practical steps to become one. Plausibility is only a minor consideration next to instant transformation, for the 'hot' blonde, ersatz and improbable, who bleaches out her own ethnic roots can expect to be admired too. Clairol's ingenious question, 'Is it true blondes have more fun?' was answered by Hollywood legend with an unfortunate twist. America's most tragic blondes, Jean Harlow and Marilyn Monroe, were patently false and celebrated as such – good time girls (as long as they lasted) of no indentifiable background, no parentage and no pedigree except for American blondeness and the egalitarian dream.

The irony was not lost on black women when Bo Derek, the blonde and perfect 'Ten,' was widely copied for her beaded braids – a style she had copied in turn from Cicely Tyson and some sophisticated black models who found the initial inspiration in African motifs. In jazz, rock music and hairdos it has been the fate of American blacks to see their originality exploited by the dominant white culture, but Bo Derek's braids caused a special black feminine anguish, for black women have suffered over their hair more than anyone else.

'Good' hair and 'bad' hair are subjective judgements that are based on aesthetic preference. 'Good' hair does not do a superior job of protecting the scalp or allowing it to breathe. 'Good' hair is silken and soft to the touch, it is full, pliant and yielding, the feminine ideal in matters of anatomy as well as in character and personality. And 'bad' hair – do we need to define that? 'Bad' hair is split and broken ends, hair that is limp and stringy, hair that is wiry and unmanageable or too thin to hold a set, hair that is coarse to the touch of the fingers, hair that is naturally wild and kinky.

'Mama' [moans Hagar], 'why don't he like my hair?'
'Milkman does too like your hair,' said Reba.

49

'No. He don't. But I can't figure out why. He never liked my hair.'

'Of course he likes it. How can he not like it?' asked Pilate.

'He likes silky hair . . . Curly, wavy, silky hair. He don't like mine.'

Pilate puts her hand on Hagar's head and trails her fingers through her granddaughter's soft damp wool. 'How can he not love your hair? It's the same hair that grows out of his own armpits. The same hair that grows up out of his crotch on up his stomach. All over his chest. The very same. It grows out of his nose, over his lips, and if he ever lost his razor it would grow all over his face. It's all over his head, Hagar. It's his hair too. He got to love it.'

'He don't love it at all. He hates it.'

'No he don't. He don't know what he loves, but he'll come around, honey, one of these days. How can he love himself and hate your hair?'

'He's never going to like my hair.'

'Hush, girl, hush.'

Toni Morrison placed this scene between a young black woman, her mother and grandmother near the end of her novel *Song of Solomon*, named after the Biblical verses of sensual love. Its mournful resolution – 'He's never going to like my hair' – has the finality of historic pain, for 'He,' whoever he is and whatever his colour, lives in white America where the standards of feminine beauty arose from a gene pool that was exclusively Caucasian and from cultural traditions brought over from Christian Europe.

Wild, springy hair was grandly positive in the African male tradition, a testament to virility and strength. By contrast the prototype feminine head was tightly cornrowed, covered or shaved. Forcibly exposed to the aesthetic and moral values of their white Christian masters, it was inevitable that American blacks would accept the judgement that this evidence of genetic heritage was difficult, shameful or bad. The celebration of Black Is Beautiful in the 1960s made pride in natural hair an easier matter for black men than for black women. Free of hot combs and straighteners, the Afro looked properly militant as a symbol of Black Power, but militance and femininity do not coexist with ease. The feminine Afro often had to be painstakingly teased to frame the face softly with a symmetrical halo.

Silky, long hair automatically inspires a cluster of preoccupied gestures that are considered sublimely feminine because they are sensuously self-involved: an absent-minded twisting of a stray curl, the freeing of loose ends that get caught under a coat collar, a dramatic toss of the entire mane, a brushing aside of the tendrils that fall so fetchingly across the forehead and into the eyes. A mass of long, soft hair is something to play with, a reassuring source of tactile sensation and a demanding presence that insists on the wearer's attention. Ntozake Shange sharply reminds us of these narcissistic feminine traits and how they exclude black women in her dramatic poem 'today i'ma be a white girl,' in which a black maid sarcastically reveals that 'the first thing a white girl does in the morning is fling her hair,' and that she falls back on flinging or swinging her hair whenever she is at a loss for something to do.

Everything is relative, of course, and white women know that the kind of hair that can be swung or flung gracefully is in limited supply. An equal amount belongs by genetic heritage to men, and most of it in the world's population belongs to Asians, but it wasn't until rock musicians and other youths of the white counter-culture let their hair grow to shoulder length in the Sixties, chiefly in defiance of militaristic values during the Vietnam war, that the 'intrinsic' feminine gestures associated with loose, flowing hair began to show their true, genderless nature.

It was too much to expect that the majority of middle-class men in the United States would risk growing their hair long in emphatic response to changing sex roles or as an expression of their sensitive nature. The militarism of the army brush cut and the corporate efficiency of the short barbered trim were too thoroughly identified with masculine power. By the late 1970s long-haired men were out of fashion (and punk rockers of the Eighties wore their hair short, tough and ugly). In addition to wanting a hard-edged, masculine look for the competitive Eighties, I suppose the former long-hairs got tired of the endless bother.

Women, of course, are not yet entitled to be free of the bother. The hairdresser's appointment is as permanent a fixture on the calendar of the female executive as the lunchtime squash date on the calendar of her male counterpart. A television anchorman ducks in and out of the make-up room before he faces the camera; his female co-host must allot time as well for the curling iron and the fluff-out before she is deemed fit to be seen by the judgemental public. An evening out on the town is ritualistically preceded by an afternoon at the beauty parlour for millions of American women, an event that would be of anthropological significance if it occurred in a distant, exotic culture. In fact, anything a woman might do that is at all public, from singing in a nightclub to attending a funeral, or simply 'going to the city,' may be preceded by an allotment of time to do her hair or have it 'done.'*

Neighbourhood beauty parlours are such an entrenched part of city life that it is hard to believe they did not exist before the twentieth century. Upper-class Roman matrons pursued the art of hair arrangement as a consuming passion, but they had their coiffures slaved over, quite literally, at home, while their husbands went daily to the public barber, whose establishment was a sociable place for conducting business that rivalled the public baths. As slaves became servants and servants became maids, women continued to have their hair done, or contrived to do their own hair, in the privacy and isolation of the home. Dressing the hair at home with the help of a lady's maid, a female relative, or a visiting artiste who arrived by appointment was standard procedure up to the 1920s, when the rebellious flapper had no choice but to go to a man's barber or ask a good friend to do the honours.

The entrepreneur who opened a small neighbourhood shop was responding directly and shrewdly to the mass appeal of short hair, for once woman was free of the coil at the nape of her neck, it became her urgent mission to seek out new ways to feminize her head. To soften the look of a practical cut, she gave herself over to professional treatment: spit curls and bangs dipped in gluey setting lotions, stiff marcel waves that were curled by hot irons, a permanent wave by electric machine, a monthly styling, a weekly set and comb-out, a shampoo and blow-dry, and as technology advanced, chemical straighteners and chemical frizzes, bleaches, lighteners, touch-ups, frostings, streakings, highlights and other permutations of colour.

Fashions in hair styles are now subject to change as rapidly as fashions in clothes, and the restless tinkering that women do is as much a product of the competitive desire not to fall behind the

* Do-does-did-done suffices for a wide range of practices that are performed in the name of cosmetic improvement. One's hair and nails are 'done' in a beauty salon; one's nose, eyes and entire face may be 'done' by a plastic surgeon. The 'done' look is sought after in the first category, but not in the second.

times as it is a reflection of female insecurity and the belief that the raw materials of the face and body are not good enough in their natural state. An artful shaping can play down a forehead that is too strong, a jaw that is too square, a neck that is too short or ears that are too large for an idealized standard of beauty. The psychological uplift that can be obtained from this feminine face improvement cannot be ignored. Nothing alters the familiar face in the mirror quite so easily as going from long to short, from straight to curly, from brunette to auburn, from grey to ash blonde. A woman will often choose to 'do something different' with her hair after a difficult crisis, for a new way of wearing the hair gives the impression of a new lease on life. A fashionable hair style can elevate the mood more successfully than any drug (although the effect may be equally temporary), a fresh look can sever the emotional ties with a person who preferred it the old way, it can offer visible proof that this spunky lady is taking charge of her personal survival, is pulling herself out of a dismal morass.

In the Sixties and Seventies the hair stylist at the top of his profession won recognition on the society page for being a friend and confidant of his rich and social clients. He went to the best parties, often as an escort, and he gave some publicized parties of his own. He was a trend setter and an acknowledged practitioner of the perfect lifestyle. He was the subject of a popular movie, *Shampoo*, and one of his number had a well-publicized love affair with a Hollywood star and went on to produce movies himself. The bond between the elite hair stylist and his elite clientele, however, was poorly understood by most men, who continued to view the relationship as a stock cliché of effeminacy, for in a sense the hairdresser was cursed with the deep strain of triviality that curses all women. Hair indeed may be trivial, but it is central to the feminine definition. A hairdresser's skills and artistic talent are devoted in a practical way to feminine illusion, and as Edith Wharton observed in 1900, 'Genius is of small use to a woman who does not know how to do her hair.'

Clothes

Who would deny that dressing feminine can be quite creative? A woman with a closetful of clothes for different moods and occasions is an amateur actress and a wily practitioner of the visual arts. A grand sense of theatre reposes on that rack of hangers, offering a choice of imaginative roles from sexy vixen to old-fashioned, romantic lady. Children of both sexes love to dress up in their mother's costumes, complete with lipstick, handbag and high heels, because they adore the game of 'Let's pretend.' Feminine clothing induces the body to strut about in small, restrained yet show-offy ways. Feminine clothing produces its special feminine sounds: the staccato clickety-click of the heels, the musical jangle of bracelets, the soft rustle of silk, or, in an earlier era, the whisper of petticoats, the snap of a fan. And the finishing touches, the makeup and the perfume, create a distinctive, sweet feminine smell.

And then there are the compliments, the ultimate reward, for men are known to be highly appreciative when a woman has taken the trouble to create an entire human being who looks and acts and smells so different from them.

Every wave of feminism has foundered on the question of dress reform. I suppose it is asking too much of women to give up their chief outward expression of the feminine difference, their continuing reassurance to men and to themselves that a male is a male because a female dresses and looks and acts like another sort of creature.

Dressing in the Fifties meant a commitment to white gloves. Worn with a strand of cultured pearls they represented impeccable refinement and upward mobility. From Elsie de Wolfe, the socialite decorator who became Lady Mendl, to Grace Kelly of Philadelphia, who became a Hollywood star and married the Prince of Monaco, the little white glove stood for class. Naturally one needed many pairs, for carrying the morning paper to work wreaked havoc on their pristine whiteness. Walking to the office was also excessively stressful on the *de rigueur* shoe with its narrow, pinched toe and spindly heel that almost invariably got stuck in a sidewalk grating. Accessories were important in the Fifties and Sixties, for they added formal grace notes to the basic dress with its hemline adjusted precisely to the middle of the calf ... precisely to the knee ... precisely to mid-thigh ... with nervous attention to Eugenia Sheppard. Of undergarments, too, there had to be a proper complement: wired bras, backless bras, full slips, half slips, elastic girdles with garter tabs, and a drawer inevitably stuffed with snagged and mismatched nylon stockings.

Along with many others, my conversion to pants at the start of the Seventies was slow but complete, accompanied by a sense of relief and relaxation. When blue jeans became the emblem of hip sophistication, I didn't understand I was riding a very short wave. Suddenly it was all right to wear pants. Then it became a feminist statement to wear pants. Never again would most women wear skirts, I thought, in the way that friends of mine have thought that the revolution was just around the corner. And here it is, well into the Eighties, and a woman who wears nothing but pants is a holdout, a stick-in-the-mud, a fashion reactionary with no sense of style.

My exile from the world of the fashionable might be easier to bear if some of those closest to me hadn't become backsliders, apologizing for their slide with the argument that they need to wear skirts for their careers because it is, after all, still a man's world and they are but feminists in it. I would never under-estimate the value of skirts and dresses as effective camouflage for those who fear that their femininity or their politics may be open to question, but I don't believe that's the entire story. I think my friends returned to dresses because they felt that life was getting grey without some whimsical indulgence in the feminine aesthetic. They missed the frivolous gaiety of personal adornment, they missed the public display of vulnerability and sexual flirtation, and they missed the promised change in appearance that a new dress – and only a new dress – can hold. Some of them had thrived on the newsiness of fashion, the keeping up, the competition. They longed to try the current look. Some of them longed to show off their legs again, and some of them, I know, missed shopping.

On bad days I mourn my old dresses. I miss the graceful flow of fabric, the gentle, gathered shapes and pretty colours. Straight-legged pants are boring. One cannot take on a new identity by changing trousers.

Then why do I persist in not wearing skirts? Because I don't like this artificial gender distinction. Because I don't wish to start shaving my legs again. Because I don't want to return to the expense and aggravation of nylons. Because I will not re-acquaint myself with the discomfort of feminine shoes. Because I'm at peace with the freedom and comfort of trousers. Because it costs a lot less to wear nothing but pants. Because I remember how cold I used to feel in the winter wearing a short skirt and sheer stockings. Because I can still call to mind the ugly look of splattered rain water on the back of my exposed legs. Because I recall the anguish of an unravelled hem. Because I remember resenting the enormous amount of thinking time I used to pour into superficial upkeep concerns, and because the nature of feminine dressing is superficial in essence − even my objections seem superficial as I write them down. But that is the point. To care about feminine fashion, and do it well, is to be obsessively involved in inconsequential details on a serious basis. There is no relief. To not be involved is to risk looking eccentric and peculiar, or sloppy and uncared for, or mannish and man-hating, or all of the above.

Who said that clothes make a statement? What an understatement that was. Clothes never shut up. They gabble on endlessly, making their intentional and unintentional points.

It is written in Deuteronomy that 'The woman shall not wear that which pertaineth unto a man, neither shall a man put on a woman's garment,' and the reason given refers to the strongest displeasure of the highest authority. Failure to abide by a sex-distinctive dress code is an 'abomination unto the Lord thy God.'

Why should the Lord have cared so intensely about clothes? Was it to keep the sexes firmly apart and discourage promiscuity? Was it to reinforce the homosexual taboo? Was it a way of saying that women were not to be soldiers and that warriors were not to sneak about in women's clothes as a ruse to fool the enemy? I've read these differing explanations and while they all may apply to some extent, they avoid the basic point. Naked as He created them, Adam and Eve could not be mistaken. Dressed in fig leaves and animal skins after they came to know shame, their gender differences were partially obscured. A sex-distinctive dress code (a loincloth for Adam, a sarong for Eve; a striped tie for Adam, a pair of high heels for Eve) created an emblematic polarity that satisfied a social need for unambiguous division, neat categories and stable order.

When a child is asked by its parents whether the naked person in the picture is a man or a woman and the child replies, 'I can't tell because they're not wearing clothes,' the joke is really quite profound. In a clothed culture the eye depends on artificial externals for its visual cues. When the cues are absent or conflicting, the psychological disturbance in the observer can be enormous. A blurring of the sartorial signposts can inspire hostility and rage. To mistake a man for a woman, or vice versa, is dangerous. An entire range of responses may be inappropriately misdirected. One's own sexual identity may be thrown into confusion, for how can we know who we are unless we are fairly certain who is the other?

Skirts and pants stand juxtaposed as the Western world's symbolic Great Divide. A traveller who does not speak a word of a foreign language can locate the male or female restroom in an international airport by seeking out a recognizable logo. A painted stick figure with a triangular skirt leads unquestionably to the women's lounge; a stick figure without a skirt is where the men should enter. I, in my pants, am grateful to know where to go – to the door with the skirt. Am I, is the world, prepared for the real basics? Stick figures with or without a triangular penis? Signposts with a pair of circular breasts?

A New Jersey NOW chapter once commissioned an educational poster showing boys and girls playing a friendly, equal game of softball, but the artist couldn't figure out how to illustrate the concept unless she put the girls in skirts. Or in pigtails and ribbons.

In certain remote parts of the globe where people are not completely influenced by Western values, trousers still carry a sex-free neutrality similar to the robes and tunics worn by the ancient Mayas and the Greeks, and of course there is the fiercely national-istic Scotsman who doggedly hangs on to his ceremonial kilts. But there is no point in stressing the exceptions. To the Western mind the grouping of men in trousers and women in skirts is something akin to a natural order, as basic to the covenant of masculine/feminine difference as the short/long hair proposition. Trousers are practical. They cover the lower half of the body without nonsense and permit the freest of natural movements. And therein lies their unfeminine danger.

Bifurcation describes the phenomenon of forking or splitting, but in the Victorian and Edwardian eras it was a euphemism for the pair of legs that women were not supposed to admit they possessed. Women's legs, or limbs (the latter term was more polite), were not perceived as an anatomical arrangement for supporting the body and for walking, but as blatant arrows that pointed the way to the seat of sex and other functions. Men might display their legs with nonchalance, but from pulpit and press there was unanimous agreement that the sight of a bifurcated woman was immodest, ungodly and sinful. The only way to avoid bifurcation was to wear a long skirt that brushed the floor.

As with most things that are categorized as masculine or feminine, it is impossible to separate longstanding concepts of sexual morality from longstanding concepts of aesthetics and fashion. Once both sexes wore fairly similar robes and tunics, but even in Greece and Rome men customarily displayed their bare legs under a tunic that came to the knees while women wore a longer, fuller drape. Leafing through illustrated histories of European costume and fashion (which, need we be reminded, are chiefly a record of what the upper class wore) it is amusing to note that during the Middle Ages men of nobility proudly showed off their muscular, shapely legs, sometimes augmented by padded stockings, while women appeared to have no legs at all. In fact, as wearing apparel was refined and embellished over a period of several hundred years, men's clothes were cut to show off their legs and thighs and where they were joined at the crotch, while women's clothes hid the legs and revealed some portion of the upper body – arms, shoulders, throat and sometimes even the breasts. A tight-fitted bodice and a long and flowing skirt was the standard feminine silhouette.

Straight-cut long pants, the modern pair of trousers, came into fashion for men at the beginning of the nineteenth century, to replace the customary knee breeches and stockings. The male retained his bifurcated masculinity, a matter of pride as well as comfort, but the shape of his legs was no longer on view. When skirts broke the floor-length barrier in the 1920s, the historic reversal was complete. Now women's legs were on public display – a distinctive new sign of the feminine.

The evolution from long skirts to short in the 1920s was an important advance in the history of women's rights. By a cut of the scissors in a dressmaker's salon, women were able to walk and move with greater freedom than they had been allowed for centuries. Gone was the dragging weight of several layers of petticoats, and yards of heavy fabric that swirled around the ankles were thrown aside in a single stroke of fashion. From breast to thighs, the torso was liberated from the restraining corset. But the transformation of women's legs from a bodily part that was hidden in modesty to a glamorous appendage that was whistled at and admired may not have been a remarkable gain. Both extremes of fashion derived from a belief in the seductive nature of female sexuality, and both sought to minimize the true function of legs.

A major purpose of femininity is to mystify or minimize the functional aspects of a woman's mind and body that are indistinguishable from a man's, and our legs have borne the brunt of this more than we care to acknowledge. Quentin Bell makes the point in his discourse *On Human Finery* that voluminous hoop skirts of the 1860s made it close to impossible for a lady to climb a narrow staircase, while hobble skirts of the 1880s were so tight that she was even more poorly equipped to mount a steep flight of steps. One hundred years later, mini-skirts presented a similar problem, but in our day the inhibition was a matter of exposure – what a voyeur might see from his vantage point down below.

A man I had some political dealings with once challenged me by questioning why my pants had a fly front. I hadn't actually thought about that before. When I was a teenager (and never wore pants except for a pair of dungarees that I rolled to mid-calf) women's slacks always zippered up the side or back. I imagine today's designers feel that pants simply fit better with a frontal close. But I hadn't given two seconds' worth of thought to the meaning behind the fly until I was challenged by somebody who obviously felt it had great meaning to him as a facilitator of sex and urination. Did he suppose I was pretending to have a penis?

Few women are reluctant to wear pants because they don't believe they have the right to wear a fly front. Some think they're too tall and might be mistaken for a man from the rear, and some think they're too broad in the beam for a pair of pants to do justice to their figure. There's no doubt that since most of the rear ends we're accustomed to viewing in pants belong to men (and most of these are covered by boxy jackets), a woman with broad, full hips will think she looks better – even gracefully voluptuous in the nice, old-fashioned sense – when she puts on a skirt. To the modern mentality, grace in pants does seem to require a slender rear end.

A skirt, any skirt, has a feminizing mission that goes beyond the drawing of a polite, yet teasing, shade over the female crotch and its functions, and of flattering or draping the rear end and stomach with graceful folds. Expansive, casual body gestures are character-ized as immodest and unfeminine when practised by women, and skirts restrict those large, free movements. One does not stride. One is perpetually reminded to be circumspect when sitting or bending down. Whatever its length, and however wide, the open-endedness of a skirt cannot help but guide the body into a set of conservative poses and smaller gestures, and the traditional femi-nine accessories that went with a skirt in an earlier era (corset, fan, muff, parasol and shawl) and the shoes and pocket-books of today have always reinforced those restrictions. But of course. Feminine clothing has never been designed to be functional, for that would be a contradiction in terms. Functional clothing is a masculine privilege and practicality is a masculine virtue. To be truly feminine is to accept the handicap of restraint and restriction, and to come to adore it.

Magnificent garments in the late Middle Ages were intentionally designed to immobilize the royal personage who wore them as much as to impress the lower orders with their visual drama, for elaborate, hampering clothes were proof that royal desires were served by the labour of others. A billowing sleeve, an immense white ruff, and luxurious layers of fur and embroidered, jewel-encrusted fabric were status symbols for kings and their courtiers even more than for queens and their ladies. A nobleman's cloak was often more splendid than his wife's. Male plumage became such a giddily competitive venture that in order to preserve the boundaries of class, sumptuary laws were enacted periodically throughout Western Europe to allocate the wearing of silk, sable, velvet and threads of gold and silver by rank and station – so many robes for a baron, so many yards for a knight, etcetera. Allotments for wives and daughters were added to the later codes as something of an afterthought. Under the energizing momentum of political revolution, industrial progress and a burgeoning middle class, a change in attitude towards clothing began to take place in the late eighteenth century. Immobilizing garments and uncomfortable accessories were out of step with the fast-moving times. Elegant men's wear began its steady advance towards functional utility and even adapted some practical ideas from the workingman's ward-robe. Gentlemen began to wear clothes that reflected the new masculine values of dynamic action combined with serious responsi-bility, expressed through expert tailoring and practical, dark col-ours. Class distinctions were maintained not by frilly impediments and ostentatious display but by a new, subtle standard of good cloth and good fit.

No such fundamental change, however, took place for women. While the design of men's clothes was streamlined and democratized to reflect the vigorous efficiency of the soot-filled age of industrialization, the design of women's clothes did not move forward at all. Although the industrial revolution employed the labour of working-class women in factories and mills, it also produced the middle-class lady of leisure with her staff of household servants and her strictly defined feminine sphere, a sphere whose parameters were motherhood, social and moral refinement, and gracious adornment of her husband's life and home. Throughout the nineteenth century, hoops, crinolines, bustles and trains might come and go, taste in colour might veer and shift, the width of the skirt, the swell of the sleeve, the location of the waist and the shape of the bust might vary with considerable imagination from season to season, but the woman of fashion remained a perishable confection, a wedding-cake vision of conspicuous consumption whose impractical clothes reflected the aristocratic values of centuries past. And she had no followers more attentive or more eager to become the Perfect Lady than the idle wives and daughters of the newly moneyed bourgeoisie with their newly acquired aspirations and pretensions, and their newly acquired laundresses and lady's maids.

In material terms – ill-paid labourers in the mills, including children, worked day and night to spin out the yardage; sewing machines were introduced to automate the stitching – this meant the piling on of ruffles, ribbons, flounces, piping, fringes, tassels, lace, beads and bows, and numerous starched petticoats to bedeck and adorn a sedate and artificially moulded figure. Perhaps one season a crinoline cage might replace the petticoats, or perhaps a hobble skirt might replace the hoop, to be replaced in turn by a bustle or train. Whatever the innovation, the latest feminine mode was usually expressed through the fashion language of a period revival.

A pattern of looking backward continues to shape the design and marketing of women's clothes in the twentieth century. New styles regularly owe their inspiration to historic costumes and the 'bringing back' is happily acknowledged – be it Dior's New Look of 1947, which brought back long skirts, crinolines and the waist-cincher, the Imperial Russian peasant look of Saint Laurent in 1976, which brought back frogging, piping and high boots, the frankly named 1940s 'retro' look a year or so later which brought back slit skirts, shoulder pads and bright-red lipstick, or Ralph Lauren's Victorian look of 1980. Except for the geometric space-age designs of Courrèges and Mary Quant in the turbulent mid-Sixties (white vinyl boots and miniskirts), new clothes and shoes for women are trumpeted each season as yet another 'return to femininity.' By contrast, fashions for men change very little from year to year and they never look back, either for inspiration or as a selling technique. A 'return to masculinity' is an unthinkable concept, for masculine is defined by the present tense. But in clothes, in attitude and in everything else, to be safely feminine – to 'retain' her femininity – a woman must look to the distant past.

Given this striking divergence in purpose between men's and women's fashions, it is no wonder that the creative design centres took root and flourished in different places. Men looked towards London, the sombre city of banking and mercantile commerce with its cautious, responsible tailors of Savile Row. Women cast their covetous eyes towards Paris, the thrillingly wicked citadel of romance and art, with its exotic perfumes, its fanciful dressmakers and ingenious corsetieres.

Although there was more than a symbolic connection between the suffocating confinements of women's long skirts and the suffocating restrictions that defined women's roles, the dress-reform movement of the 1850s became an excruciating personal torment and a political mortification to the American heroines of women's rights. All told, not more than one hundred suffragists dared to appear in public wearing 'the rational dress,' as it came to be known in health and hygiene circles. Among the pioneers were Elizabeth Cady Stanton, Lucy Stone, the Grimke sisters and the self-effacing Quaker organizer Susan B. Anthony, who later recalled this time in her life as 'a mental crucifixion'.

It was popularly named the 'Bloomer' costume because Amelia Bloomer, a Seneca Falls neighbour of Mrs Stanton, took up the cause in the pages of her reformist newspaper, *The Lily*, and because 'Bloomer' sounded so ridiculous and funny. But the suffragists simply called it 'the short dress' and they were punctilious about giving credit where credit was due – to Mrs Stanton's cousin Elizabeth Smith Miller, the daughter of abolitionist Gerrit Smith.

Mrs Miller's creation, which she had originally stitched up for working in the garden, had a somewhat Turkish look. The lower part consisted of a pair of ankle-length pantaloons with an overskirt that came to the knees. To the knees! No trailing skirts to get caught underfoot, stepped on, ripped or soiled. No undulating petticoats to gather up and hold with dainty grace while turning a corner or sitting down, in order to avoid a mishap. On a visit to Seneca Falls, Lizzie Miller gave Lizzie Stanton a practical demonstration. She showed her cousin how confidently she could walk up a flight of stairs with a baby in her arm and an oil lamp balanced in her other hand, without fear of tripping. Mrs Stanton, who already had four of her seven children, was instantly converted. With the bounding enthusiasm for which she was famous, she applied the scissors and needle to her own long skirts and began to evangelize among her many friends in suffrage and abolition, offering to make a present of the short dress to Susan Anthony, a promising new ally from the temperance movement. Miss Anthony replied that she would never put it on.

'We are like the poor fox in the fable, having cut off his tail,' Mrs Stanton wrote to her cousin. 'We can have no peace in travelling unless we cut off the great national petticoat . . . Stand firm.'

There were many exhortations from one feminist to another in the years 1851 and 1852 to stand firm. Wrote Ida Husted Harper, '. . . the press howled in derision, the pulpit hurled its anathemas and the rabble took up the refrain. On the streets of the larger cities the women were followed by mobs of men and boys, who jeered and yelled and did not hesitate to express their disapproval by throwing sticks and stones.' Many a votes-for-women rally turned into a circus when an unruly mob invaded the hall to gawk at the Bloomers. What began as a personal convenience had turned into a painful political principle, the right of a woman to wear comfortable clothes. In December 1852 while visiting with Mrs Stanton, Susan B. took the plunge, shortening her skirts and cutting her hair to make a total statement. 'Well, at last I am in short skirt and trousers!' she anxiously wrote to Lucy Stone. She was the last of the great suffragists to adopt the style. Within one year, she would be among the last to still wear it.

Despite the support of her husband and father, who believed that dress reform was the key to women's emancipation, Elizabeth Smith Miller lowered her skirts with each passing season. She wore some variation of her Turkish costume for seven years, as did

Amelia Bloomer. Elizabeth Cady Stanton's bloomers became an unpleasant issue in her husband's campaign for the state senate, inspiring a bit of verse from the opposition: 'Twenty tailors take the stitches, Mrs Stanton wears the breeches.' Her son Neil wrote from school begging his mother not to wear the short dress when she came to visit. In less than two years Mrs Stanton capitulated. She let down her hems and urged her movement friends to full retreat, writing to Susan B. Anthony and Lucy Stone, 'I know what you must suffer in consenting to bow again to the tyranny of fashion, but I also know what you suffer among fashionable people in wearing the short dress; and so, not for the sake of the cause, nor for any sake but your own, take it off!'

Anthony and Stone conferred quickly by letter. From Stone: 'I have bought a nice new dress, which I have had a month, and it is not made because I can't decide whether to make it long or short. Not that I think any cause will suffer, but simply to save myself a great deal of annoyance and not feel when I am a guest in a family that they are mortified if other persons happen to come in. I was at Lucretia Mott's a few weeks ago, and her daughters took up a regular labour with me to make me abandon the dress. They said they would not go in the street with me . . .'

Susan B. replied in agitation, 'If Lucy Stone, with all her powers of eloquence, her loveliness of character, who wins all that hear the sound of her voice, cannot bear the martyrdom of the dress, who can? Mrs Stanton's parting words were, "Let the hem out of your dress today, before tomorrow's meeting." I have not obeyed her but have been in the streets and printing offices all day long and have had rude, vulgar men stare me out of countenance and heard them say as I opened the door, "There comes my Bloomer." O, hated name! I am known only as one of the women who ape men – coarse, brutal men! Oh, I cannot, cannot bear it any longer.'

The failure of the Bloomer movement can be laid at many doors. Mrs Stanton conceded years later that pantaloons under a knee-length skirt were 'not artistic,' and Mrs Bloomer ruefully acknowledged that new ideas in women's fashions did not arise from reformist journals but from the romantic fantasies draped and sewn for the Emperor's ladies in France. Among the denizens of the water-cure resorts and the partisans of the 'improved' spelling, the rational dress had its devoted champions – they tried to rename it the 'American costume' – but these women were on the fringe, determinedly unfashionable, and the suffragists needed to win the hearts and minds of the nation. Where the suffragists saw a short skirt and a modest leg covering that allowed them to move with an ease and freedom they had never known, others saw only a pair of obtrusive pants that confirmed their worst fears – that suffragists were women who really wanted to be men.

In Victorian England, where femininity was enshrined in ribbons and bonnets and Alençon lace, reform-minded women also formed a Rational Dress Society to press for the divided skirt. But the real drama lay with a group of working-class heroines who fought desperately from 1850 to 1877 to remain in trousers, for their livelihood depended on rugged clothes. These were the colliery workers of Lancashire, Wigan, Birmingham and South Wales, the hardy pit-brow lasses and mine-tip girls who sifted and loaded the coal after men brought it up to the surface. (The women had already been banned from working the mine shafts and tunnels.) Dressed in trousers, clogs and sacking aprons, the coal haulers laboured in twelve-hour shifts, and by all accounts they were fiercely proud of their grimy independence. Newspaper exposés and government subcommisions periodically deplored the colliery women in their 'disgusting habiliments,' and repeated efforts were made to oust them from the mines on the pious ground that their work clothes rendered them 'unsexed' and degraded.

History is enlivened by a number of women of ambition and talent who chose to masquerade in men's clothes, or who wore some essential part of the forbidden costume in order to work in comfort. Whether it was to take up arms and fight for her country, like Joan of Arc, to lead escaped slaves through Southern swamps to freedom, like Harriet Tubman, or to carouse at night in raffish cafés for research and adventure, like George Sand, a bonnet and skirt would have imposed a ridiculous bar. They are a mixed bunch, these purposeful cross-dressers, these illustrious women in serious drag, having little in common besides a profound need for self-realization and unstoppable courage. The list includes Rosa Bonheur, who received official permission from the Paris police to dress in men's clothes when she went to sketch horses at the slaughterhouse, Calamity Jane, who drove a stagecoach in the American West, and the eminent landscape designer Gertrude Jeykl, who wore army boots and a workman's apron to supervise the planting on England's great estates.

No woman was more stubborn in her refusal to bow to the conventions of feminine dress than Joan of Arc, and no woman in history paid a higher price. In the glorious days of her triumph the Maid had exchanged her peasant's red skirt for a page's costume of grey and black; her pride was a suit of shining white armour for leading her troops in battle. After her capture Joan was beseeched by her jailors to put on a gown, but she would not comply. Her Voices had not told her that her mission was over, and besides, it was safer to dress as a soldier in a prison administered by men. Joan's inquisitors pondered obsessively on her masculine attire. Receiving the sacrament while dressed like a man was one of the crimes with which she was charged. A woman's gown was brought to her cell after she broke down and made her sworn confession. Joan put it on, then took it off. God's soldier could not bear the humiliation. Her relapse into masculine clothing sealed her fate, for this was proof that her mind had not submitted. Joan was taken to the stake and burned in a skirt and bodice, an additional triumph for her captors.

Spinsters, lesbians, bisexuals, women of ambiguous, androgynous sexual persuasion? Decadent showoffs and publicity hounds? Artists and actresses playing with roles? The divine Sarah Bernhardt posed in a jacket, foulard and trousers when she announced her intention to give up the stage to devote her life to sculpture. What did it signify when the rebellious actress and writer Fanny Kemble, opposed to 'tight stays, tight garters, tight shoes, tight waistbands, tight armholes and tight bodices,' put on a vest and breeches to spend the afternoon with a woman friend? When Colette grinned rakishly for the camera in a stylish man's suit, a cigarette burning between her fingers, was this not the time between husbands when she was conducting her outrageous affair with the very mannish Missy? We know from her diary that Vita Sackville-West disguised herself as a boy, running and jumping and vaulting over gates 'in the unaccustomed freedom of breeches and gaiters,' when she was madly in love with the seductive Violet.

When celebrated achievement or dazzling beauty can be added to the visual effect, the world smiles more kindly on women who dress in men's clothes. Even within Natalie Barney's lesbian circle in Paris between the wars, the stylish grace of actress Renee Vivien and Romaine Brooks, the artist, when they dressed in high drag, set them apart from friends who were less physically blessed and less notably accomplished – Una, Lady Troubridge, in her monocle and cravat, and Radclyffe Hall with her ill-fitting suits and laboured writing. Deborah Sampson Gannett, who dressed as a boy and soldiered in the American Revolution, would be a more acceptable role model if she had saved a platoon or captured a city. Dame Ethel Smyth, the British composer and champion of suffrage, might have worn her swallowtail coat to better effect if her figure were less stocky, and her music more tuneful. And to bring matters up to date, the 'Annie Hall look' that Diane Keaton created for the movie of the same name proved not so easy to pull off when women less winsome than Keaton affected a slouch hat, vest and baggy pants.

This much can be said: Some women have worn men's clothes to accomplish their work. Some women have worn men's clothes to indicate their temporary or permanent sexual attraction to other women. Some women have worn men's clothes to experience the power and freedom of being a man. Some women have worn men's clothes because they hated their female bodies. Some women have worn men's clothes because they looked so adorable in them. Some women have worn men's clothes because they sought an alternative to the confining clothes they were expected to wear, and expected to delight in, as women. *Orlando*, Virginia Woolf's novel of 1928, may be read not as a witty story of a woman who undergoes a change of sex, but as a metaphorical essay about a woman who undergoes a change of clothes (the book is dedicated to V. Sackville-West).*

In the 1930s and '40s Hollywood accomplished what the earnest movements for dress reform and the individualistic rebels had never been able to manage – an acceptable image (one that men found sexy) of a glamorous, vulnerable, patently heterosexual, sophisticated lady in slacks. As the glamorous ballroom dancer Irene Castle had feminized and popularized short hair in the 1920s, the frail figure, plucked eyebrows, heavy mascara, bright-red lipstick, platinum hair and high-heeled shoes of Marlene Dietrich feminized

* Woolf's autobiographical pieces, published for the first time in 1976, reveal a woman who felt terror when buying a new dress – from 'looking-glass shame' in the fitting room to self-consciousness and dread when she finally wore it. Miss Virginia Stephen had come from a family of famous beauties. Within the rules of Victorian manners that she and her sister followed, 'During daylight one could wear overalls; work,' but in the evening in her father's drawing room, 'Dress and hair-doing became far more important than pictures and Greek.'

and made palatable the threatening image of a woman in a man-tailored jacket and trousers. Dietrich on screen, and Garbo, Hepburn and Bankhead off-screen, were photographed repeatedly in pants, as was America's first androgynous sex symbol, the high-flying aviator Amelia Earhart. Ah, Amelia. Wearing a brown leather flight jacket and grinning shyly from the cockpit of her aeroplane, she appears to soar high in androgynous freedom. Of course Earhart would be an appealing heroine with her easy good looks and mysterious death. Not like the dour, unstylish Susan B. Anthony, or the brilliant George Eliot with her lace-trimmed blouse and her corkscrew curls preposterously framing her homely, strong face.

But it is Dietrich's image and not Earhart's or Keaton's that permits the fashionable young woman of today to wear her fly-front trousers. As long as she gussies them up with high heels, painted fingernails, 'done' hair, plenty of jewellery and makeup, her feminin-ity will not be challenged. Compensatory femininity extracts its due in the form of fancy embellishments to modify the suspect masculine model. This is known in the trade as 'the softening effect' – an interesting phrase, since there is nothing soft about spiked heels and long red fingernails, except that they reduce functionalism, hint at masochism and alter the natural, normal motion of the sophisticated lady in pants. 'Heterosexualizing effect' would be a more accurate description, and what a sad commentary it makes on the tenuous relationship between the sexes that a woman must resort to a string of intricate deceptions in order to prove her heterosexual good will.

Winter and summer, touches of nudity are another proof of feminine expression. It is chic to bare the skin, to play the tease, however unwittingly, between the concealed and the exposed. A reluctance to show a thigh or reveal a midriff is construed as prudish timidity, old-fashioned dullness and a lack of confidence, or else it is circumstantial evidence of flaw: thick legs, flabby skin, a hideous, deforming scar. I am sympathetic to the argument that a woman should be free to wear what she wants without moral judgement or accusations of inviting assault (no study has ever shown that rapists seek out those who are provocatively dressed), yet I am not unmindful that the argument usually comes from very young women in the happy phase of exploring fashion with a pioneer spirit, and who look ahead to new frontiers. Those who resent gratuitous nudity are usually older, at an age where the flesh is less firm and the attitude less liberal. Because older women are placed automatically on the losing side of the competition to look sexually appealing, they are in possession of knowledge that escapes the young and the physically blessed. Exposure of flesh is not a mere matter of style, insouciance and modernity; it is a contest by which women are judged.

Was it inevitable that the movement for dress reform should have passed so blithely from the battle against restrictive clothing to a glamorous rivalry over how much nudity could be revealed? Erotic attire has often served as a smoke screen to deflect female consciousness from a lasting understanding of the nature of oppression. The décolleté ball gowns of the rich and the peekaboo costumes of whores historically shocked the industrious, God-fearing poor with their prideful displays of pampered flesh. Mrs Grundy may have been a stereotype of conservative bourgeois values, but she was created by men of the bourgeoisie who wished to escape their own background. Her opposite number, the 'liberated woman,' is assumed to be a *femme fatale* in scanty dress. It is not accidental that as soon as women were freed from tight corsets and heavy, hampering clothes they were heartily encouraged to express the feminine difference in terms of exposure, for exposure was always the issue as the moralists saw it. Decency was thought to reside in the length of the hemline, or more coyly in the lace hanky stuffed into the cleavage. So if Suzanne Lenglen made tennis headlines in 1919 when she appeared on court in a mid-calf dress and long stockings, and if Alice Marble shocked Wimbledon in 1933 by playing barelegged in shorts under an unbuttoned tunic, there is logic of a sort in the hullaballoo in 1948 over the famous lace panties of Gorgeous Gussie Moran. Gorgeous Gussie, I suspect, was only trying to feminize a practical, and consequently sexless, costume – but no matter. The right to move freely has always been a dangerously unfeminine issue; the right to be titillating has greater appeal.

Veils are a worldwide symbol of mysterious feminine sexuality, presumably because they conceal some frank aspect of a woman's appearance. As popular wisdom has it, the erotic life of the veil resides in the imagined beauty of the hidden face, yet a person with any sense of history must know that even when the slot for the eyes is richly embroidered, the veil is a shroud of silence, anonymity and restriction that is used to keep women secluded from the active world of men. Efforts in Moslem countries to throw off the veil meet with a frightening amount of resistance from men who howl about the destruction of their traditional values. In Afghanistan the proposed unveiling of women by a Marxist government was one threatening factor that inspired the revolt of fundamental rebels. The return of women to the chador was one of many disturbing aspects of Islamic nationalism promoted by the Ayatollah Khomeini's regime in Iran. 'Taking the veil' remains the customary expression in Christianity to describe a woman's act of renouncing the temporal world and a sexual life to enter a convent. Whatever their religion, women in veils are a mummified caste whose sexuality is hidden so it cannot threaten the social order of men.

By sentimental tradition, the act of unveiling the bride at the close of the wedding ceremony announces the lawful permission to deflower the virgin within the sanctified union of marriage. As the bride wears a veil of white, the widow once shrouded herself in veils of black to signify, among other things, the passing of the active phase of her sexual existence. Devised as a feminine cloak of moral virtue and protected status, the veil could also impart a message of intrigue and illicit sex. Swathed in heavy veiling in order to visit her clandestine lover, an adulterous woman in the nineteenth century might view her disguise as a titillating prelude to the amorous assignation, and so might her lover. The veil is perceived as erotic when sexual guilt is perceived as erotic. Favoured by milliners of the twentieth century to give a froufrou touch to their original creations, the peekaboo veil on a fanciful hat became a glamorous artifact of submission, ambiguously ladylike and provocative in its vestigial drape of black net.

At this particular moment in history when the ratios of sexual preference seem to have gone awry and vast numbers of homosexual men and straight single women are roaming the range in search of love, sex and meaningful relations, it is obvious that these two groups dress up to enhance their sexual attraction while lesbian women and heterosexual men dress more carelessly or to conceal their bodies, having no urgent need to attract the judgemental male eye. Intense concern for appearance in the gay male culture – working out, keeping thin, looking young, wearing strategic, form-fitting clothes – may be evidence of an aesthetic sensibility, but the sensibility is an all-out effort to win the sexual interest of other men. This circumstance lends credence to the point of view that women do not dress for other women, except to show off their stuff competitively, and furthermore, that 'homosexual designers' cannot be blamed for the uncomfortable, unrealistic fashions they 'foist upon' women, for the whole show is produced for the approval of heterosexual men.

Many gay men, as straight women often observe, are very attractive. There's a lot to be said for tight pants on a good body in excellent condition. However, the effort is seldom made on our behalf, except by a handful of rock stars and movie actors who absorb themselves in this colourful, sensuous manner – the word is narcissistic – because appearance and audience play a crucial role in how they earn a living. Most straight men do not need to rely on sexual plumage, either to earn a living or to entice a woman, and masculine tradition of the last two centuries has taught that sexualized clothing on a man is undignified and foppish. Men of action and power are colourless by choice, it would seem, when their status is unchallenged and secure. Only those most likely to be ignored or discounted, or who possess a special need to be noticed (a broad category that might include women, blacks, gay men, short men, men on the make and entertainers) are demonstrably more colourful and fashion-conscious.

Gays nevertheless have had a marked effect on men's fashions, chiefly because the new emphasis on slim-line jackets and close-fitting pants has reopened the question of pocket-books and pockets. Women's clothes are rarely designed with functional pockets (the nineteenth century feminist Charlotte Perkins Gilman wrote passionately about this) because the necessary objects a real pocket might be expected to hold – money, keys, comb, eyeglasses, pen and all the feminine etceteras – would spoil the graceful, smooth line. Influenced in part by European designers, a pioneering number of American men have persuaded themselves that it might not be too great a blow to their masculinity if they carried a shoulderstrap bag. Not a clutch or a handbag – that would be too feminine and inconvenient – but a neat, tailored carryall that is flat and unobtrusive. Perhaps the day may arrive when the pocket-book ceases to be a feminine symbol (how will the Freudians cope with that?), or perhaps this brave new accessory will prove too encumbering for general masculine appeal. Realistically, it is harder to imagine legions of women without their pocket-books than legions of men with them, for men have a definite biological advantage when it comes to stowing a packet of cigarettes and a wallet. An inside breast pocket, or an outside breast pocket for that matter, is no place for a woman to carry anything.

If dolls are given to little girls to train them for motherhood, they also train little girls to become fashion consumers. Blissful hours spent dressing and undressing a Barbie Doll with her wondrous costumes are preparation for little except the department store and the shopping mall, the dreamy, habit-forming world where the adult woman is encouraged to feast on the sensuality of texture, shape and colour and bring into her life the romance and illusion she is expected to embody: a trench coat suffused with foreign intrigue, a negligee of satin and feathers for the romantic, candlelit evening, an après-ski suit even if one doesn't ski. Shopping is indeed the woman's opiate, yet the economy would suffer a new crisis if the American woman dropped her feminine interest in clothes and ceased to be a conspicuous consumer.

As far back as the Bible and the writings of the early Christians, women were denounced as prideful and whorish for indulging in the extravagance of fashion. Entire he-man industries – baleen whaling, fur trapping and the like – were built on a woman's need to look feminine and appealing, and yet when the fashion peaked or the supply was exhausted, the conceit of womanhood was blamed. Women were blamed for the annihilation of whales to make stays for their corsets, women were blamed for the near-extinction of egrets to put feathers in their hats. Women were blamed for the miserable conditions of the Belgian lacemakers and the Japanese silkworm workers, and women are blamed today for the murder of baby seals and rare leopards. Yet the point of it all was usually to please a man, for it accrued to his success that his woman was arrayed in such majestic finery.

Few women today are in a position to exempt themselves from productive labour, but none of us is exempt from a standard of feminine dressing that still includes evidence of conspicuous consumption. A hardworking woman who pays her own bills now puts aside some money or sets up a charge account to treat herself to the fur coat or piece of jewellery that a husband or lover might have bestowed on her in an earlier age. Lillian Hellman poses in *The New Yorker* for Blackglama mink and Lauren Bacall exhibits the gold bracelets and diamonds she bought for herself in a Fifth

Avenue store. Are these superficial values or an enviable example of American success, a tribute to the financially independent woman? Probably neither. So long as society measures a woman's status by the evidence of luxury on her person, no individual woman may be faulted – or applauded – for hankering after jewellery and fur. But neither will it be understood automatically that her finery was hardwon by her honest labour.

A woman 'dripping in fur' is still perceived as a woman who has acquired an expensive gift, and the credit is thought to reside with her devoted, successful husband or in her liberally bestowed sexual favours. The sable and the mink are known to breed a masculine fantasy: a desire to make mad, passionate love to a naked woman wrapped loosely in fur. Indeed, a fur coat possesses a sexual aura that is not entirely the product of its warmth or luxuriant softness. There is a history to women in fur: mistresses opening the gaily wrapped gift box with squeals of joy, 'Take Back Your Mink,' fluffy white bear throws and tigerskin rugs, chorus girls and stage door Johnnies, 'I'd rather sin with Elinor Glyn on a tiger skin than err with her on any other fur,' and there is even a pornographic classic, *Venus in Fur* by Masoch of sadomasochistic fame. There is, as well, a moral probity attached to not wearing fur. Accused of financial wrong-doing in his 1952 Vice-Presidential campaign, Richard Nixon assured the nation in his Checkers speech that wife Pat wore a 'good Republican cloth coat.'

Like the religious moralists before them, New Left radicals of the Sixties used the expensively dressed woman as a hated symbol of selfish disregard for the ills of the world. What one chooses to wear may well be an indication of economic status, class aspirations and political and moral values, but the woman's situation is doubly complicated by the feminine goal of appearing expensive, frivolous, sexy, vulnerable and refined in one package. Some women of the Old Left doggedly wore their fur coats at demonstrations in the Sixties against the Vietnam war because they wanted to show a doubting nation that the peace movement was filled with people of substance. A decade later and at the other end of the political spectrum, Fascinating Womanhood groups encouraged their members to surprise and delight their husbands when they came home for supper by dressing up like floozies. Whatever a woman puts on, it is likely to be a costume, whether it is fur, white lace, a denim skirt or black leather pants.

Serious women have a difficult time with clothes, not necessarily because they lack a developed sense of style, but because feminine clothes are not designed to project a serious demeanour. Part of the reason many people find old photographs of parading 'suffragettes' so funny is that their elaborate dresses seem at odds with marching in unison down the street. Team spirit has always relied on a uniform dress code for maximum effect, as generals and bohemians well know. Despite the proliferation of advice manuals on what the up-and-coming young female executive should wear to the office, dressing feminine remains incompatible with looking corporate, credible and competent, and no dress-for-success book has been able to resolve the inherent contradictions, or provide the extra time and money that maintaining a feminine wardrobe requires.

Men resigned themselves to a lack of individuality in clothes a long time ago, but women still hold out the hope for clothes that are comfortable, feminine and appropriate for work in one all-purpose outfit. Major airlines periodically commission top designers to perform this feat for their flight attendants with mixed, and often peculiar, results. The US Army has yet to resolve the weighty matter of the right kind of shoe for its female recruits. In tradition-minded occupations where women are breaking employment bars, an appropriate dress code seems particularly elusive. How should a woman dress for her job in a symphony orchestra where the men perform in regulation black tuxedos? At one concert I attended, the flutist wore a floor-length black skirt, the violinist wore a knee-length black skirt, and the cellist opted for black trousers. They managed to play harmoniously, and that was important.

In corporate law and finance, two conservative fields where ambitious women have established a tenuous foothold, the conventional uniform for the new female executive is the dull-coloured jacket and matching knee-length skirt, suggesting a gentlemanly aspect on top and a ladylike aspect down below. Pants are not worn, except by an occasional secretary, for they lack the established tradition, and bright colours do not signal efficiency, responsibility and steadiness on the job. Calling attention to the breasts by wearing a sweater or a silk shirt without a jacket is unprofessional on the executive level, especially since men persist in wearing regulation suit jackets to show their gentleman status. Few think it odd that the brave new careerist must obscure her breasts and display her legs in order to prove she can function in a masculine world and yet retain some familiar, comforting aspect of the feminine difference. Tradition in clothes may well outlast tradition in occupation. When Sandra Day O'Connor was sworn in as the first woman to serve on the United States Supreme Court, there was no mistaking which one she was in the formal group picture. Eight smiling justices wore trousers and long black judicial robes that came to the ankles and one smiling justice wore a specially hemmed robe that came to the knees. Justice O'Connor was the one in nylon stockings.

Voice

A boy's voice breaks in puberty. This celebrated milestone in the pathway towards manhood is reached after a surge of testosterone has induced a stepped-up division of cells in the thyroid gland and in the cartilage of the larynx. After the voice box enlarges, the vocal folds vibrate more slowly. They resonate through the nasal and oral cavities (also larger in the male) to produce a sound that is deeper and stronger than in women and children. A girl's voice also lowers in puberty, but the mild transition may go unnoticed. Only men have Adam's apples, those knobbly protrusions of cartilage at the front of the neck. Their absence in women has been celebrated in art, poem and metaphor: a white swan's neck with a delicate arch, a smooth expanse of vulnerability. One could argue that an Adam's apple looks vulnerable too.

Once the larynx is enlarged, the effects are irreversible, unalterable by physical castration or large amounts of oestrogen. Castration jokes about a suddenly high-pitched male are unscientific and silly, reflective though they are of masculine fear. Castration before puberty is another matter, ritualized in music as late as the eighteenth century by the sweetly singing Italian castrati. An Adam's apple can be a dead giveaway in a male-to-female transsexual, for removal of the throat bulge by surgery is a difficult operation that is usually avoided. A man who wishes to approximate a woman is stuck with his larger vocal chamber and deeper voice. He must practise like an actor to pitch his tones high. But since an enlarged voice box is induced at puberty by androgen, a woman who wishes to approximate a man can develop an Adam's apple and a deeper voice through testosterone treatment, just as she may grow a beard.

On the average, the difference in pitch between men's and women's voices is almost a full octave, a true example of sexual dimorphism that is about as consistent as size. A typical female sound in conversational speech corresponds to three halftones below middle C on the piano. A standard male sound registers one octave and a halftone below middle C. Trained singers can stretch their normal range into upper and lower reaches from coloratura soprano to basso profundo, but most people have a speaking range that rarely exceeds one octave. There is a fractional overlap between the usual male and female tones.

Child, grownup, man, woman: biology gives us fairly reliable auditory clues, and our ears are attuned to the signals. We expect to hear certain sounds from certain bodies; we are perplexed when they do not meet our expectations. Failure to identify the sex of a telephone caller is oddly disturbing, for the information is the first stage in a subconscious process of naming and placing. Sexual dimorphism in voice is an important guideline, a reassuring indicator of the natural order. Those whose voices fall mainly within the overlap are mistaken for the other sex too frequently for comfort. When audio cues fail, the burden of proving gender lies more heavily on the male, for the low-voiced female is allowed a trick: she can soften the edge of her tones with breathiness to make her speech sound sultry. A high-voiced male is given no relief; he cannot make sexual capital of his vocal situation. Falsetto mimicry is a slander at manhood, a slur on the testicles, not on the larynx.

Most animals produce sound and communicate in a rudimentary way among themselves, but interest in singing chimps and chatty dolphins aside, only humans are capable of true speech. Speech is the distinguishing feature of civilization; language is the crucial achievement of the Homo sapiens brain. By studying brain-injured people, neurologists discovered that speech capability, including reading, writing and analytic functions, is located in the brain's left hemisphere, while the right sphere holds the capacity for visual orientation and spatial concepts, which extends to artistic and musical skills. But there, perhaps, the matter does not rest. Recently a theory has been put forward claiming that the human brain itself may also be sexually dimorphic.

Clinical tests show that from infancy onwards little girls excel in verbal skills while boys move ahead in spatial skills during adolescence. Girls begin to talk earlier, are quicker to speak in fluent sentences. They begin to read sooner, have a larger pre-school vocabulary and perhaps a better memory than boys. When they reach adolescence the boys become more adept at solving geometry problems and three-dimensional puzzles. At every age level more males than females stammer and stutter (the ratio is four to one).

What does all this mean? Are the test score patterns merely

reflective of societal expectation and pressure, of parental reward and practice, or are they reflective, as those who hold to the theory of the male/female brain believe, of basic neurological differences that are genetically programmed and hormonally shaped? And which alternative explains the stuttering males? Science as yet can make no determination. In the next fifty years it may well be proven that the left half of the brain is innately more responsive in females and the right half is ordained to develop more fully in males, but hardly enough evidence is in today for me or anyone else to cast a wise ballot for or against a sexually dimorphic brain. For the time being it is enough to say that Woman the Communicator has had her capacity to speak, acquire and transmit knowledge squelched, hindered, restricted and scoffed at in every age, in the name of the feminine ideal.

The sad history of prohibitions on women's learning is too well known to be recorded here. Without access to knowledge half the world's population could instantly be eliminated from the competitive lists – one need look no further for the underlying reason. In much of the world women still are barred from advanced knowledge and technical training. Germane to this book are the theories offered as an excuse to keep women dumb, for they bear on a cluster of feminine qualities as men have defined them, and that women seek to fulfil.

Shakespeare wrote that a voice soft, gentle and low was 'an excellent thing in woman,' yet the public voices of women in his day, except for the Queen, were nonexistent. Females were barred from the stage in Elizabethan England. Lower-class dialects were merrily amusing to the British elite, but when the harsh, untutored accents were spoken by women, they grated on upper-class ears as particularly strident and shrill. The fishwife hawking her wares in the market went into the dictionary as a coarse, vulgar-tongued woman; her husband the fishmonger remained a mere seller of fish. If Eskimos have several words for snow because snow looms so large in their daily lives, what may we conclude about the English, who devised so many words to define a woman with a loud, unpleasant voice, a short temper and impertinent speech? The fishwife is joined by the shrew, the harridan, the magpie, the virago, the termagant and the scold.

Dickens has a teacher of manners instruct Little Dorrit to mouth the words 'prunes and prism' when entertaining a room because the effect on the lips is so pleasing. In Shaw's *Pygmalion*, Henry Higgins transforms a street vendor, Eliza Doolittle, into a fair lady by modulating her cockney tones. Fifty years ago elocution lessons were the rage in Brooklyn for immigrant Jewish families who wished to give their daughters the right advantage; sons were prepared to study medicine and law.

The great French and German philosophers of the eighteenth century addressed themselves with vigour to the questions of female education and feminine deportment. Rousseau theorized in *Emile* that the purpose in educating a girl was to render her 'agreeable to man,' because women by nature were 'framed to please, to live in subjection.' Rousseau's educational theories were designed to perfect a winsome creature who was spotlessly clean, inherently modest, naturally polite, and a bit of a coquette. Her feet were quite small, and in matters of food she preferred tiny sweet cakes to meat. To gild this delightful lily, Rousseau instructed that she should be given lessons in singing but not in the reading of music. She should be allowed no 'books of genius' that would tax and upset her mind. There was no point in teaching her abstract mathematics, nor in taking her to Paris, for she would find the loud noise of that city distressing and would want to go home. Attention, he instructed, should be paid to her elocution, to encourage her 'pretty manner of prattling' and animated face. There should be practice in the pleasing art of the curtsy, and perhaps in the harpsichord, to best display her pretty hand. Proper training should be given in 'cooking and the buttery,' in needlework and lacemaking, especially in lace, 'because there is none that gives a more agreeable attitude to her person, or in which the fingers are employed with more dexterity and grace.'

A girl so educated would have 'taste without study, abilities without art, judgement without learning.' She could then be called by Rousseau's highest accolade, 'Oh lovely ignorant fair!' and be a fit wife. 'She will not be her husband's tutor, but his disciple; instead of desiring to subject him to her taste and inclination, she will enter into his. Such a wife will be better and more suitable by far to him, than if her head were filled with learned lumber.'

Ah, Rousseau. He struggled to fill his own head with learned lumber. He taught himself music and developed an original system of notation. He studied mathematics, he travelled to Paris many times. 'Reader,' he asked, 'which would you prefer . . . a woman with a needle in her hand . . . or a female genius, scribbling verses and surrounded by pamphlets of all sorts?' Rousseau was true to his ideals. No pamphleteer for him. He hooked up with an illiterate servant girl who bore him five children that he put in a foundling home.

'Oh lovely ignorant fair!' In *A Vindication of the Rights of Woman* Mary Wollstonecraft hurled herself against Rousseau – she could not contain her rage. From a more secure position in the twentieth century, we may now explore with dispassionate neutrality the thinking of Immanuel Kant, who also read *Emile*, and who never had an intimate relationship with any woman. Within the stiff sentences of this German philosopher of the beautiful and the sublime lies a critique of pure femininity that education would damage.

In Kantian logic, charm and a beautiful nature form a feminine essence that is inborn but rather easily bruised. Women have 'very delicate feelings in regard to the least offence.' They 'love pleasantry and can be entertained by trivialities if only these are merry and laughing.' Good-hearted, sympathetic, compassionate and friendly, women at all times 'prefer the beautiful to the useful,' are 'intolerant of commands' and do things 'only because it pleases them.' What pleases them most is 'adornment and glitter.'

The feminine characteristics that Kant describes are not very different from the set of virtues that American plantation owners in sentimental moments ascribed to their slaves, who were also denied education, but the reasoning behind the denial of knowledge to women is somewhat different: in Kantian logic a woman's gentle, sensitive nature must not be marred by 'painful toil.'

Overcoming great difficulty in the drive for success is noble and sublimely masculine, according to Kant. 'Deep meditation and long-sustained reflection . . . do not well befit a person in whom unconstrained charms should show nothing else than a beautiful nature. Laborious learning or painful pondering, even if a woman should greatly succeed at it, destroys the merits that are proper to her sex. A woman who has a head full of Greek, or carries on fundamental controversies about mechanics, might as well have a beard.' Abstract speculation and useful but dry knowledge upset her 'finer' feelings. 'A woman therefore will learn no geometry . . . In history they will not fill their heads with battles, nor in geography with fortresses, for it becomes them just as little to reek of gunpowder as it does the males to reek of musk.'

Kant and Rousseau have a point. If one accepts the idea of inborn feminine qualities, and believes they were placed in the 'fair' sex to render them pleasing to the 'noble,' then one shouldn't tamper with human nature. One should stay far away from geometry, mechanics and the history of battles – as most women have. Deep meditation will earn us frown lines above our fair brow. Laborious learning will get us squint lines around the eyes and a pair of glasses, and we know what Dorothy Parker says about girls who wear glasses. To sustain membership in the fair sex one should never carry on a fundamental controversy over anything. Knowledge is power, and the lack of it is charmingly feminine. Between the bluestocking and the dumb broad, there is no doubt who lies closer to a natural feminine state as men have defined it.

A variety of curious theories were floated in the campaign to keep women from knowledge. In the Victorian era it was not woman's charm but her uterus that was in mortal danger from geometry and Greek, as doctors sought to convince their patients that a woman's reproductive system could be upset by intellectual stimulation. But the femininity argument, the danger to the traits that men find pleasing, has been woman's own compelling fear.

Belief that the feminine nature could be coarsened by learning has been coupled in history with the idea that it is in woman's nature to talk too much. Loquaciousness in the female sex has been remarked upon, not surprisingly, by the most voluble of men. Woman's wagging tongue was discussed by Aristotle, Aristophanes, Juvenal, the Babylonian Talmud, Swift, Ben Franklin, Shakespeare and Milton. Her silence was counted a virtue by Sophocles, Plutarch, Saint Paul and Samuel Johnson. Babblers, tattlers, gossips, chatterboxes, nags and scolds: the descriptions apply to one sex only and suggest a severe defect of character. It is said that women gush. We run on about insignificant matters, and when entrusted with something important, we can't keep a secret. The din is infernal. What's a man to do? A popular pub in London, The Silent Woman, named for the Ben Jonson farce, has as its tavern sign a headless female torso, the final resort.

'One tongue is enough for a woman' was the excuse the blind poet Milton offered his friends for why he would not teach his resentful daughters Latin and Greek, although he had them read aloud to him from the classics without understanding. A biographer rallied to Milton's defence with the explanation: 'It was a masculine jest, with centuries of satirical laughter behind it; but later ages, more conscious of woman's emancipation than of her traditional garrulity, have sometimes heard it with a literal mind.'

Centuries of satirical laughter have not been an aid to women's confidence in speaking, but the attempts to silence the woman's voice have gone further than satire. In Orthodox Judaism a woman is exempted from synagogue prayer because of her motherhood duties; if she chooses to go to a house of worship, she is required to hide behind a curtain or screen. Although women were active as prophets and preachers during the early years of Christianity, Saint Paul put an end to their work when he told the Corinthians, 'Let your women keep silence in the churches, for it is not permitted unto them to speak.' During the Protestant Reformation, William Tyndale, the Bible translator, took on Saint Thomas More to argue that women should be allowed to preach, baptize and administer the sacrament. Tyndale did not prevail.

During the Middle Ages, Christian theology, as well as chivalric custom and secular law, condoned wife beating for such offences as lying to a husband or scolding him before others. *The Book of the Knight of La Tour-Landry*, which set forward the duties and customs of upper-class society and was the most popular manual of its kind in medieval Europe, favourably mentions a husband who broke his wife's nose for scolding him in front of others 'with evil and great language.'

Writing on indictable offences against the public order in eighteenth century England, Sir William Blackstone makes reference to the common scold, provides her with a Latin name, *communis rixatrix*, and adds the witty aside, 'For our law Latin confines itself to the feminine gender.' A common scold was a woman who disrupted the peace of the neighbourhood with her ribald speech or abusive tongue. She was punished by confinement in a ducking stool and plunged into a river, lake or pond. The scold did not have a male counterpart, and although the ducking stool was utilized for other offences, the ignominious punishment was identified in the public mind with noisy females.

Ducking stools 'for the correction of unquiet women' were celebrated hilariously in popular English ditties. One poetic example: 'There stands, my friend, in yonder pool/An engine called the ducking stool/By legal power commanded down/ The joy and terror of the town/ If noisy dames should once begin/ To drive the house with horrid din/ Away, you cry, you'll grace the stool/ We'll teach you how your tongue to rule/ No bawling wives, no furious wenches/ No fire so hot but water quenches.'

An iron muzzle with a triangular bit that fitted the mouth, known in Scotland as 'the branks,' was another device to silence an idle tongue during the Middle Ages. Locked into the branks, an offender was chained to a post or led through town for all to witness her shame. Male blasphemers and some paupers also were sentenced to wear the branks, but like the ducking stool, the scold's or gossip's bridle (its other familiar names) went down in history as a punishment reserved for raucous, troublesome women.

English colonists brought the definition of a scold to America where, according to historian Alice Morse Earle, the ducking stool was in great favour in the cavalier colonies of the South and in Quaker Pennsylvania, set up near the local courthouse along with the pillory, the stocks and the whipping post. She quotes a Virginia statute: 'Whereas oftentimes many brabling women often slander and scandalize their neighbours, for which their poor husbands are often brought into chargeable and vexatious suits and cost in great damages, be it enacted that all women found guilty be sentenced to ducking.' Eyewitnesses reported many duckings in Virginia. A letter written in 1634 describes the ducking of 'one Betsey wife of John Tucker who by ye violence of her tongue has made his house and ye neighbourhood uncomfortable.' Betsey Tucker was ducked five times before she was penitent, and she was the third such case that summer. In colonial Philadelphia the ducking stool was considered a 'just punishment,' but a visitor to Boston in 1686 found that 'Scolds they gag and set them at their own Doors for certain hours together, for all comers and goers to gaze at; were this a law in England and well executed, it would in a little Time prove an Effectual Remedy to cure the Noise that is in many Women's heads.' (It is worth noting that a woman with a gag in her mouth is a staple of present-day hardcore pornography.)

'Meekness is ye choicest ornament in a woman' was a popular saying in colonial times. Women were not permitted to speak or hold office in the Church, and there was even some question as to whether they should be allowed to sing the psalms, under a literal reading of Saint Paul. Yet as the country grew, organized religion was unable to silence a number of impudent females who founded their own sects or who preached their own brand of evangelistic worship. The list includes Anne Hutchinson, who wished to remove the stigma of original sin from Eve, and was banished from Massachusetts, Sojourner Truth, forty years a slave and forty years free, who earned her living as an itinerant preacher and raised her voice for women's rights, Mother Ann Lee, who founded the Shakers, Ellen G. White, who formulated Seventh-Day Adventist doctrine through her revelations, Aimee Semple McPherson and a continuing procession of charismatics, faith healers and visionaries, and Mary Baker Eddy, who founded Christian Science. More typically, devout women were content to be moved by the Spirit within the church choir; yet even there Mahalia Jackson and others won international recognition as gospel singers.

The verbal capabilities of women have been hindered in every age: by legal restrictions on higher learning, which go back as far as ancient Greece, by prohibitions on devotional public speech in church, which effectively banned female contributions to thought and doctrine in the world's major religions, by the infliction of humiliating physical punishment for the use of strong, rebellious language, by wicked ridicule in poems and plays for alleged verbosity, and by imposing in the name of femininity a self-conscious emphasis not on content but on modulation, elocution and pleasing facial expression. Further, the historic division of work into male and female roles has had its own effect on choice of words and imagery. Add to these realities the continuing imbalance in the power relationship between men and women, and the fear of women that their femininity may be found wanting, and it is no wonder that men and women may speak the same language, but they speak it with a difference.*

In *The Woman Warrior*, Maxine Hong Kingston wrote of her childhood struggle to sound like an American girl: 'Normal Chinese

* Many languages of the world use masculine, feminine and neuter genders in their grammar. In the dim origins of speech when few words and sentence constructions were in circulation, it is possible that grammatical gender had an actual basis in perceptions of sexual difference. This tantalizing thought has occupied the reveries of language historians. But a principle that explains to one linguist's satisfaction why the Spanish words for city and mountain are feminine (they are round and large) fails miserably when applied to German or Hebrew. Otto Jespersen, a renowned philosopher of language, was forced to conclude that no single principle governs the chaos of grammatical gender.

women's voices are strong and bossy. We American-Chinese girls had to whisper to make ourselves American-feminine. Apparently we whispered even more softly than the Americans. Once a year the teachers referred my sister and me to speech therapy, but our voices would straighten out, unpredictably normal, for the therapists. Some of us gave up, shook our heads, and said nothing, not a word. Some of us could not even shake our heads. At times shaking my head no is more self-assertion than I can manage. Most of us eventually found some voice, however faltering. We invented an American-feminine speaking personality.'

For Kingston an American-feminine speaking personality had its own coordinates. These coordinates are now the subject of intense research by a handful of feminist linguists, psychologists and sociologists: Barrie Thorne, Nancy Henley, Cheris Kramerae, Robin Lakoff, Mary Ritchie Key and Sally McConnell-Ginet, among others. In the next several pages I have drawn on their research and combined it with my own observations.

Speaking 'in feminine' – or speaking 'in masculine,' for that matter – is an imitative process that begins early in life. Like the clothes we put on each morning, the rhythms of our speech, in a sense, have been chosen for us. Some styles seem appropriate and some do not. Speech is an assertive act, sometimes an aggressive one, and male and female are schooled in different ways.

Right from the cradle, girls and boys are spoken *to* somewhat differently, as they are handled differently, by their gender-conscious parents. Mothers and fathers tend to use a higher singsong register with baby girls, a sweet coo of 'Isn't she pretty?' as opposed to a brisk, jovial 'Hey, how's the little feller?' and 'Look at the little guy!' Children are great imitators – how else are they going to learn? – and the process of mimicry in the child helps to set the speech pattern for the adult.

When men's and women's voice tones are compared with the respective size of their vocal tracts, the tonal differences are greater than the physical differences warrant. In feminine speech the voice is pitched towards the upper end of the natural range, the decibel level is reduced and the vowel resonances are thinned. Writes Jacqueline Sachs, who is pursuing this line of research, 'Men may try to talk as if they are bigger than they actually are, and women may talk as if they are smaller.' The boarding-school voice of the debutante, a breathy vocalization of poor-little-rich-girl helplessness, is a case in point. Sometimes a minor impediment – sibilance, a mild lisp, a gentle stammer – conveys an impression of feminine charm, much as the hesitant speech of a child is heard by grownups as cute. Far from working against their success, the controlled impediments of two top female broadcasters, Barbara Walters and Jessica Savitch, actually may have given their delivery a softened feminine edge that men unconsciously find appealing. Not necessarily in contradiction, precise articulation of word endings ('loving' not 'lovin' ') is also a feminine mode, cultivating the impression that a woman is more refined than the men of her class: ladylike, or as some might say, affected.

Speaking in feminine also produces wavering tones within a syllable and a careening range of pitch within a sentence to dramatize shades of meaning. Heard critically, the speaker sounds overly emotional and insecure. Exaggerated to the stereotype, this is the 'speaking in italics' familiar to readers of *Cosmopolitan*: 'I have this *wonderful* boyfriend and my *favourite* magazine says it's *perfectly okay* that he's *married*.' (The masculine stereotype is a cool, terse monotone, the 'Yup' and 'Nope' of Gary Cooper.) Ruth Brend, who diagrammed feminine intonation patterns, reports that they often end on the upswing. Swoops and glissandos, she believes, build into a sentence structure elements of politeness, surprise, hesitation and good cheer, and seem to beg for outside confirmation. Brend finds most men avoid speech patterns that do not terminate at the lowest level of pitch.

Some men do incorporate musical swoops and rising inflections. Indulgence in campy speech by portions of the gay male community is a puzzle to straights, who think they are imitating women. Those who speak camp might disagree. Whatever the underlying reasons, campy speech allows a male to be extravagantly emotional and sensuous about everyday things in a manner that is normally permitted only to women. 'It is to *die*!' I heard a young man in my neighbourhood exclaim in front of a pastry-shop window. An emotional response to a piece of pastry is out of keeping with heterosexual manhood, but when the dessert cart rolls around in a restaurant the ladies are expected to ooh and aah, and they usually comply.

It is not that the speech of men must be flatly without emotion. Skilled orators like Winston Churchill, Billy Graham, Martin

Luther King, Fidel Castro and Hitler learned how to wring emotion from their audience by embodying passion in their own extravagant inflections – but politics and religion are certifiably masculine themes. The feminine, and gay masculine, infusion of passion into the stuff of everyday life is considered trivial, weak and sometimes unstable by heterosexual men.

On occasion they have a good point. Vocal expressions of passionate interest in clothes are objectively no less significant or understandable than emotional outcries over a football game, but how can a man relate to the woe, the utter tragedy, of 'I just ruined a nail!'? Unless a person has invested daily time, patience and work towards the creation of a perfect set, a broken nail is a peculiar cause for wailing. Feminine speech is charged with sudden upsets and crises ('I've got a run in my stocking!'; 'I'm getting a pimple!'; 'I gained two pounds!') that are inexplicable to those not engaged in the struggle for feminine perfection.

Fashion and shopping add fanciful touches to feminine speech. Subtle gradations in colour bear succulent, romantic names. A woman speaks in familiar terms of taupe and oat, of plum, aubergine, mauve and mulberry, of tangerine, salmon, cerise, coral and peach, while a man may take inverse masculine pride in the broad generalities of light brown, purple and orange. A feminine colour vocabulary is filled with hues and shades that most men have little occasion to learn or would hesitate to say aloud for fear of being called effeminate or superficial. Significantly, more than ten times as many men as women are colourblind to some degree (this is a sex-linked characteristic). Colourblindness in a sizable portion of the male population, particularly the white male population, where 6 to 10 per cent see a limited spectrum, offers a possible explanation for professed masculine disinterest in the refinements of colour. But if a man earns his living as an artist or in the fashion business, knowledge of colour is not considered unmasculine at all.

If one outstanding characteristic marks feminine speech, it is the reluctance to voice a declarative sentence – 'I say this' – with certainty and strength. Robin Lakoff, a pioneering theorist of feminine inflections, devised a classic masculine-feminine exchange to demonstrate how women routinely turn a declarative into a faltering question:

MAN: When will dinner be ready?

87

WOMAN: Oh . . . around six o'clock . . .?

'It is as though [the woman] were saying "Six o'clock, if that's okay with you, if you agree,"' writes Lakoff. 'Here we find unwillingness to assert an opinion carried to an extreme.'

But of course. It is not feminine to express a strong opinion, even about something as controversial as when the roast might come out of the oven. Women are not supposed to be authoritative. By reputation we are not even supposed to be able to present a set of facts in a rational, cogent manner. (Analytic thinking, however, is believed to be a process of the left side of the brain.) A female opinion strongly expressed is often considered emotional or bitchy. In the Fifties, when a woman criticized another woman – easier in mixed company than criticizing a man – she might find herself greeted by a chorus of meows. Meow, meow, her observation was dismissed as catty.

Even when a woman is a forthright, assertive, highly confident and successful performer on the stage of life, she may temper her speech patterns to fit a less challenging mode. Commands and directives that come from her lips will be modified with little grace notes, qualified with an extraneous phrase to take the edge off the expression of power. 'Would you like to get that for me?' is a feminine turn of phrase. The underling may have no choice: he will get that memo on her desk first thing in the morning or be fired for incompetence, but the command has been softened, the power relationship disguised, the male ego left intact.

Except when dealing with children, women are rarely comfortable issuing a command – not only because we have had fewer opportunities to be in a managerial role, but because commands and orders are blatantly unfeminine. A command uses a minimum amount of language; it need not be couched in terms of politeness. Politeness is required from underlings but not from rulers. A command may be barked, but a woman must coo. 'Would you do me a favour and . . .?' It is not surprising that insincerity is a charge that is levelled at feminine speech.

Few fault the Southern belle for her insincerity, however. Insincerity is part of her flirtatious charm, as long as it is directed towards the gentlemen in the form of compliments and feigned, wide-eyed interest. 'Let's go over and fluff up Uncle Hubie,' Luci Baines Johnson, the eager student, told Barbara Howar at a

Washington party where Vice President Humphrey was holding forth. 'Fluffing up,' the Southern belle strategy, is a highly success-ful, vivaciously feminine conversational mode, redolent of magnolia blossoms, tinkling laughter and soft breezes on a summer night: the perfect style, short of silence, for women who are extraneous to a male-oriented, power-driven society. Flirtation allows for some pert audacity but it never goes for the jugular or engages in 'Can you top this?'

Self-centred interest in personal experience and feelings is another charge that is levelled at feminine speech. According to psychologist Nancy Henley, a number of research studies find that women do disclose more personal information, 'just as subordinates in general are more revealing.' She continues, 'Self-disclosure, including emotional display, is not in itself a weakness or a negative behaviour trait. Like other gestures of intimacy, it has positive aspects, such as sharing of oneself and allowing others to open up, when the self-disclosure is voluntary and reciprocal.' By contrast a masculine verbal strategy avoids personal admissions, confessions of weakness and failure, and displays of emotion that reveal vulnerability and dependence. This is considered a wise, defensive manoeuvre in the competitive arenas of business and warfare.

'Loose Lips Sink Ships' was a popular motto during both World Wars. A commercial advertisement of the Forties, 'Don't Talk, Chum; Chew Topps Gum,' had a patriotic slant that confused me when I was eight years old because by that age I knew that chewing gum was not a feminine habit. But the point is that trading baseball statistics, discussing the physical attributes of women or negotiating deals is considered appropriate conversation among men, and being tight-mouthed about information that others can use to their advantage is considered a masculine virtue. Women devoted to the lifelong pursuit of romance and relationships cannot help but rely on their emotional feelings and the private lives of others as the backbone of their conversation. They accuse men, often unfairly, I think, of being uncommunicative and closed off. Men, for their part, are quick to assume that an intense conversation among members of their own sex is probably a theoretical discussion or a serious conference, while women engaged in earnest conver-sation most likely are exchanging love lives, recipes or gossip.

Is gossip trivial, reprehensible and malicious by intent? Having worked in the news business for many years, I can say that reporters are enthusiastic gossips in private conversation, not only because they love a good story but because their job is to make coherent sense out of the way the world functions by putting together odd, seemingly trivial pieces of fact. Trying to substantiate a rumour is a beginning step in investigative reporting. As a sign of the changing times, what once had no place in honourable journalism among men – who sleeps with whom, for example – is now considered morally pertinent to biography and politics. Gossip is feared because it is disrespectful of the mighty when it exposes personal behaviour at odds with public pretence.

Women have a tough time getting listened to, except by other women. The Sphinx, who had the head and breasts of a woman. talked in unfathomable riddles; Cassandra was fated by the gods to see the truth and not be believed; female prophets in the Church were squelched as unseemly. And Sigmund Freud lifted up his head to inquire, 'Dear God, what do women want?' A touch of madness, or silence, or coquettish uncertainty have been the feminine strategies when answering men.

In mixed company there's no question which sex has cornered the market on long-winded chatter. Men readily interrupt the speech of women, and women allow the interruption. In one systematic analysis of taped conversations between men and women, the men did 98 per cent of the interrupting. Sociologist Pamela Fishman concluded that men are the talkers and women provide the support work that keeps a conversation going. In Fishman's study of male-female conversations, when women tried to initiate new topics, it was mostly without success. They generously followed male-suggested topics, they asked nearly three times as many questions as the men to draw them out, and they interjected frequent little boosts like 'Oh, really?' to keep things perking. (Women also employ more body language than men to indicate conversational interest. Head bobbing, a flurry of little nods to show support and agreement, provides a visual accompaniment to the feminine task of animated, emphatic listening.)

There are many reasons why men interrupt the speech of women and get away with it. For one thing, more men have been trained to be verbally aggressive. In law school an argumentative, disputatious style is practised in the classroom to sharpen combative skills. Courses for salesmen include training in how to make an effective stand-up presentation and how to be persuasive. But more to the point, boys grow up assuming they have valuable information to impart. By tradition girls were instructed by their mothers and advised by their teen magazines that the most appreciated quality in a young lady is her ability to listen, to play dumb on dates and to act impressed in male company. In all-female company, a church mouse can turn into a nightingale – I've seen it happen.

Then there is the very real question of how well female voices carry. A deeper male voice can drown out a lighter female one, and a woman has to work extra hard – truly assert herself – to override an interruption. Once again, a natural biological difference between males and females works to female disadvantage. A deeper voice seems more authoritative, like taller stature. Advice on how to train a dog usually includes the suggestion to lower your voice register to impress your pet with the seriousness of the command. I always used this procedure on my sensitive collie and it worked – the dog hopped to. A deeper voice means business.

But there is just so much lowering of the voice a woman can do. I never had trouble getting my devoted dog to sit or stay, but hailing a cab is another matter. When waving the arm fails, one must resort to 'Hey, taxi!' A guttural shout – Dustin Hoffman's funniest moment in *Tootsie*. Ladies aren't supposed to shout. Neither are they supposed to whistle. Whistles and shouts are as unfeminine as belches, snores and loud sneezes. Of course, no lady should ever be in the bereft situation of needing to hail her own cab, should she? 'Hey, *taaxiii*' strikes momentary terror in my heart. As I hurl the ringing words aloft I simultaneously worry that my voice won't carry, the cab will speed by, and someone on the street will think, That certainly is a loud woman.

When hailing cabs it might be inspirational to remember the Great Call of the gibbon, the monogamous primate who is our fourth-closest relation, for vocal dimorphism in gibbons refreshingly gives females the centre stage. The female's Great Call dominates their morning territorial display, and the pair of apes perform their gymnastic stunts during the Great Call's climax. A gibbon male has a short *hoo-hah* that he interjects between renditions of the female's aria, but her opening notes command his silence. 'The female gibbon can utter the short calls of the male,' Joe and Elsie Marshall reported in *Science*. 'The male, however, never sings the Great Call.'

That's how gibbons do it. Actually I'm good at hailing cabs and

I hold the floor well in male-female conversations. I say this not to toot my own horn – 'A whistling woman and a crowing hen are fit for neither God nor men' – but to make the point that when my reputation for authority does not precede me, my gibbonesque arias get drowned out accordingly.

Women know how to laugh appreciatively; indeed, smiling and giggling are acknowledged feminine skills, but most of us are rotten at telling jokes. And many have learned to censor the belly laugh and the risible guffaw with a hand that daintily covers the open mouth. The aggression in humour is well known. A stand-up comedian takes conscious risks that are incompatible with feminine propriety. He holds centre stage; he delivers a punch line. (Get it? A *punch* line.) He ridicules the manners and customs of others. 'Let me tell you about my mother-in-law . . .' Would the reverse be funny? Erma Bombeck, a very funny woman, sits down to do her humorous riffs, and while she uses herself, the car, the washing machine and the children as subject matter, I have never heard any father-in-law jokes. Or many husband jokes, either. Comedic women are usually self-deprecatory, in the Phyllis Diller–Joan Rivers tradition. With few exceptions, female guests on the Johnny Carson show present themselves as dizzy dames. Encouraged by Johnny, feminine dippiness became a talk-show routine in the late-night hours. Madcap femininity with a touch of instability is a saleable female commodity, as Hollywood discovered. Bright comediennes with the knack for playing dumb, vulnerable dips are quickly stereotyped, like Judy Holliday, Shelley Winters, Goldie Hawn. (It helps to be blonde.) Aware of the damage in this feminine stereotype, Jean Stapleton, who played slow, simple Edith Bunker on television for many years ('Stifle yourself, Edith!'), took pains to disassociate from the role when she campaigned for the Equal Rights Amendment. In a sense, men are right. The women's movement has no sense of humour.

Using expletives is another mode of expression that runs counter to femininity and the power relationship in the most basic of ways. To no one's surprise, studies show that men use more four-letter words than women do, but younger women are narrowing the gap. I doubt whether liberation will bring us to parity in this regard. Something more than a disregard for politeness is involved in the classic obscenities of Anglo-Saxon origin. They are anti-female in intent and cannot be used by women with convincing authority.

The shock value of the words may be an affront, but the power behind the basic image, the ability to follow through, is sorely absent when a woman says 'Fuck you up your ass, buddy.'

Achieving parity in jokes and curse words is obviously not the cutting edge of the movement for equal rights, but being listened to is crucial. Sitting in a close circle and speaking in turn by 'going around the room' became the first rule in feminist consciousness-raising sessions, to make sure that every woman, the reticent, the diffident, the shy, would be heard. The technique can work only in a small group, and there are some who claim that the leaderless small group best suits a woman's style of communication, rather than the hierarchieal principle of an auditorium with a raised podium at one end.

'Give me a balcony in every town and I can take over the country,' a Latin American dictator once said. Speaking to the multitudes from a certain removed height is a technique that few women have mastered, or tried to master. Eva Peron aside, demagogic manipulation of the masses has been a masculine province. A woman on a soapbox with a microphone in her hand, even is she is perfectly coiffed, will still be called strident, hectoring or 'somewhat shrill,' as the American press said of Margaret Thatcher the week she took office. Electronic amplification of a high voice annoys many listeners, and it doesn't help that audio equipment is set for lower tones, or that speaker's podiums are routinely built to the specifications of male height.

For one brief and shining moment in world literature, writing 'in feminine' gave women an edge in creative expression. Japanese nobility during the tenth-century Heian period believed the Chinese language was superior to their own. They reserved Chinese for higher study barred to women, and they attempted to write their serious works in Chinese as well, in much the same manner that Western scholars used Latin and Greek. While they struggled to master the square, formal characters of a foreign language, women of the court were free to use *kana*, a simplified, phonetic script, to set down the language they actually spoke. Permitted a fluidity and a native idiom that men denied themselves, Murasaki Shikibu (Lady Murasaki), author of *The Tale of Genji*, and Sei Shonagon, author of *The Pillow Book*, produced the lasting masterworks of their age.

There is something very Japanese and very feminine in the story of Shonagon and Murasaki skipping past their fellow writers with a brush stroke light and true. Their experience was not repeated elsewhere. In European ghetto culture, Jewish men of learning reserved Hebrew for themselves while others made do with Yiddish, but no Lady Murasaki emerged in Yiddish, or if one did, his name was Sholem Aleichem.

But writing in feminine does not usually refer to the genius of Murasaki. It refers to the stereotype, to sentimental prose that is scented with lavender, that is vapid and suffocatingly enclosed. A feminine sentence is said to gush rather than roar; it lacks muscle and lean strength; it is precious and insubstantial; it limps along to inconclusion like an unstressed final syllable, inferior and weak. It suffers from italics and from excessive quotation marks when it tries to be slangy. When it seeks to break from its mould and be strongly declarative it is said to raise its voice and become strident and shrill.

Do women write in a feminine style? If there is evidence that women speak in a feminine manner, how can this not carry over into writing, since the rhythms of a written sentence reflect the cadences of oral speech? The feminine environment has been a world of closed interiors, imposed limitations and cramped space. It would be strange in some instances if claustrophobia, desperation and self-consciousness did not seep on to the printed page. In *A Room of One's Own* Virginia Woolf toyed with the notion of a distinctive feminine sentence, one that was not without positive virtue, but she did not define it, and her own style of writing, except in her diaries, was an extreme attempt to shake loose of gender. (Towards the end of her life she grew to detest her early essays and blamed their politeness and sidelong approach on 'my tea-table training. I see myself handing plates of buns to shy young men and asking them, not directly and simply about their poems and their novels, but whether they like cream as well as sugar.')

To be accused of a feminine style has haunted the psyches of women who write, for the accusation means critical dismissal, not chivalrous regard. George Eliot, the Bronte sisters and George Sand did not care to reveal their sex on the title page; a masculine pseudonym gave protective coloration to their words, and that was the only chivalry they required. Earlier in the nineteenth century Jane Austen had coped with the identity problem by publishing her first novel as the work of 'A Lady,' alerting the reader, suggests critic Rachel Brownstein, that here is a 'distinctly feminine and well-bred voice, the voice of a genteel maiden' who desires to please. As recently as a decade ago a university study attempted to gauge reader response when the sex of an author was attached to a piece of writing. When the writing bore a woman's name, readers felt it was a less competent, less significant work.

A professor of English named Mary Hiatt put excerpts from the works of one hundred contemporary authors into a computer to see if any general principles of feminine writing might emerge. The women in her sample wrote shorter sentences than the men, had a tendency to overwork the word 'really' in an effort to be *really* convincing, thereby betraying the fear they would not be believed, and they displayed an overall tendency to play it safe with language. Caution is what marked the writing style of women.

I understand the tendency to play it safe when one feels grateful to be allowed to play at all. 'Literature cannot be the business of a woman's life,' Robert Southey sternly reproved Charlotte Bronte, who had the courage to withstand his opinion. A more feminine woman – a less certain woman, one without egotistical belief in her own worth – would surely have acquiesced. She might have been imitative rather than original in the effort to prove that the business of literature could be hers. Or she might have chosen to scratch off a very small piece, a modest, negligible portion, to claim as her own: she would deal in the miniature, the cameo, the sketch. A more feminine woman might have given up thought of publication altogether, to pour her passion into her diary where she could express her emotions as freely as she wished, and never face up to the unfeminine task of pounding her thoughts into hard-edged shape. The hope, of course, would always remain that one day a reader would discover her soul.

Skin

During a season of public exposure when I travelled the country in leaps and bounds, one pale, imperceptible hair on my chin, lighter than an eyelash and less significant than a freckle, abruptly multiplied into two, then four, sturdy dark bristles that thrust themselves forward with pushy vigour. This uninvited quartet grew more swiftly than any hair that had ever been mine. Offended, I wiped the slate clean with a razor. Two days later the stubble reappeared.

Stubble! Only men had stubble on their chins! I was growing whiskers! One night I dreamed that a stiff black moustache had sprouted above my articulate mouth, a dream so frightening that I awoke in panic.

In the neutral light of a hotel mirror I contemplated my mortification. Were the hairs on my chin a warning or a retribution? Had my unholy ambition tapped some dormant source of testosterone within my system? Had I unlocked a reserve tank of hormonal assertion to which only men were allowed the key? Whatever the cause, I knew with certainty that I would now be packing a razor whenever I travelled, and that I would feel for the trace of coarse hair in odd moments, just as a man absently strokes his chin for signs of five o'clock shadow.

Some months later I furtively visited an electrologist. She peered through a magnifying glass and pronounced her judgement: 'It's a mole.'

A mole is a great relief when a woman fears that her drive for success has sprouted whiskers.

Beyond the many diseases of the skin itself, from psoriasis to venereal infection, a change in complexion may indicate a threat to life. There is the ashen face of a person in shock, the blue coloration of cardiac failure, the jaundice hue of a liver infection, the pigmented moles of cancerous melanoma. A ravaged, pitted skin marked the survivors of the virulent smallpox epidemic that decimated populations and affected the course of world history.

Skin also functions as a means of social communication. Newborn babies that are not picked up and held may die. A rash or an outbreak of pimples can indicate an emotional upset or an allergic reaction. Profuse sweating and strong odour are a common response to stress. Hairiness that is normal for one ethnic group may be aesthetically offensive to another. Job and housing discrimination on the basis of skin colour has been codified by private covenant and public law.

A four-year study of skin disease in the United States reported the following: Nearly one-third of all Americans suffer from some sort of skin condition; pathology increases with age; and more males than females are subject to major and minor disorders, for reasons of heredity and hormones. Yet to judge from the multi-billion-dollar cosmetics industry, the persistent rash of books on skin care, and the popularity of dermatologists, plastic surgeons and skin clinics that cater to the problems of beauty and ageing, improving the texture and quality of the skin is a basic feminine obligation, while for men it remains an optional or irrelevant concern.

Fair skin of the sort that poets have praised – pale beauty, white shoulders, a complexion of peaches and cream – is more than a matter of health and cleanliness, although the anxious regard for a clear complexion found in descriptive reports sent to kings in search of a royal wife no doubt was inspired by fear of the pox and its deadly contagion. Beautiful skin – sweet-smelling, lily-white, rosy-cheeked, soft and dewy and free of blemish – is a sentimental attribute of virginal innocence and aristocratic fragility, historically defined by that complex mixture of exaggerated anatomical difference, evidence of a sheltered life and male sexual preference for a serene young female in mint condition.

'The Princess and the Pea' by Hans Christian Andersen tells of the wonderful good fortune that befalls a bedraggled young girl who knocks on the door of a castle during a rainstorm. She is shown to a bed piled high with twenty mattresses stuffed with feathers under which the queen has placed a single pea. In the morning the girl confesses to having spent a sleepless night. Her entire body is black and blue, and, without wishing to offend her hosts, she thinks she must have been lying on something hard. The king and queen are filled with joy. They have found a proper wife for their son at last, for 'Nobody but a real princess could have such delicate skin.'

As told by the brothers Grimm, the story of Snow White is

similarly instructive. *Mirror, mirror on the wall, who's the fairest of us all?* The queen had grown accustomed to a reassuring answer. *You,* the mirror always replied, *You are the fairest of them all* – until that terrible day when the mirror spoke another truth: *Snow White is fairer than you.*

This happens predictably to ageing queens. They are no match for dewy-skinned challengers. The mirror does not lie, and emollients, moisturizers and wands of magic colour are insufficient measures for dealing with crow's feet around the eyes, furrows on the brow, enlarged pores, brown spots and loss of elasticity. But for the young as well as the old, advertisements for commercial skincare preparations and advice columns in the women's magazines spell out an impossible prescription: Clear, fresh, firm and youthful. Soft and smooth in texture like a baby's. Lighter in colour than a man's. No freckles, no pimples, no blackheads, no wrinkles, no frown lines, no dryness, no sag. No oily condition, no sallow complexion, no glisten and shine of perspiration, no bags or shadows under the eyes. No scars, no birthmarks, no pits, no pockmarks. No bulging blue veins, no broken red capillaries, no liver spots, no white spots, no open pores, no blotches. No unsightly facial hair, no hair on the legs and other proscribed places. No crepy neck, no scaly, calloused heels, no coarse, rough elbows, no dishpan hands. In short, a skin that shows no sign of physical maturity, hard work, aggravation, exhaustion, hormonal changes, the effects of pregnancy or the normal wear and tear of daily living.

Minor skin troubles are a fact of life for more men than women, but they are rarely a disqualifying factor in terms of sexual appeal. A boy may suffer acute social mortification from a severe case of blackheads and pimples, but the pits and scars of his youthful acne may be perceived as ruggedly masculine when he reaches maturity. A girl will have no such respite. She will pathetically try to hide her 'angry' eruptions under a thick cover of makeup that is guaranteed to aggravate her condition, and later on may become an eager candidate for medical dermabrasion. Similarly, the deep furrows that signify concentration, sensitivity and interesting experience in a man of middle years are the subject of massive emergency measures at their first sign of appearance in a woman, who embarks on her desperate maintenance programme of moisturizers, facial masks, wrinkle creams, and perhaps some subcutaneous injections of silicone or collagen and a facelift. In a culture that glorifies youth, men are hardly immune to the anguish of ageing, but they have yet to resort in large numbers to the illusory feminine procedures for stopping the clock, even as they continue to judge women by standards they would not be foolish enough to apply to themselves.

Belief that a woman's skin should be lighter and more perfectly smooth than a man's has had a tenacious hold on aesthetic convention. A dark/light palette to indicate sex differences was used for ancient Egyptian wall paintings; yellow pigment was applied to female bodies and reddish brown was the standard colour for males. A flawless shell-pink body was the romantic convention for female nudes in Western art, while earthier flesh tones portrayed the masculine complexion. To this day, theatrical makeup remains divided into a range of shades by sex.

In biological fact there is no natural difference in skin colour between men and women. Darker skin has a greater concentration of the pigment melanin in the epidermis, but while melanin has an obvious genetic correlation with race, a connection with gender does not exist. A comparative study of skin tones in a sample population in Michigan reported that men did appear to be somewhat darker about the chest area than women but concluded in its wisdom that men often worked or sunbathed without a shirt while women did not.

Spending more of the day out-of-doors obviously contributed to the artistic convention of the 'naturally' darker male, but even more significant to the evolving values of femininity was the earnest conviction that persons of royal heritage possessed a lighter, more delicate skin than commoners. This flesh-tone convention of the Middle Ages and the Renaissance can be seen in Spanish and Venetian art, in the brilliant portraits of nobility and their servants by Goya and Pietro Longhi, where a pale, glowing skin visually directs the eye to the people of importance, an artist's trick of great technical merit. An elitist approach to skin colour was not restricted to the painted canvas. In real life, the aristocrat's fair complexion was a lofty sign of noble lineage and gentle breeding, as opposed to the dim, thick-skinned lower orders, the swarthy peasants who laboured under the sun. 'Sunburnt' carried the meaning of rude and uncouth, as 'red-neck' does today.

Ladies and gentlemen powdered their faces (and often their hair) to achieve the starchy whiteness that symbolized their elevated station. To preserve or encourage a fine, noble pallor, complexion masks of paper and cloth were worn out-of-doors to protect the fair face from the rays of the sun while a creamed, perfumed glove protected the fair hand from roughness and chapping. For cases where a dusting of white lead powder could not disguise certain misfortunes of birth such as ruddiness, freckles or an olive complexion, there were recipes for blanching the skin with a glaze of egg white, tartar, lemon juice, mercury and the sap of the birch. Elizabeth of England was so intent on preserving her whiteness, a quality she shared with her father, Henry the Eighth, that in her old age she painted blue veins on her royal forehead to promote the illusion of translucent splendour.

Parasols and sunbonnets were standard regalia for would-be ladies in the American colonies who sought to emulate the upper-class customs of England and France, and both sexes in the upper reaches of society powdered their hair and their faces. It is difficult to pinpoint the precise moment when men abandoned whiteness as a mark of quality – the French and Industrial Revolutions were urgent catalysts in the decline of extravagant dress and cosmetics as symbols of masculine power – but by the late nineteenth century a fair, light skin was exclusively and enviously feminine.* If an 'interesting pallor' could not be achieved by powder, tight-lacing and strict avoidance of the sun, some desperate beauties resorted to eating small quantities of arsenic, a cause for alarm in the medical journals.

Associating pale skin with aristocratic refinement was not restricted to white-skinned people. Ivan Morris records in *The World of the Shining Prince* that among the nobility in feudal Japan, the physical ideal was a round, white face and a heavily perfumed body, removed in countenance and scent from the sweaty, sun-scorched labourers of the rice fields: 'In paintings of gentlemen and ladies of the court, it was conventional that people of higher rank had fairer faces. Since nature could not always be relied on to respect these distinctions, generous amounts of powder were used in order to produce the fitting degree of pallor.' The sun parasol that is such a charming fixture of Japanese art was used by both sexes, and as

---

* In the twentieth century, pale skin remains a proud symbol of lofty aims and spiritual masculinity in Orthodox Jewish communities, which still value the pallid, pasty-faced Talmudic scholar above other men.

late as this century, long after upper-class men had given up the convention for themselves, Japanese peasant women covered their faces when they worked in the fields to preserve a light complexion, a custom they shared across continents and cultural barriers with identically swathed peasant women in Italy and France.

There are many poetic terms of praise in India for the light-skinned woman, who is highly valued for her beauty, an aristocratic tradition that predates British rule, but the emphasis on light-skinned feminine beauty among American blacks has been one of the bitter fruits of racism, the imposition of one culture's values on another.

In slaveholding America, within one generation light colour became a pragmatic asset, as it subsequently did for Cubans and Puerto Ricans, since looking 'more white' was a passport to economic and social mobility. Black aristocracy in Harlem and elsewhere had always been light; however, for women 'bright-skinned' or 'high yaller' (those semi-contemptuous, semi-approving Southern terms) meant being singled out for sexual attention, a boon or a misery depending on circumstances. But the passport of light skin was held by only a few; for the majority of black women in America, a general negation of good feelings about their dark looks found expression in the lyrics 'What did I do to be so black and blue?' 'All the fellers go for the high yallers.' Billboard and magazine advertisements in the 1940s and '50s for Nadinola and other skin lighteners held out the romantic promise 'Now you can be lighter than he,' in the same way that Adler Elevated Shoes assured men, 'Now you can be taller than she.' According to Michele Wallace, author of *Black Macho and the Myth of the Super-woman*, despite attempts by cultural nationalists in recent years to extol the image of a dark African Queen, and despite the success of a few dark-skinned actresses, models and singers, in white America a light-skinned beauty remains the ideal.

My own claim to beauty, I learned at college, was an unusually pale skin which bruised easily and did not tan, presenting a striking contrast to my dark hair and darker disposition and wardrobe. To my romantic satisfaction, I was known on campus as 'the white-skinned girl,' an extraordinary tribute at an Ivy League school of ten thousand students and many blondes. My tendency to bruise, a perpetual crisis in childhood whenever I came home from the playground, was elevated, largely by me, to an emblem of fragile sensitivity of the sort that marks a sisterhood of heroines in sentimental novels, and my whiter-than-white complexion was compared favourably by some clever boyfriends to the Spanish royalty painted by Goya and to the stark, sophisticated models in the black-and-white pages of *Vogue*. Needless to say, I gloried in my delicate coloration, expecting the compliments to continue over the years as a matter of course. Sadly for my femininity quotient, my porcelain complexion, my alabaster loveliness, darkened with time to an average colour.

In Pride and Prejudice the jealous Miss Bingley had scoffed at Elizabeth Bennet for her coarse, brown complexion while the loyal Darcy staunchly defended his ladylove's right to the summer tan she had inadvertently acquired on walks in the country. Lively, athletic Elizabeth was a woman ahead of her times. It wasn't until the 1920s that the rich overcame their historic aversion to the sun's effects and took up the pastime of soaking up the summer rays at their seaside resorts and watering spas. The sybaritic novelty of toasting to perfection on the Riviera or lying on a beach blanket at the Lido was strictly for the summer months, and the women's magazines of that era still featured advertisements for skin whiteners and freckle creams to improve the feminine complexion. By the 1960s, however, the superior femininity of lily-white skin had become an outdated concept, replaced by the healthy vision of the golden California girl and the tawny glow of the international jet set who followed the sun, never fully unpacking their Gucci bags. An expensively acquired Caribbean tan became an enviable winter status symbol when compared to a dull office pallor. Quick to capitalize on middle-class aspirations, cosmetics companies began to feature tawny makeup and rosy blushers for the winter season so a secretary or file clerk could look as though she'd been somewhere interesting, at least in her imagination.

But just when a ruddy complexion was no longer the mark of a low-class labourer or the exclusive dominion of lean, hard masculine strength, dermatologists sounded the warning (the alarms were especially loud in *Vogue* and other women's magazines) that nothing ages the Caucasian skin more rapidly and irreversibly than prolonged exposure to the sun. If large numbers of women become convinced that the leathery, wrinkled look of a sea captain, or skin cancer, may be in store for them rather than a permanent extension of a sunny vacation, we may see a reemergence of the alabaster lady who eschews the noonday sun, although PABA lotions and sun blocks may deter a wholesale return to the romance of the parasol and bonnet.

Because of their higher levels of androgen, more men than women suffer from acne, especially in its severest forms, but the sheer panic a woman goes through at the eruption of a single pimple has led to a common assumption that breaking out is a female problem. It is, but the problem is strictly social in origin, for a solitary pimple standing in wretched bas-relief on a woman's cheek is a total repudiation of the ideally flawless feminine complexion. That a woman's skin often erupts on a monthly cycle, because of increased androgen and lower oestrogen at those times, has contributed to the belief that female hormones are somehow to blame. Oestrogen actually has a calming effect on the skin because it reduces oil-gland production, as many women on birth-control pills have discovered. But tinkering with the body's natural hormone levels can have unpleasant permanent effects on the complexion, as women on the pill have also discovered to their feminine chagrin. Giant freckles on the face and chest, known medically as melasma or chloasma, have appeared in perhaps as many as 30 per cent of all women who have taken birth-control pills for long periods of time; as with blood clots, the pigmentation was an unexpected side effect about which they were given no advance medical warning.

Despite the old canard that a woman never looks better than when she's pregnant, dramatic changes in oestrogen and progesterone levels during pregnancy commonly cause a blotchy pigmentation on the face and stomach, freckling, darkening of the nipples and areolae, varicose veins, unwanted face and body hair, mild balding, inflamed gums, stretch marks, itching, swelling and other assorted skin afflictions. Some of these side effects disappear in time and some, like stretch marks, do not, despite cocoa butter, exercise, massage or whatever. Pregnancy and childbirth are prime, incontrovertible expressions of biological femaleness, and the effects on the skin are so nearly universal that they cannot be considered abnormal, even though in medical terms they may be considered adverse. In societal terms, however, they are a feminine misfortune, signs of a used and slightly worn body, a negation of the youthful, unblemished ideal. I would like to meet the woman who is proud of her stretch marks as the sign of a job well done.

Pimples and stretch marks are trivial concerns compared to the pitted, pocked skin that permanently disfigured survivors of epidemic smallpox, the periodic scourge of Europe and the United States until Jennerian vaccination brought it under control in the nineteenth century. To honour a lady by praising her milkmaid's complexion was no mere poetic fancy, for the milkmaid, as Edward Jenner discovered, had been immunized by catching a mild form of the pox from her cows.

Smallpox, like syphilis (the great pox), was no respecter of class. Lady Mary Wortley Montagu, a controversial figure in eighteenth-century England for her presumptuous forays into the masculine field of writing, had survived the disease in childhood. She was broadly ridiculed by Horace Walpole and others for her excessive use of cosmetics, her thick and artless facial plaster. Whether or not the ridicule was justified, heavy makeup to cover her pocks was one of Lady Mary's passions. Her letters from Turkey, a rare account of life within the harem, are filled with admiration for the concubines' adept ways with jars of cream and pots of colour, and she brought home many samples. Always the first to try something new, Lady Mary Wortley Montagu introduced the smallpox inoculation to England. Her son was the first to receive the serum.

Thick enamel was one contemporary solution to the aesthetic problem of a pockmarked skin; another was the Parisian fashion called *les mouches* – patching the face with little black stars and crescents of velvet or paper to hide the disfiguring pits. The contagion of patching spread among ladies and dandified gentlemen even faster than the pox, but while two or three black spots charmingly affixed to the cheek, chin or forehead were admired, an evening at the theatre afforded the amusement of counting patches on those who were more intent on camouflage than fashion. No other period in history has been so heavily made up as the eighteenth century, concludes Fenja Gunn in her history of cosmetics, *The Artificial Face*.

Hair on the face, or any part of the facial topography beyond the eyebrows and lashes, is definitely off-limits to the feminine woman. Bearded women have been exhibited as sideshow freaks in the circus, where they are jokes for the rubes on summer evenings. 'You should be women, and yet your beards forbid me to interpret that you are so.' With this famous challenge, Banquo addressed the three witches in *Macbeth*. While a student at Oxford after the first

World War and an active participant in militant feminist campaigns, the English writer Vera Brittain nearly suffered a breakdown, convinced she was growing a witchlike beard.

At the beginning of the new feminist movement, when many of us rebelled for the first time in our lives against artificial beauty from girdles to lipstick, I saw the emergence of several bearded women. Peach fuzz, really, not the sort of stuff that could develop into a patriarch's full beard, but nonetheless a groundcover of surprising, dense growth. I was shocked and wished they would do something about it – continue to do whatever it was they had been doing – depilatory creams, strip wax, electrolysis, plucking, bleaching, the daily shave. The women with hair on their faces were asking for support, but a lifetime of social conditioning ordained my aesthetic aversion.

A beard is defined as a male secondary sex characteristic because it arrives at puberty, separating the men from the boys and the males from the females in Mother Nature's perfect order, which is never so perfect and never so orderly. Men and women within a family, race or ethnic group have a fairly equal number of hair follicles on cheek, chin and upper lip, but a rush of androgens in adolescence makes the difference in male growth. But not the entire difference, for hairiness is also an inherited characteristic. Whites are usually more hairy than blacks; Mediterranean, Celtic and Arab populations are usually more hairy than other whites; American Indians and Asians are the least hairy of all. This genetic pattern holds true for body hair as well as hair on the face, and for women as well as men, and has nothing to do with androgen levels.

In *War and Peace* the little Princess Bolkonskaya, an acknowledged beauty and the toast of St Petersburg, was famous, as Tolstoy describes her, for the downy hair on her upper lip. White women are endowed genetically with more facial hair than the modern Western aesthetic would care to admit. Hair on the chin and upper lip has a statistical frequency of 10 to 28 per cent, depending on ethnic origin, compared to a zero incidence for Japanese women. Although a hormonal imbalance may be the cause in a small number of cases (too much androgen or over-sensitivity to androgen can turn a smooth-cheeked woman distressfully hirsute), excessive hair is medically defined as 'more hair than is cosmetically acceptable to a woman living in a certain culture.' Facial hair in American women is socially defined as unpleasantly masculine in appearance, and it is psychologically feared as abnormal.

Quite understandably, the beard has not been significant in the mythology of the American Indian or in African cultures. By contrast, Western and Middle Eastern tradition is full of beards and their weighty importance. The mighty pharaohs, including Queen Hatshepsut the obelisk builder, come down to us in monumental portraits wearing false, formal beards, and it is difficult to visualize Moses or God the Father without their patriarchal growth. Hairs from the chin of the prophet Mohammed are celebrated as holy relics in Moslem shrines.

One of the more bemusing aspects of male-biased and white-biased anthropology has been an obsession with beards and their evolutionary importance to male domination. Identifying their interests, or the hair on their chins, with the whiskers on the male baboon and the glorious mane on the lion, some impressionable men have asserted that by presenting a stern and fearful visage, the bearded male makes a better hunter and fighter. When George Schaller reported from the Serengeti in 1969 that the female lion did 90 per cent of the hunting, that took some of the starch out of the King of Beasts and his magnificent mane. Nowadays one mostly reads about the glorious silverback mane on the male gorilla, who is a leaf eater anyway. Speculation as to why females are beardless has also crept into anthropological doctrine. One imaginative authority has offered the thought that this 'evolutionary adaptation' took place because it was nicer for the baby to cuddle up to a hairless cheek.

Whatever the advantages or disadvantages to having a beard, in people of bearded stock the ability to grow facial hair is a proud sign of normal development and virility in men – even if they choose to shave every day – and a cause for deep social alarm and insecurity in women, upon whom aesthetic tradition imposes a childlike state of hairlessness that is truly the unnatural condition. Masculine appearance may fluctuate from clean-shaven to full moustache and beard, but women consistently winnow away the scant amount of facial hair allotted by nature to establish a feminine look even further removed from the emblematic hairiness of men. A demure and placid feminine expression was achieved in the Middle Ages by totally obliterating the eyebrows and plucking an inch of hair from the temples and nape of the neck to create the oval face of pious chastity that is seen in the works of Memling, Pisanello, Van der Weyden, Van Eyck and others.

There has rarely been an age in which the eyebrow tweezer has not been a necessary feminine aid, either to clean up a scraggy line or to compose a thin arch of perpetual serenity and pleasant surprise. Women have tampered with their eyebrows in practically every permutation of ideal beauty, even today when the thick dark brows of Brooke Shields are considered chic. One could argue that tweezing the brows is merely the feminine equivalent of masculine face design *vis-à-vis* the moustache and beard, but a plucked brow that retains only a faint reference to the muscle that lies underneath it functions to reduce the intensity of facial expression. Unruly eyebrows that are thinned to a delicate arch and spaced wider apart than nature intended can effectively turn a bold, forthright stare into a pampered, shy glance that is coyly flirtatious. Tweezed brows can transform a knitted furrow of effort and concentration into a mild, even gaze of inscrutable blankness; they can dilute the severity of a negative thought into a tremulous flicker that might be mistaken for timid approval. For these artful reasons, the tweezer remains a keystone of feminine disguise and good grooming.

Reduction of body hair follows reduction of facial hair, for here again, there is no absolute difference in the distribution of hair between the sexes, there is only a difference in amount or degree. Males and females grow a coarser type of hair at puberty because of target-tissue sensitivity to the normal amounts of androgen we routinely produce. As with hair on the face, the gradation is significant enough to be called sexually dimorphic, like muscularity and height. Body hair on men usually is more profuse and it covers a wider area, and that is a basic hormonal fact. Body hair on women is subjected to the closest aesthetic scrutiny, and most normal manifestations are thought to be at odds with feminine appeal.

According to an electrologist's chart, there are nine common areas where the presence of hair may be cosmetically superfluous or indelicately offensive on a woman's body: underarm, lower arm, between the breasts, around the nipples, lower back, abdomen, pubic zone, thigh and leg. Since femininity in all respects is a matter of containment, a woman whose hair exceeds the aesthetic limits of her culture probably will employ some depilatory procedure to bring her body into line.

I remember when the fine, downy hair on my legs began to darken over a summer vacation. I was startled and not altogether pleased with what was happening, but I knew what to do. Remove it. I purloined a razor and hurriedly shaved the emergent fuzz off my legs as fast as it appeared – even faster, so entranced was I with this grown-up rite of passage – and begged my mother for a pair of nylon stockings. Smooth, shaved legs were sexy. Now I could be a pinup girl, Betty Grable. The hair under my arms got scraped away too, even though that hurt, and putting on deodorant, a finishing touch to the careful procedure, caused a nasty sting.

Newly vigilant, I embarked on the classic American-feminine mopping-up operation that soon ceased to be an exciting ritual of glamour and became a time-consuming, repetitive chore vey similar to housework. No matter how well I performed the required scouring, within a few days the telltale signs of embarrassing neglect showed through. During the many years I dutifully trimmed and clipped my natural landscape, I couldn't help but feel that the insistent new growth was some sort of repudiation of my work, and also that the work itself was patently hypocritical, an elaborate ruse to pretend that the skin on my legs was naturally smooth and that no dark shadow ever fell across my pale underarm. If the evidence had to be wiped out on sight, a proper female body shouldn't be growing the stuff at all. Why did I need to lock myself in an aesthetic convention that denied my physical reality? There was nothing wrong or unnatural about the hair that grew back in the places where I tried to will it away. It had a perfect biological right to be there. It had a perfect female right to be there. What it did not have, however, was a feminine right.

Thought to be a vestigial remnant left over from a time when humans or our precursors were completely furry, body hair in modern times has lost whatever protective function it once may have had. Since the coarse patches that appear under the arms and about the genitals are synchronized hormonally to puberty, they boldly signify sexual maturation and once may have served as a mating signal. J. M. Tanner, a British authority on anatomical development, has theorized that the so-called sexual hair may have provided a handy clutch for an infant when carried under its mother's body, as apes and monkeys carry their young. Perhaps. We know for a fact that pubic and underarm patches require only small amounts of androgen at adolescence, and all normal adults have some hair in these places, even the least hairy ethnic groups whose leg hair, especially on women, is sparse. We also know that body hair in both sexes diminishes with age, while hair on the face increases. Tanner's intriguing theory of the parental function of body hair, which I'll admit a fondness for, is at odds with other anthropological speculation which fixates on the relative hairlessness of females in comparison to males.

Darwin once claimed, and others continue to echo in abysmal ignorance of modern endocrine research, that hairless skin in females has been an evolutionary end product of sexual selection because of its keen attractiveness to males. In other words, men preferred to mate with less hairy females and chose them over the hairier types, and eventually hairlessness became the genetic norm. Darwin was surely a genius, but he was wrong about many things, and why females have less hair than males was one of them: yet this specious teleological reasoning lives on. In *The Naked Ape*, Desmond Morris proposed that females may have lost their body hair 'to make sex sexier' by revealing their shapely outlines and by enhancing the gratification of touch, ultimately tightening the pair-bond by intensifying copulatory rewards.

We don't require a Charles Darwin or a Desmond Morris to tell us that men may be put off by a hairy woman. Centuries before these gentlemen gave us a clue to their own personal preference, Ovid the love poet had jauntily compared the hair on a woman's legs and under her arms to that of a rude goat. As it happens, hairlessness in newborn babies and puppies does look innocent, vulnerable and non-threatening, while unkempt hairiness in werewolves, witches, barbarians and madmen appears uncontrolled and fierce. The animal-like aspect of body hair, to a very refined sensibility, and the fact that women under detention were denied their razors, undoubtedly led a pioneer criminologist of the nineteenth century named Cesare Lombroso to propose that the body type of the female offender was characteristically hirsute. A similar claim was made for female schizophrenics, nymphomaniacs and prostitutes. Under these hairbrained theories, Mediterranean women ranked high in all categories: oversexed, violent and mentally unstable.

The biological truth that males are hairier than females, and that a lack of hair is sometimes connected with faulty maturation, gives credence to the myth that vigorous growth, especially on the chest, is evidence in men of superior virility and courage. Phrases like 'This'll put some hair on your chest' are now without effect, and many a smooth-chested teenage boy has been hauled off to a doctor by his over-anxious parents. Genetic propensity, however, does not unfailingly cooperate with cultural myth. Given the ethnic diversity and individual differences among American men, a smooth or hairy chest is evidence of nothing at all. As for women, the presence of hair around the nipples is also related to ethnic stock (a study conducted in Wales reported an incidence of 17 per cent; this would be high for other ethnic groupings), but all prevailing images of the beautiful, bountiful breast are so faultlessly smooth that a 'normal' feminine appearance cannot tolerate the existence of a solitary speck.

Ballet dancers of both sexes customarily shave their body hair and wear flesh-coloured tights, for hair does obscure and detract from the purity of shape and design. Black net stockings and pink tights were essential to the suggestive cancan costume in an age when women did not shave their legs and were fleshier than today. Without the mesmerizing apparition of near-nudity in synchronized motion (thanks to the tights there would also be no jiggle in the thighs), the high-kicking chorus line would never have got off the ground. To think of 'Swan Lake,' a Busby Berkeley routine or the Rockettes' precision drill with leg hair is a ludicrous notion. When a leg is shaggy, who can tell if the knee is dimpled, the calf is shapely and the ankle well turned? Unshaven it remains a utilitarian limb, not a heightened, artistic vision of feminine flesh on erotic display.

Leg hair was not a problem to American women before the 1920s because the legs of most women were never on public view. When a change in attitude towards recreation, fashion and female emancipation during the prosperous, post-war Jazz Age made it socially acceptable for women of all ages and classes to expose their limbs, modesty regarding the propriety of showing legs was transformed with astonishing rapidity into a dainty self-consciousness regarding 'unsightly' hair. As depilatory advertisements reminded their audience in the women's magazines, the classic Greek ideal of feminine beauty appeared hairless in sculptured white marble. More to the point, perhaps, the show-girl's smooth, leggy glamour, the sleek, hairless models in the fashion illustrations, and the changing rules of etiquette at the beach had upped the ante of feminine competition.

Before the Great War, voluminous, skirted and bloomered bathing costumes for ladies desirous of a refreshing dip were modestly worn with long, dark stockings. A woman did not swim; she bathed. Not until the Twenties, notes costume historian Claudia Kidwell, did social attitudes permit women the same full use of water as men. Inspired by the advanced ideas of Annette Kellerman, Gertrude Ederle and other aquatic celebrities, when women did take up swimming, a brief, functional swimsuit gradually came into vogue. Alert to a trend, one depilatory ad took notice that 'Women who love swimming for the sake of sport find stockings a great hindrance to their enjoyment.' The new craze for sunbathing, pursued with passionate interest on the Riviera by the smart set of international socialites in beachwear designed by Patou and Schiaparelli, had a trickle-down effect on brevity in and near the water. Unable to resist the tide, public beaches in the United States began to ease their long-stocking regulations. At the decade's close, an abbreviated swimsuit with knitted trunks that bared the thighs had won popular acceptance and was being mass-produced by the new ready-to-wear trade.

Short dresses for street wear and the national craze for dancing also encouraged a sleekly groomed leg. Abandoning her corset, the flapper rolled her stockings with a circular garter when she did the Charleston, cutely exposing a flash of bare knee. While the spunky flapper was perpetual grist for the Hollywood mill, the movie makers threw back at her a winning image of femininity that was even more daring, glamorous and exacting in its cosmetic demands. Film historian Marjorie Rosen records that from 1920 to 1930 Hollywood memorialized the prancing, leggy chorus girl in more than one hundred movies. There wasn't a trace of 'superfluous' hair in sight.

Within the unprecedented exposure given the feminine leg, the stocking trade went through a revolution of its own. At the turn of the century, when skirts touched the floor, 88 per cent of women's hosiery had been woven of durable cotton typically embellished with clockwork, embroidery, lace insets and colourful patterns. Eleven per cent of the market was in heavier, serviceable wool. A lasting image from the Gay Nineties remains the multiple white petticoat and the opaque striped stocking. Perishable silk in brilliant colours, which represented only 1 per cent of all hosiery sales, was reserved for the upper class, for Sunday best, and for hussies. But with the vogue for short skirts and the popularization of bare legs at the beach, the stocking of choice in the Twenties was silk, flesh-coloured and as sheer as the looms could make it, to give the illusion of nudity in an impeccable, luxurious casing.

By the end of the Twenties, silk stockings in service weights and sheers had taken over the women's hosiery market. The silk stocking era with its dependence on Japanese imports, its symbolism of prosperity and glamour (even through the Great Depression) and its aggravating crooked seams and costly, frustrating holes and runs, lasted until the shrewdly orchestrated introduction of nylon on May 15, 1940, a date that is famous in hosiery annals for consumer mob scenes in the department stores and other retail outlets. After a wartime hiatus when those without access to a black-market supply were forced to make do with inferior rayon or leg paint and an eyebrow-pencil seam, the triumphant reappearance of the nylon stocking at the nation's hosiery counters and on the feminine leg was welcomed with all attendant hoopla as one of the sweet fruits of peace.

Although nylon was sheerer than silk and without the imperfections of the natural fibre, the new technology did not resolve the problem of snags and runs; but it did eliminate the embarrassment of a crooked line up the back of the leg, with a seamless stocking that held shape through a couple of washings and was less prone to wrinkling at the ankles. Still, the subtle tyranny of the nylon stocking over the minds and actions of women for the next twenty years – until it was partially overthrown by the anti-bourgeois fashion revolution of the Sixties – should not be forgotten. Sheer, see-through nylons were the *only* leg wear that met the test of both sex appeal and conservative refinement in rain, snow, bitterly cold or brutally hot weather. Not only did their exquisite transparency serve to remind a woman that she needed to shave every couple of days in order to wear her stockings, but their fragility dictated a certain cautiousness and restricted movement that the girdle with garter tabs compounded. The illusion of satiny skin and impeccable chic that a pair of nylons engendered could be destroyed in an instant by an ugly snag, and stockings could snag on the most innocent of objects, such as an office desk. One could even have the depressing experience of seeing – and feeling – a run while putting on a new pair fresh from the box. The imposition of a special cosmetic vulnerability that did not exist in nature was the price that had to be paid for a pair of acceptable feminine legs.

Hair under the arms was confronted by depilatory companies in the 1920s as though they were missionaries to a leprous population. 'Perhaps, because of an old-fashioned scruple, you have hesitated to rid yourself of the disfigurement of underarm hair,' ran the copy for Neet in *The Delineator*, a popular magazine for middle-class women, in October 1924. 'Are your arms constantly pinned to your sides? Or do you scorn to wear the filmy or sleeveless frocks that the vogue of the day decrees? In either case, *He* is apt to think you lifeless and behind the times. He will notice you holding yourself aloof from the swing of convention . . .' Ads for Zip had already employed a similar message: 'When you go to the beach this summer, are you going to be afraid to raise your arms? Are you going to shrink from the scrutinizing glance of your friends?' Alas for Zip and Neet, the swing of convention was towards the use of a safety razor, fashioned to a smaller, 'more feminine' size.

Zola's Nana had thrilled a Parisian audience in the 1860s when she raised her white arms to reveal a nest of golden hairs. Loretta Young epitomized the new American bathing beauty when she posed for *Vogue* in 1930 like a vertical odalisque with the hollows of her armpits as perfectly hair-free as her shapely bare legs. When a friend of mine tried to read *Nana* during the 1950s, she put the book down in confusion when she came to the vivid picture of Nana on stage. Underarm hair was vile – how could Zola write such a distasteful scene? she wondered. To a young American girl in the Fifties, sexuality and underarm hair were mutually exclusive.

Americans frequently have been accused of a Puritan attitude towards sex. If the removal of body hair is an indication of an unnaturally fastidious, overly refined and repressed sexuality, then Americans deserve their reputation. Influenced by Hollywood's sexpot starlets, only in the last twenty years have European women followed the American lead and begun to denude their underarms and legs. In her autobiography, Shelley Winters recalled her mortification in Rome during the Fifties when she realized that in a roomful of women wearing formal, strapless gowns, she was the only one whose underarms were pink and hairless. Today at a similar event a woman who neglected to shave would probably be mortified by her conspicuous breach of good taste and grooming.

113

A hairy armpit casually exposed by a sleeveless blouse, a bathing suit or the barest of summer dresses remains an indecorous violation of airbrushed feminine glamour. The natural hair seems oddly out of place in the context of artful fragility, and its unfamiliar presence calls attention to certain unpleasant facts of life concerning armpits – that they have a normal but unfeminine tendency to sweat and smell.

'Horses sweat, men perspire, but ladies glow.' Biologically a woman has fewer functional sweat glands than a man and she also has a slightly higher sweating threshold except when pregnant. So women as a rule do perspire less than men, but this minor difference has not been deemed large enough to distinguish the sexes. A lady is not supposed to sweat at all.

Telltale beads of moisture that form on the palms, forehead, the upper lip, the soles of the feet, the underarms and elsewhere are normal expressions of intense physical effort and emotional stress, as well as a regulatory response to heat. A sweaty palm (which in the history of evolution may once have been an aid to arboreal gripping) may be an embarrassing indicator of inner turmoil and social anxiety for both of the sexes, but rivulets of dampness that soak the shirt and mat the hair are honourable emblems in a man of action who earns his bread by the sweat of his brow. If a man perspires in the course of hard work or sport, or in response to physical danger from which he emerges triumphant, he may sweat profusely without a loss to his masculine image. On the contrary, his sweat is proof of heroic exertion: every pore announces that he is giving his all. To work up a good sweat at the gym is a vigorous, manly goal. Only if the sweat runs freely without gruelling effort or a victorious outcome – e.g., the sweating coward – is it a distasteful sign of the weak.

But there is no situation in which perspiration enhances the feminine aura, despite the obvious model of biological femaleness presented by the woman in labour who sweats to give birth. Strenuous endeavour in which every pore is utilized in a meaningful struggle is thought of in strictly masculine terms. Sweat on the brow defeats the attempt to look untouched and untroubled. Beaded moisture on the lip does not give the impression of sweet, quiet grace. A patch of wetness spreading under the arm is incompatible with genteel refinement, with fresh spring-flower loveliness that is calm, cool and collected. Compounding the problem, perspiration causes ugly fissures in the polished and perishable feminine veneer: caked make-up, the fallen hairdo, a ruinously expensive dress with a permanent underarm stain. Bring on the moisture-proof eyeshadow, the extra-hold hair spray. Sew in a dress shield, don't raise your arms. A sweating woman is a wrecked illusion. In her wildly successful Broadway comeback Lena Horne brought the house down with a monologue about sweat while she wrung out her hair and pointed with satisfaction to the drenching wetness that discoloured her white gown in the course of a demanding performance. The humour derived from its being such an outrageous subject for an elegant star whose name has been synonymous with impeccable glamour during a long and admirable career.

Eccrine sweat glands secrete the watery substance that evaporates on the skin to regulate heat. The other type of sweat gland, the apocrine, is more problematic. Located under the arms with the eccrines (and also around the pubic zone and the areola of the nipples), the apocrines release a sticky fluid during excitement and stress that mixes with local bacteria to produce the characteristic, stale body odour that society abhors. Because the apocrines lie dormant until puberty, their link to sexual attraction has been speculated on, but if the glands once performed some pheromone function, it is now emphatically vestigial. To judge by the deodorant market, no one, male or female, cares to be known by an unmistakable pungency under the arms. As it happens, the feminine convention of shaving does act to inhibit the development of odour, as hair is a retainer of sweat. In obsessively odour-conscious America, home of the vaginal deodorant spray and the little mint mouth freshener before kissing, women are given an olfactory as well as a visual reason for keeping their underarms bare.

Beyond the fairly universal agreement that roses smell sweet and the defecation of others may be personally offensive, the entire question of pleasant and unpleasant odour is tempered by familiar likes and aversion to the unfamiliar that is affected by sanitary customs, food habits and the oils and greases that may be used on the hair and skin in a particular culture. Unpleasant odour is an accusation that is levelled against other races, and given as a reason for avoidance – Japanese have claimed that whites 'smell bad'; whites have claimed that blacks 'smell bad' – and it lurks behind the belief shared by large numbers of both sexes that women are more attractive to men when they mask their human scent with the fragrance of flowers.

During that time in Western history when bathing was rare and contagion-ridden towns and cities smelled of horse manure, raw human sewage, the unwashed labouring masses and the pervasive stench of death, the solution of the upper classes to health care, offensive odours and sensual refinement was to carry a scented handkerchief, a perfumed glove or a pomander ball wherever they went. Today, when none of the above applies, a woman is persuaded not only to scrupulously rid her body of all natural smells, but even to replace the fresh, clean smell of soap and water with a brand-named perfume. That it is considered feminine and erotic for a woman to smell like a bouquet of flowers while a fragrant man is considered decadent and foppish presents a marketing problem to those who sell men's perfumes, but the serious issue remains an acculturated aversion to the natural odours of femaleness and sexual arousal.

Left to stew in their own juices, adult males and females do give off different odours. Mixed sweat and semen is appreciably distinct from the odour of sweat mixed with vaginal secretions, and menstrual blood has its own unique scent. Furthermore, body odours in others strike us more sharply than our own. Animals routinely sniff each other to ascertain a sexual message, but the true biochemical signals among humans are at once too vague, too intimate, too closely related to animal behaviour, and altogether too funky, in the original meaning of the word, to have retained much sex appeal in a sanitized world imbued with upper-class aspirations.

A primitive tribe that reeks of cow dung is convinced that its odours are pleasantly tolerable to others. Similarly, most men are not self-conscious about giving off too strong an impression when they engage in activity that is certified as manly. A man's aroma can accommodate fresh sweat, beer, horses, leather, pipe tobacco and cigar smoke with no detriment to his masculine image, and some of these odours are thought to enhance his virile status, but he is probably of the opinion that the opposite sex is best served by a dab of perfume behind the ears. 'The girl that I marry,' sings the all-American cowpoke, 'will smell of cologne,' even if she spends her days changing nappies, chopping onions and feeding slop to the pigs. No work that a woman does, even cooking, can enhance her aroma, for femininity exists on a plane of enchantment where the air is rarefied and sweet.

The narrow range of scent that is acceptably feminine does not seem so limited or lacking in imagination when it is sold by the ounce in a brilliant array of crystal bottles that promise to release the voluptuous powers of love and desire in an atomized mist of fine French elegance or an exotic cloud of oriental sophistication. Despite my uneducated nostrils, I cannot ignore the claims of my women friends that not only can they discern an expensive scent as distinct from a cheap imitation, but their pleasure is heightened when they indulge their senses in a whiff of their favourite fragrance. Nor would I make light of the sacred act of anointment, solemn and joyous in one graceful gesture, a moment akin to the last rites in the feminine ritual of preparing body and soul to meet the unknown.

'Why shouldn't a woman want to smell good?' a friend of mine asks, and I would like to answer: If you think that perfume makes you smell good, and you feel more feminine when you put it on, then wear it. A bottle of Chanel plays no direct part in the subjugation of women; it merely extends the prescription of sweetness to the olfactory senses, where pretence is easier than in matters of character and disposition, at least on first impression.

Yet I can never convince myself that perfume is just a harmless pleasure. I've heard too many nasty jokes, I suppose, like the one about the blind man who tips his hat and says 'Good morning, ladies,' when he passes a fish market. Dread that the female scent needs a mask for sexual confidence is frankly exploited in commercials for vaginal deodorants, or feminine-hygiene sprays as they are called euphemistically. (Perhaps not so euphemistically. Hygiene refers to the practice of health and cleanliness; in the context of a douche-like product, the word conveys the age-old charge against women, 'Unclean, unclean.')

As for the dab behind the earlobes – why, if perfume is such a universal delight to the senses, do men prefer to indulge themselves at one remove, and why is the gift of perfume from a man considered such a tribute to the soul of womankind? I have never been delighted to receive a bottle of perfume. On the contrary, I have always felt mildly affronted, as if the human distance had been pointedly increased. Oh, I know that was not the giver's intention – he was complimenting my sexual nature by catering to the charming enigma of my feminine affinity for luxury and froth. Women are supposed to adore good perfume and be touched by a gift that pays homage to their alluring vanities and trifling desires.

Efforts by the perfume companies to penetrate a resistant male market have been nothing short of astonishing in recent years. Are men being sissified in a decadent plot of capitalist expansion? Is the pursuit of sybaritic leisure in economically uncertain times a significant factor? Or are there now sufficient numbers of men no longer morbidly afraid of overstepping the bounds of masculinity who will venture to buy a cosmetic product that supposedly will enhance their physical appeal? And to whom is the sweet-smelling, newly liberated man appealing? I suspect that he wants to appeal to another man in the competitive scramble of the gay community, but no doubt there has been some fragrant spillover to straight men who also wish to spruce up their grooming now that the male sex is being assured by judicious advertising that 'a man's cologne' surrounded by images of polo, karate, the great outdoors, a Stetson hat, riding boots, grey flannel suits, etcetera, is a safe world apart from the stuff in the other bottle that belongs to women.

In an age devoted to personal gratification and self-improvement, the boundaries of masculine-feminine can shift with ease to permit an equality in artificial scent. Perfume is, after all, a gloss that requires little time or effort, that is rarely noticed in its absence, and that does not inhibit the capacity to function. For these reasons its usefulness as a delineator of the feminine may be on the wane. Body hair, or the tireless elimination of it, is another matter, for here the tradition rests on a true biological difference in gradation and on the lofty aesthetic of high art.

Before the dawn of twentieth-century modernism, the female nude in Western art was never blemished by pubic hair anymore than she was by underarm hair, leg hair, a spotted complexion or wrinkles. Seamless perfection was the artist's goal. It is not possible to say with authority whether actual custom influenced this shorn-lamb vision of feminine beauty. Although conscientious plucking of the pubic region was practised by Roman courtesans and high-born ladies, and Moslem women diligently plucked themselves bare and still do, body depilation has been inconsistent in other cultures. Not so, however, in art. Historian Anne Hollander has written, 'From classical times onward, the harmony of the female body seemed to require the absence of pubic hair whereas the opposite seems to have been true for male beauty.'

So while Michelangelo graced his David with sculptured curlecues in marble, honouring the golden age of Greece and Rome as well as his own predilections, Botticelli's Venus rises from the sea with a hairless crotch demurely obscured by a hank of her golden tresses. The fleshy nudes of Titian, Raphael and Rubens seem baldly plucked or oddly sparse in the context of their languorous thighs and indolent bellies. Ambiguous shading, a pallid stroke, the strategic cover of a hand, a thigh, a drape of cloth – by these devices the natural look of a realistic woman never confronts the charmed observer. Ingres did a study of Perseus and Andromeda with full pubic hair, but in the finished oil it was absent. Courbet, notes Hollander, 'did specifically pornographic paintings showing very thick pubic hair, but these were for private patrons.'

Seeking to explain the hairless convention, Hollander and others suggest that because the erotic essence of a female nude is a harmony of curves that are softly rounded, a thatch of dark pubic hair could become the unintentional focal point of a painterly composition. By contrast the highly visible male genitalia could absorb a thatch without disruption. This is a clever, painterly excuse, but I can't help thinking that the great artists felt their omission was a definite improvement over the stuff of real life. Pubic hair is coarse hair, no matter how fine the woman, and an allegorical, idealized woman can have nothing coarse about her.

The hairless nude persisted into the twentieth century until pioneers like Degas, Toulouse-Lautrec and Eakins – who did not deny they were painting mistresses, models and prostitutes, not Venus, Diana and Eve – chipped away at the convention that Modigliani and Picasso bravely discarded. Coincidentally, with the development of the camera, nude photographs without pubic hair were statements of high art, while nudes with hair, or women with hair peeping out below skirts that were coyly lifted, signified picture-postcard pornography, designed to shock the viewer with a realism that was vulgar and naughty. In an interesting turnabout, the hairless vulva has now become pornographic in a genre of magazines catering to fetishists enamoured of prepubescent girls, and sexual sophisticates like to scoff at early issues of *Playboy* with their airbrushed centrefolds that look to the modern eye neither honest nor arty.

But of course we are talking about a weightier matter than the showing of some springy, coarse hair. Female genitals are not visible unless the body is posed in what the skin magazines prosaically call a spread-shot, and because of this anatomical reticence, pubic hair has always been a stand-in for the hidden female mystery, the ultimate secret. Venus plats (Aristophanes in translation) and woody grottoes and sweet bottom-grass (Shakespeare) were literary euphemisms for what lies within the tangled thicket, like today's slangy allusions to 'beaver' and 'bush.' 'Push, push in the bush,' a disco song of 1979, got a lot of play on the airwaves because its message was rife with ambiguity and suggestion.

Tampering with the appearance of the female genitals in a given society is more than a matter of cultural aesthetics. In the legends of the Trobriand Islands as told to Malinowski by his male informants, there once lived a race of beautiful, wild women who walked in nakedness and did not shave their pubic hair. Fierce with insatiable desires, they imperilled any sailor who was stranded on their shores. The custom of total depilation that is practised in some Moslem countries is consistent with more serious measures (such as clitoridectomy) to tame female sexuality and keep it in line. In the Western world, where the rights of women have a happier history, expectant mothers have shown resistance to the routine hospital procedure of antiseptic shaving, demonstrating a genuine fondness for their pubic hair as part of their bodily dignity and mature sexual image. Yet even in Western countries, where genital hair is a familiar component of sexual expression, the amount of hair and its boundaries are subjects of intense, self-conscious feminine concern.

In a majority of women the pubic hair confines itself generally to an upside-down triangle, often with a slight spread past the crease of the inner thigh. This is known in clinical literature as the 'horizontal' or 'classically feminine' pattern. Fifteen per cent of all women and 80 per cent of all men have a spread that goes further down the thigh and up towards the navel in an irregular configuration. Since it is socially acceptable for a man to have hair on his thighs and torso, the demarcation of his pubic growth is not particularly noticeable, nor does it become a worrisome problem of indecent exposure. Yet on a smooth-thighed woman, one single curlecue that escapes the bikini line is a gross affront to feminine modesty, almost as if her genitals were showing. In one of the strangest games ever played in fashion, present-day string bikinis and some one-piece suits cut high on the inner thigh are designed deliberately to cover less hair than most women have. Those who feel their feminine charms are heightened when they wear the most revealing attire must play along with this curious rule by which a bathing suit sets the limits on the pubic zone, providing women with yet another arena in which to feel imperfect as they shave or wax or undergo extensive electrolysis to fit a designer's concept.

Ah yes, indeed, but if I happened to have hair that crept down my thigh or up my stomach, I know I'd be knocking at the electrologist's door. Women do what makes us feel normal and pretty and competitively equal, and the historic taste-makers in art and fashion have imbued us with the notion that beyond a certain arbitrary cutoff, body hair is a flagrant violation of feminine beauty and sexual appeal, if not an outright repudiation of gender. When the boundaries get switched around or narrowed, they present an exacting new challenge to those most eager to please.

As a matter of principle I stopped shaving my legs and under my arms several years ago, but I have yet to accept the unaesthetic results. The prettiest clothes rely on hairlessness to complete their effect, and there are many designs I no longer can wear. Actually I've reached an accommodation with the hair under my arms, at least when I'm not wearing a sleeveless blouse, and especially when I'm not wearing anything at all, since it balances nicely with the hair down below, but I look at my legs and know they are no longer attractive, not even to me. They are simply legs, upright and honest, and that ought to be good enough but it isn't – not when they are viewed against the smooth, sleek limbs of high art and high fashion or the high-stepping gams of a chorus line. To ease my dilemma, in the summertime I bleach my leg hair to a golden fuzz, a compromise that enables me to avoid looking peculiar at the beach. Sometimes I wonder if I'm the only woman in the world who puts colour into the hair on her head while she takes colour out of the hair on her legs in order to appear feminine enough for convention. To defy the rules and still get by is a worthy intention. However it seldom works.

'Colour her feminine.' Colour her eyes, colour her lips, colour her cheeks, colour her fingertips and toenails. To dress up grandly for the first day of high school, I put on a lipstick called Tangee

Natural. On the second day, when the boy sitting next to me in Latin leaned over to whisper, 'Hey, you forgot your makeup,' I knew I had crossed a significant bridge into the world of grownup masculine expectations. And so for the next twenty years I coloured my lips pink, orange, wine red or frosted, according to the current fashion, making the classic faces into the mirror, pressing and blotting, wiping the smear off my teeth, repairing the damage after a meal, removing the smudges after a kiss, etcetera. Although I delighted in the thick, gleaming tubes of pure, intense pigment and can reel off the names in sequence, of my next five shades (Pixie Pink, Goubeau No 2, Cherries in the Snow, Snow Rose, Where's the Fire?) while I remember nothing of Latin declensions, I never believed that a brightly painted mouth did anything positive for my face, my conversation or my kissing.

From lip colour it was an easy jump to fooling around with foundation, powder, and rouge, to compacts, tweezers, eyebrow pencils, lash curlers, liner, mascara and eye shadow, to moisturizers, pancake and liquid bases, eye creams, night creams, glosses, blushers, nail polish, perfume, *et al*. But while I've bought each of these items at least two times and some of them many times over a period of many years, selecting the most famous names and the prettiest jars and bottles, except for lipstick I've never really worn makeup at all. At the start of the women's movement I put away my crayons and paints and haven't bothered with them since, although I keep a bottle of Revlon Touch and Glow and a blusher stowed away in the medicine chest for use on stressful occasions, since I know by the face that stares back at me in the mirror that a few strokes of base and a blush of colour on my cheeks can mask the human failings of my skin and help to hide the characteristic signature of my features, a weariness under the eyes.

There is no getting around the fact that I have an anti-makeup bias, believing with as much objectivity as I can muster that I have one of those faces that simply do not benefit from an application of paintbox colour. Long before there was a women's movement to reject artificial beauty or to decry the judgement that a woman needs to 'fix herself up' through camouflage and trimmings, I had come to detest the stuff and the convention that said I had to wear it.

An unadorned face became the honourable new look of feminism in the early 1970s, and no one was happier with the freedom not to wear makeup than I, yet it could hardly escape my attention that more women supported the Equal Rights Amendment and legal abortion than could walk out of the house without their eyeshadow. Did I think of them as somewhat pitiable? Yes I did. Did they bitterly resent the righteous pressure put on them to look, in their terms, less attractive? Yes they did. A more complete breakdown and confusion of aims, goals and values could not have occurred, and of all the movement rifts I have witnessed, this one remains for me the most poignant and the most difficult to resolve.

If women's faces are supposed to benefit from cosmetics, the underside of the equation is that the wearer of makeup dislikes her face without it, believing she is wan, colourless, uninteresting, flat, an insignificant blob of blemished skin with eyes that are too small, a nose that is too broad, cheekbones that are non-existent and a mouth that fails of its own accord to whisper of sexual desire. This is the central contradiction of makeup, and the one I find most appalling. Cosmetics have been seen historically as proof of feminine vanity, yet they are proof, if anything, of feminine insecurity, an abiding belief that the face underneath is insufficient unto itself.

As it happens, some women look good in makeup – in societal terms I will even say that they look *better* in makeup; I'll grant them that, for who among us has not been trained to discern beauty in women in terms of professional, expensive glamour – the actress, the model, the President's wife? When my cosmetically adept friends complete their conjurer's art of creating their faces, I marvel at the finished picture, the makeover, the transformation: an even, glowing skin, a widened eye, a richly defined and luscious mouth. In short, a face that has responded to the age-old injunction of man to woman: Smile. A made-up woman does not need to be inwardly happy to give the impression of ecstatic pleasure, nor does she require expressive, mobile features to project the illusion of vibrant, animated life. To the contrary, facial mobility is a detriment to the made-up face, and makeup in turn inhibits genuine facial mobility. This is why, I think, the best models usually have vacant expressions and why it has become the fashion for them to scowl when they pose for the camera. A scowl on an artfully made-up beautiful woman may look petulant or cute, but it cannot be construed as a serious emotion or an unpleasant threat.

Of course there is nothing wrong with wanting to look attractive. I am the last person in the world who wishes to look like a little grey wren, and I take many steps to keep up my appearance, but I think I am right to prefer my own authentic countenance and the authentic countenance of others – with breathing pores, a living map of human experience and admitted vulnerabilities – to the impersonal cosmetic mask of smooth polish and bright colour. Makeup has been touted for centuries as basic feminine allure, but the allure is homogenized and distanced through the medium of routinely processed markings. Are men less fearful of women when they come all done up in festive wrappings?

My made-up friends are defiantly pleased with their feminine tricks of beautification. They are in step with the Eighties, brave and chic, women on the go, and I am the one who feels defensive and left behind, suffering from self-doubt. My unadorned face, the free spirited look of a decade past, now appears stick-in-the-mud, frumpy and prim: I am the dowdy feminist, the early Christian, the humourless sectarian who is surely against sex and fun. My congratulations to the cosmetics industry – they weathered the storm. Makeup doesn't even have to look 'natural' any more. Women are proudly celebrating the fake.

It was probably inevitable that the anti-makeup forces should lose. We were bucking too much of history. To tell people not to do something that makes them feel better is always suspect, and to suggest that women throw away their mascara and file down their nails in the name of liberation casts the feminist movement in a repressive light. In past centuries and present totalitarian regimes, those who have harangued against cosmetics have been grim moralists who have sought to control or crush the sexuality of women, equating the age-old tools of feminine decoration with worldly decadence, immodest pride and the devil's lure. By contrast, the artifice of cosmetics has represented good times and luxury, an emblem of physical indulgence for its own sweet delight.

'War paint' is a snide term for cosmetics that women dislike, for it brings to mind one version of the battle of the sexes in which the conniving female prepares her trap to ensnare and capture the unwitting male. The ritual of making up has only a vague connection with the primitive painting of face and body before the hunt or the fight, arming the warrior with magical signs to ensure his survival. For women the armour of cosmetics is more typically a defence against imperfection and ageing, against looking plain or tired or defeated. In the 1920s, rouge was fondly called 'the little red box of courage,' a tribute both to Stephen Crane and to the secure feeling that comes from putting on a good face.

A notion that one is doing something constructive, something beneficial, is another part of the cosmetic urge. When the ancient Egyptians, man, woman and child, rimmed their eyes with kohl, the effect was stylized and sensual, but it also reduced intense glare from the desert sun and was believed to ward off infection. Purveyors of tinctures and lotions always trade on the hope and promise of scientific improvement, of medicinal wonders. Consequently, they have often been charlatans with a grand disposition towards mumbo jumbo and unsubstantiated claims. The modern business of cosmetics has its own Horatio Alger story: the young woman blessed by nature with extraordinary skin who parlays a face cream, her 'aunt's original recipe from the old country,' into a vast, lucrative empire. With a slight variation in scenario, these heroines became known, in fact, as the Cosmetics Queens: Madame Rachel, Helena Rubinstein, Elizabeth Arden, Estée Lauder, Irma Shorell, Madame C. J. Walker and others.

Cosmetics and perfumes were used by aristocrats to preserve a haughty appearance and to indulge the aesthetic sense, but they and the aspiring gentry who copied their manners were not the only people who set themselves apart by style and scent from the dreary, unwashed masses. Face painting was a practical tool of the trade for two risky occupations that existed outside the formal class structure – the actor and the whore. The professional actor studied the art of greasepaint as he studied body movement and voice, to perfect his craft of character transformation and visual illusion – a craft that included the impersonation of women, who were not permitted to display themselves on stage. And borrowing the tricks of the theatre for the singular role she was permitted to perform on the street and in the brothel, the professional prostitute blatantly coloured her face and perfumed her body to present the boldly magnified impression of gaiety and erotic appeal that by an equally venerable tradition has advertised the selling of sex and sexual fantasy from the hetaerae of ancient Greece to the hookers of Times Square.

From its beginnings, Christianity stood opposed to the brothel, the theatre and cosmetics, often treating the three as if they were one composite evil. Preachings by Saints Ambrose and Cyprian and the writings of Tertullian exhorted against cosmetics, jewellery and bright clothing as a sign of the whore; a virtuous, submissive woman did not call attention to the lures of her sex. A similar theme was expounded by Puritan moralizers in Elizabethan England: painted women were shameful, dishonest Jezebels and the cause of worldly sin. In fashionable Paris or in decadent Venice where the Renaissance spirit inspired cosmetic decoration, worldly Catholics might be immune to the idea that makeup was akin to moral looseness, but in stodgy Protestant England and its American outpost the suspicion prevailed. In the nineteenth century, a proper Victorian maiden made do with a blush of modesty, or surreptitiously pinched her cheeks to bring out the colour. Powder and rouge were wickedly French and belonged to the arsenal of the fading beauty, the outrageous actress and the lady of doubtful reputation, the demimondaine.

What can match the powder puff as an enduring symbol of femininity, even in an age where powder, loose or pressed, has given way to liquid foundations, and the cottonwool ball, the sponge, the sable brush or the tips of the fingers perform the delicate veneer work that once required that celebrated round pad of pink or white fluff? Thirty years have passed since powdering the nose was the quintessential feminine gesture, but there are still Powder Rooms and Powder-Puff Derbies, and in certain parts of the former British Empire the street term for homosexual is still 'poofter,' although the jest I remember from my childhood, 'Hey, hit him with your powder puff!,' is probably forgotten. Once the shiny nose was considered to be womankind's chief affliction, to be remedied several times during the course of a day with a dusting that rendered, if it didn't streak, a dull matte finish. Powder is now passé; its association with upper-class whiteness and the courtesan's wiles has been superseded by the skin that glows with tawny colour, cosmetic 'proof' in modern times of vibrant health, expensive travel and adventure. (Rouge, too, is passé, but only in name. Identified too intimately with jaded ladies of a certain age, rouge does better on the cheek and at the cash register when it goes by the bright young name of blusher.) Femininity suffered an identity crisis when the powder puff lost its place on the vanity table and the little mirrored compact for touching up the shiny nose became a relic of the past. Lipstick has been the all-purpose replacement, the modern portable expression of the feminine soul.

When Sarah Bernhardt applied her lip rouge in public with the imperious manner she adopted to shock the dull bourgeoisie, she pioneered a breakthrough in cosmetic convention. The grand tragedienne was doing for an audience what she had trained to do backstage, and what celebrated beauties did privately in the sanctity of the boudoir – she was making up her face for the fun and drama of it, in the pursuit of excitement and pleasure. Half a century later, the Twenties flapper would also declare that the world was her stage, and she too would put on bright lipstick in public to shock her parents' staid generation, sometimes going so far as to dab the colour on her newly exposed knees. But the flapper herself was a bourgeois creation, occasionally a deb but more often a shopgirl, a daughter of the working class, and her lipstick did not come from Paris or the theatre: it was a standarized, mass-distributed product that she purchased in a drugstore.

What the flapper began, Hollywood took over – and magnified on the giant silver screen with the aid of newly indispensable makeup artists. Vamps and sirens, the stereotypic no-good women of the silent film, wore heavy eye makeup and lip paint to indicate destructive sexuality. By the 1940s, the American motion picture was successful in projecting an image of erotic femininity not necessarily connected with badness that still managed to drip with dark-red lips and the latest sensation, a set of perfectly manicured, brazen nails. Hollywood's glamour girl of the war years (her acting was secondary) was never without her pancake makeup, false eyelashes, fake nails and matching lipstick and polish, and from the moment she made her stunning impact as the GI's pinup and hubba-hubba queen, the very words 'glamour' and 'glamorous' when applied to women became synonymous with the razzle-dazzle of cosmetic glaze as much as with a curvaceous figure, high heels and revealing clothes.

Glamour was good for wartime morale, and Rita Hayworth seemed more appreciated in the foxholes than the factory work of Rosie the Riveter. On the home front, writes historian Fenja Gunn, 'the whole image of glamour created an unprecedented demand for cosmetics,' and the demand was from women of all ages and all social classes. A luxury tax was placed on an entire range of cosmetic items in the United States because of the petroleum shortage, and in England and France lipstick became a black-market commodity along with silk stockings. Inside the Third Reich, where German women were not recruited for factory labour because it might affect their child bearing, Hitler could barely bring himself to shut down cosmetics and hair-dye production in favour of armaments. (Albert Speer, who reports this fact in his memoirs, also records that he was made uneasy by the heavily rouged face, in private, of Hermann Goering. The perception of glamour in women and decadence in men often turns on a few strokes of artificial colour.)

By the time I was old enough to identify my femininity with a Revlon colour chart in the 1950s, lipstick was a redoubtable emblem of the American way of life. While the poor Soviet woman had to make do, we heard, with only one shade – a muddy yellowish brown produced by the State – we in the free world were codifying our sexual mores, guilt-ridden and trophy-oriented, according to the bright-red smear. A girl of thirteen who put on lipstick after school was fast and headed for trouble. A girl of fourteen who wore too much lipstick was boy crazy. Lipstick on a cigarette butt was a sign of a dangerous, sophisticated woman. Boys who came home from a date without lipstick on their handkerchiefs hadn't been able to score. Lipstick on a shirt collar was evidence of a straying husband.

Intimately connected with those aspects of sex that were forbidden, smirky or hypocritical (in actual practice why should anyone think of lipstick or any cosmetic as anything but a barrier to the touch of skin on skin?), it is not surprising that the effort towards sexual honesty that characterized the Sixties and Seventies should have had an anti-makeup bias. If women in the Eighties now find they are returning to makeup as feminine camouflage, even as they continue to raise their expectations, they are saying that the competition – not with men, but *for* them – is so intense that the historic lure of bold, bright colour and the teasing sexuality it signifies cannot as yet be abandoned.

Putting on makeup well is an exacting craft that requires a sure hand, a knowledge of theatrical effects and an aptitude for composition. Those who appear on camera utilize professional makeup artists as a matter of course, yet the average woman is expected to have skill enough for her daily routine of facial decoration. As street makeup grows increasingly elaborate in imitation of professional techniques, cosmetics companies disingenuously promote the myth of amateur proficiency with colour charts, diagrams and fine-point brushes, while those who can afford the expense increasingly rely on the professional salon. The professionalization of skin care and makeup for women who are not theatrical performers is another indication of the pressures of competitive femininity. It is not simply that the rich can pay for luxury and service, but that the rich can obtain a professional standard of cosmetic beauty that is beyond the scope of most amateur efforts.

From all parts of the media the professionally cared for face of the celebrity (it doesn't matter in what field the celebrity is famous) beams at us incessantly as the face we must measure against our own. Obsessional worries about keeping up their looks that have traditionally haunted actors, actresses and models now are shared by politicians, executives, magazine editors, television-news reporters, talk-show moderators and their assorted guests who, even when they are not in show business, are judged by performance values. The media images we have grown used to are of the young and the extraordinarily good looking, the exceedingly successful and the remarkably well preserved, whose preservation methods include the finest cutting and sewing that plastic surgery can offer.

Pressures on a woman to keep up her looks are far more imperative than they are for most men. Lately there has been talk among dermatologists that women appear to age more rapidly than men because oestrogen cumulatively thins the skin and decreases its collagen content, causing a swifter loss of elasticity in the connective tissues. While the thinning effects of oestrogen may turn out to be a concrete, biological factor in the promotion of wrinkles and sag, an inner sense of success or failure probably affects skin tone and vibrancy more emphatically than any hormone or palliative cream. If a man's work has gone well for him, tangible achievements and the satisfaction of power may give him a radiating glow of personal success in his middle years, but in a culture where the chief criteria of feminine success are ephemeral youth and beauty, a woman's sense of failure is likely to begin at the moment she is perceived by others as no longer young and desirable. Society offers a woman few objective reasons to feel successful as she grows older. More insidious, perhaps, society offers her few ways to *look* successful as she enters her middle years. Regardless of her accomplishments, which may be substantial, given the conventions of feminine appearance there is little chance for her to escape the look of defeat that is read into the face of a woman who is 'over the hill.'

How much of this is subjective? It is telling that the fine creases of age that define the mature face are known in the beauty books as frown lines, for the etchings on a woman's forehead and the tracery at the corner of her eyes and mouth seem to project an impression of harshness and dissatisfaction. Gravity pulls the features downward into what might be construed as a glower. Would the effect be as devastating if feminine charm were not measured in terms of unblemished radiance and the simple emotion of an uncritical smile?

'After forty it's all patching, patching, patching,' the actress Mary Martin once observed with rueful candour; but the art of preservation begins for the female when the bloom of youth is still on her. Thirteen years of age, *Seventeen* magazine once intoned, was not too early for a girl to begin the nightly practice of creaming her eyes. On the warning track before she has reached the prime of life, each succeeding year brings fresh anxiety, a new dilemma before the mirror, and the recognition that an upstart Snow White is making her debut. How different things are for men. The spectre of a wave of youth eager to displace them is no comforting thought, but the younger men must prove themselves by feats of achievement, not by a dewy cheek. The irrational dislike that sometimes overtakes a mature woman when she sees a vision of loveliness many years her junior is based on a realistic understanding that this is her competitor in a contest whose outcome has been preordained. There is little solace in the knowledge that the new Snow White's season will also be brief.

Of course the 'correct' moral posture should be that mean spirited jealousy of the younger woman is unseemly in a person of generous character and sweet disposition, just as attempts to conquer the reality of one's own diminishing attractiveness through extreme procedures of cosmetic surgery should be beneath the dignity of a serious mind. But the irony of the facelift is that it has become a logical extension of every night cream, moisturizer, pore cleanser and facial mask that has gone before it, for the preservation of youthful beauty is one of the few intense preoccupations and competitive drives that society fully expects of its women, even as it holds them in disdain for being such a narcissistic lot.

Movement

Athene, goddess of wisdom and goddess of war, protector of cities and patron-inventor of the technological arts, also invented a remarkable flute. Pleased with her accomplishment and its beautiful music, she played one day at an Olympian banquet, expecting a generous round of applause. Instead, she noticed Hera and Aphrodite laughing behind their hands. Repairing in confusion to a stream in the woods, Athene picked up the flute and watched her reflection in the water. Suddenly she understood. In the strain of transforming her breath into music, her cheeks puffed out comically; her features were distorted. Athene threw away her fine invention with a curse. (According to scholars of classical Greek, this story comes late in the cycle of myths.)

My mother gave me curtsy lessons before I was five. At the drop of the cue, 'And this is our daughter, Susan,' I'd gather the ends of my short, pleated skirt – elbows *in*, wrists *down*, fingers *up* – and fall to the ground on one tender-skinned knee. Grownups were enchanted. So was I, for Shirley Temple, Deanna Durbin and all the storybook princesses stood at my side. I had mastered my first serious training in feminine movement, and found it was something at which I excelled.

I always excelled in feminine movement. I'm lissome, I'm fluid, even in trousers. Want to see me raise my eyebrow? I used to practise for hours in front of a mirror. Notice how I roll my eyes when I say something clever and crinkle my nose when I laugh? Teen queen flirtation, consciously applied. The slight tilt to my chin? Copied from Paula E——, the most popular girl in grade school. The arch of my neck, the curved alignment of my raised arm and hand? Poses I learned from ballet. My fluttery wave goodbye? An adaptation of Queen Elizabeth in a motorcade. I never jab a finger – Mother always said 'Don't point,' and I still relax on the sofa in a kittenish curl.

Inspired by classical sculpture, Chinese ivories and Florentine art, I'm an adept practitioner of the oblique gesture, the softened motion, the twisting torso, the widening eyes. I rarely stand straight, preferring to lean sideways from the waist with one knee slightly flexed, one hip extended. I lower my shoulder when I lift my arm, adjusting the balance of elbow, wrist and fingers, breaking the line at each critical joint. Without conscious effort I smoke a cigarette, eat a sandwich, regard my hand, climb into a taxi with full assurance of the feminine effect. I've been doing it for a lifetime; I never forget.

Or do I? What about when I hurry through a crowded street, when I lose myself in a heated discussion, when I make a wisecrack that is aggressively cutting? Hunched shoulders, clenched jaw, narrowing eye and head thrust forward like a lowering bull. Torso rigid, neck strained, thumb jerking strongly. Nothing is feminine about these postures – where did they come from? I shrink from the knowledge that my reliably trained body can slip so easily over the line, and I remind myself to watch it. Even the best of actresses can let her performance slide, and I perform now without props and from memory.

What a stroke of good fortune that my basic equipment is right for the part. What anatomical dumb luck, what a happy accident of genetics, that my physical characteristics fall within the idealized norm. Suppose my shoulders were broader or my fingers were stubby? Suppose my joints weren't supple and I didn't possess a limber, flexible spine? What if I weren't small-framed and light-boned? What if my reflexes were sluggish, my coordination a bit slow? Suppose I was big-framed, hefty and stiff through the middle? The answer must be acknowledged. I doubt that I would have got away with being me. My disinterest in children, my dislike of makeup and jewellery, my inability to cook a good meal or embroider a pillow – what a terrible record of unfeminine traits to pile on top of strong ambition. If I hadn't felt secure in the way that I move, something else would have had to give.

For in truth I could not have pushed forward in life without some signal part of the feminine standard to claim as my own. I'm too competitive and eager to please. Biological femaleness never left me in doubt as to which sex I belonged to, and I've always been pleased with the luck of the draw, but gender alone does not suffice to convince the judgmental. One must demonstrate that one glories in being a woman or suffer suspicion. In the illusory, demanding art of the feminine, I've let my physical gestures prove my credentials.

And now for the hard part. The four-year-old who practised her curtsy, wore an opal ring on her finger and walked with her small fists tucked in a little fur muff wanted to be the best little girl in the world. Being best, she discovered, was relative and complex. The spirited twelve-year-old was elected captain of the girl's punchball team, but her pleasure at socking the ball out of the schoolyard was tempered by her worry that she might develop muscles. The teenage romantic, stuck on boys, gave up sports and bought a baton to practise twirling. She hoped to become a drum majorette, performing at half-time. She devoured the etiquette columns in *Seventeen* magazine. She waited for her dates to open the door for her and walk on the kerbside when they went to the movies. Her dates, alas, were not up on the etiquette columns. There were bumps and confusions, not the stately minuet of manners of which she had dreamed. She found that stepping to one side while her date bought the movie tickets was humiliating. She toyed with her hair and studied the movie posters, but that didn't help.

Complications soon multiplied in fast order. She who could execute an arabesque with grace was incapable of taking her partner's lead in a foxtrot or lindy. Mother's curtsy lessons and the ring and the muff had not thoroughly prepared her for following a boy. She had learned only half the required course and she resented the other half, although she didn't know why. She liked being touched but she didn't like being handled. Thus began her difficult time of testy resistance, when the boys at the dance would say, 'Relax,' which was guaranteed to make her nervous. She gloried in her feminine movements in solo performance, but in a one-two-three dip she had two left feet and felt diminished.

'And mind you,' the shantywoman told Huckleberry Finn, on the lam and dressed in a calico frock, 'when a girl tries to catch anything in her lap she throws her knees apart; she don't clap them together, the way you did when you catched the lump of lead.' The shantywoman had seen through Huck's disguise and was trying to give him some helpful pointers. He didn't know the first thing about threading a needle; he tossed a lump of lead sidearm like a boy when he should have thrown it overhead on tiptoe; and he had beaned the rat squarely instead of missing his target by six or seven feet. But Huck's worst mistake had come when she dropped the lead in his lap. To convincingly imitate a girl, Huck should have spread out his skirt to receive it.

This is a famous scene in Mark Twain's great novel, remembered by those who read it when they were young as a vivid explication of the difference between girls and boys. The scene has nagged at my mind for thirty-five years. Mark Twain got it wrong. Girls surely learn to thread a proper needle at home or at school (I had), as boys are taught to throw sidearm – I've heard more than one anxious father yell at his son not to 'throw like a girl' – but no girl, no matter what she was wearing, could deny such a basic reflex action as clamping her legs together when a lump of lead was dropped in her lap. Throw the knees apart? Not likely, not for any human being. Physiology can be compromised only so far.

When the imaginative choreographer Tommy Tune taught a cast of actresses how to walk and sit like men, he told them to imagine they had something dangling between their legs. This adjustment, along with a suit and some direct, forceful gestures, was all the actresses needed. No mysterious bundle of tricks is required to impersonate a man, for masculine movement flows naturally from physiology with little modification. Female impersonation, however, relies on a suitcase full of special effects: a wig, a dress, a brassiere and a set of falsies, jewellery for the arms, neck and ears, a makeup kit with lipstick, rouge, eye shadow and false eyelashes, a girdle, nylons and a pair of high heels. Not only must the impersonator deck himself out in full regalia to create his illusion, he must familiarize himself with the workings of each and every item, for women are all female impersonators to some degree.

See him on stage. He fluffs up his wig with a hand that is ringed and manicured with false nails. Body pitched forward on wobbly heels, his rear end juts upwards as he minces to and fro. Deciding to sit, he perches one hip on a stool in a dainty manoeuvre. Smoothing the folds of his gown, he crosses his shaved, stockinged legs and twirls one ankle. Resting elbow in palm, he shakes a wrist to jangle his bracelets. Absently he fondles the pearls at his neck, then touches an eyelash with one polished nail to free a bit of mascara stuck to his lids. Feather boas, fur wraps and diaphanous shawls work nicely for him. The elbow rotation required to drape them protectively across the chest induces a winsome motion. A professional calls this 'working with pieces,' and the art demands that he practise with each separate piece.

I am entranced when I watch a female impersonator at work, particularly one who wears street clothes and is attempting to pass. Sometimes the effect is uncanny. The head turns with piquance, the fingers are never splayed, the wrist is never held rigid. The penis, I know, has been strapped back with care (or surgically removed), the breasts are augmented by hormones and silicone or padding, and all the tell-tale signs of male hair have been thoroughly denuded. It wouldn't do for a drag queen to feel for his five o'clock shadow.

But no matter how good the act, and sometimes it's very, very good, it is easy to notice a foot that is improbably large, a calf muscle that is oddly sinewy and hard, a set of shoulders that are impossibly broad, buttocks that are too high and flat, and biceps that are too thickly developed. Whenever a female impersonator does something awkward, incontrovertible biology usually gives him away. Men who imitate women are generally too big and muscular for the part, and they began to practise too late in life. Their gestures have an exaggerated, overly energetic, overly calculated look. But then, many observers are willing to accept a few tokens, a flash of some familiar signals. Author James Morris, who took the hormonal, surgical voyage to a more peaceful state of mind called Jan, has written, 'I soon discovered that only the smallest display of overt femininity, a touch of makeup, a couple of bracelets, was enough to tip me over the social line and establish me as a female . . . The more I was treated as a woman, the more woman I became . . . If I was assumed to be incompetent at reversing cars, or opening bottles, oddly incompetent I found myself becoming.'

Women do move in ways that are different from men. The anatomical difference lends to routine activities such as walking a marked ambience that we identify as gender-specific, for size and shape have a profound effect on objects in motion. A hundred-pound woman who is five feet two, with large breasts, short legs, a wide pelvis and a low centre of gravity will hurry across the street with a natural gait that is quite unlike the stride of a two-hundred-pound man who is six feet tall with long legs, large biceps, wide shoulders and a high centre of gravity. But this, of course, is an exaggerated example; physical difference between the sexes is usually less extreme.

When it comes to bones, a female skeleton is lighter and thinner than a male skeleton of the same age and height. Fleshing out the bony frame, an average woman is 25 per cent fat and 23 per cent muscle; an average man is 15 per cent fat and 40 per cent muscle.

This is a hormonal difference. Centimetre for square centimetre of muscle, a woman might be as strong as a man, but this seems to be a moot point. Taller and heavier – in absolute weight, in muscle weight and in bone weight – and carrying less fat, which is dead weight in terms of strength and motion, adult men usually have one-third more physical power than adult women. Most of this extra power resides in the upper body. With a rigorous training programme, a female athlete's leg strength can equal the strength of a male athlete's leg, with adjustments for size and weight, but her arms, chest and back muscles will remain comparatively weak.

Legs perform the same function in men and women, but a woman has functional breasts with the capacity to nurse, and musculature in her upper body takes second place to the capacity for lactation. There may be cultures still extant in which a woman serves as beast of burden while her man sits under a tree and takes his repose, but in terms of biological efficiency, it is the male of the species who is usually best suited for lifting and carrying the heavy load.

With one big exception. To successfully hold a growing foetus in place and to force it down and out at birth, the uterus possesses a powerful set of muscles. This grand, intricate muscle mass that expands in pregnancy and contracts with giant heaves during labour is of no use in athletic competitions or in measuring the comparative strength of women and men. But labour is what the uterus does, the bone-wearying work of pushing and bearing down until exhaustion, even though it may be called upon infrequently or not at all.

A related aspect of femaleness is a large, bony pelvis that must accommodate safe passage of a baby from uterus to birth. A female pelvis is shaped like a bucket. With similar structural functions (supporting the upper body, housing the abdomen and securing the hipbones) but without room for a birthing channel, the narrower pelvis of the male resembles a funnel. In consequence, a female's hip bones are set at a relatively greater distance and the angle of the sockets allows for a wider range of motion. A woman can execute a split with greater physical ease, but when walking or running she must shift a bit farther to keep her centre of gravity over the weight-bearing foot. (This contributes to the slight roll and sway that sometimes distinguishes the female walk.)

Limberness and supple gestures are also characteristic of the female anatomy in motion. Compared to men, women usually are more flexible throughout the spine, in the hamstrings that control the knee and in the joints of the elbow and fingers. Looseness in these specific joints is probably an oestrogenic effect.

Small, light bones and agile fingers give the female a greater aptitude for fine motor coordination of the hand. This is useful, interestingly enough, in traditional women's work such as weaving, sewing, knitting, quilting and crocheting, in making pottery, nets and baskets, and in hand-painting miniatures and china plates. In the division of labour by sex in early hunting and gathering clans, nimble fingers were a female asset in harvesting roots, seeds and fruit. In the permanent settlements that later evolved, deft, flying fingers would help in sowing, planting and weeding, but not in clearing the land and breaking the soil, where muscle strength in the hands, arms and back is required.

Adroit small motions are useful in routine office procedures such as filing, sorting and typing, and in the assembly of small parts and microscopic chips on a production line – jobs that are considered women's work. Similar skills are an advantage in film editing, a craft that is popular with women in Europe, though not in America, where union discrimination has been rank. The advantage should hold for playing the piano – especially if the keys were narrowed to better suit the female span – and the woodwinds and strings. Musical instruments were passionately approved of for young ladies in the drawing rooms, but not on the concert stage. The sole exception has been the harp, for which graceful plucking gestures are a visual component of pleasure, as they are for the Japanese samisen and the ancient Greek lyre, also favoured for beautiful young women. Rapid finger motions and graceful coordination are helpful in the varied, exacting chores of the kitchen. Shelling, plucking, fine slicing and chopping, stirring, whipping, and kneading bread and decorating cakes and cookies have been traditional feminine pursuits in the home, but not, however, in the restaurant. And finally, skilful, fast, light fingers should put many women with diagnostic acumen at the top of the field in neurosurgery, and in all kinds of surgery for that matter, where the accolade of 'golden hands' stands for deftness at cutting and stitching – aptitudes required for dressmaking as well.

Grace has subtly entered the discussion, since grace may be defined as an aesthetic value that we place on fluid, coordinated motion. The female hand makes a poor fighting fist because of small, light bones and limited strength, but it lends itself well to supple articulation. Fingers that flew over a piece of embroidery sent the philosopher Rousseau into rapturous praise for the graceful feminine gesture; it was he who suggested that a dutiful daughter be trained in needlework to best display her pretty hand. Finger dexterity is probably the basis for the famous, or infamous, arched pinky gesture when holding a cup of tea that was once considered genteel when women did it, and so effeminate and unseemly when practised by men.

A feminine hand is chiefly admired these days not for its skill at embroidery, or its grace at the typewriter, or for its heroic service in the kitchen, or even for its gentle touch on another's body, but rather for its manicure, the artful shaping of the fingernails and the daily creaming to banish roughness that creates a look and feel so different from the strong, blunt hand of a man, or the work-worn hand that signals a woman's unprivileged station. Dexterous fingers are relied on to perform routine functional acts like changing a baby, grasping a suitcase, dialling a telephone or typing a letter with the self-imposed handicap of nails that are grown to excessive length.

Hollywood's contribution in the late 1930s to the concept of seductive glamour (with antecedents among Balinese dancers and Chinese mandarins), a set of protruding, enamelled nails transforms the simplest gesture into the contrived, the self-conscious, or in some cases the impossible or the to-be-avoided-at-all-costs. Seeking an explanation for their renewed popularity in the Eighties, David Kunzle, author of *Fashion and Fetishism*, suggests that restrictions on manual dexterity imposed by long nails are comparable in their erotic appeal to the narcissistic transformation of feminine motion imposed by a corset and high heels. This is not necessarily what women think, for women are notoriously unaware of how their feminizing effects may be perceived. (No woman seriously entertains the idea that her lipstick-reddened mouth is a provocative symbol of her vagina, as the porn magazines suggest.)

On men and women the cared-for hand is a sign of money, vanity and social refinement, but modern feminine psychology goes further. Growing long nails is a proud achievement, proof that a woman has triumphed over her personal shortcomings and the realistic odds. Cultivating a uniform set of ten individual nails is a project akin to the propagation of tender seedlings. One need not be a horticulturist or a nail-biter to understand the hazards or to seek out professional aids: the emery board, the cuticle stick, the gelatin packet, the liquid hardener, the creamy softener, etcetera. Other women manage to grow beautiful nails, why can't you? The feminine competition of nail-growing woman against herself, woman against nature, and woman against other women, is so absorbing that accounts of the struggle, which read like the triumph over polio, have been written by Shirley MacLaine and Helen Gurley Brown, among others.

And the results are indeed a tactile sensation. Thumb against nail, nail against palm, finger against doorbell, the merest gesture gives reassurance of the feminine difference, while a jagged, broken end is evidence of public failure and a stern imperative to begin again. Gaily enamelled fingertips tap out a romantic desire for a life free of drudgery and manual chores. In an extraordinary inversion of the function of hands, the improbable nails are flourished aloft as sophisticated symbols of feminine labour, for hard work, vigilance and creative care go into the maintenance of each forefinger and pinky. Even when they are glued-on fakes. Fakery may not be chic but nevertheless it is a permissible resort. The House of Revlon was built on the legend that a woman of glamour possessed long, perfect nails that never broke, chipped or cracked. (In an embarrassing repudiation of the Revlon myth, Suzy Parker once lost a false nail during a presentation of the new fall colours.)

The buffed and manicured feminine hand is admired for its sparkling conveyance of material status: the engagement diamond that flashes a husband's financial worth, the plain gold band that signifies marriage, the trinkets and baubles that trill a love of wealth, fun and drama. Once kings and popes loaded their fingers with jewelled rings that were kissed as symbols of absolute power. In the age of democracy it is a woman's hand that bears the encrusted brilliance to convey the message that manual labour lies whimsically beyond its reach, while protruding fingernails and jewels on men are shunned as signs of decadent effeminacy.

A pliant wrist is supposedly another sign of grace in women and effeminacy in men, but laboratory tests show no difference between the sexes in ability to flex the wrist joint. Yet the limp wrist has been caricatured so often and so wickedly that it has become the defining gesture of swish and the woman. Heterosexual men seem to guard against natural wrist flexibility, except when throwing a ball or swinging a racquet, in the interest of preserving a forceful, dynamic, straight-line masculine gesture (as evidenced in a vigorous, manly handshake) while women and gay men, in the interest of expressing emotion, practise less constraint in their gesticulations. In *The Homosexual Matrix*, C. A. Tripp expounded, 'A hand movement which may be gracefully soft when done by a woman can gain so much energy and speed when done by a man that it becomes swish – the very word denotes the rush of air around a high-speed motion. The exaggerations of swishy effeminacy . . . that can make it look like caricature . . . are the result of rounded, highly animated motions being transposed into the more muscular and aggressive repertoire of the male.' In any event, biologically speaking, a floppy wrist has no gender-related basis.

Authentic limberness in the female may be demonstrated in the ability to bend from the waist and touch the palms to the floor. Trunk and hip flexibility, which includes lateral motions, and loose elbow joints and hamstring muscles are an advantage in certain physical pursuits that girls traditionally have shown a preference for, and have been directed towards by their parents, such as ballet and figure skating, and, more recently, gymnastics and yoga. The splits, bends, arches, twists, leg extensions and elbow rotations that a limber female body can coax itself into with less difficulty than the male have led much of the world (Nureyev and Baryshnikov might disagree, but Balanchine, I gather, would not have) to consider woman the more graceful of the two sexes. Beyond flexibility, there is something about a small, light body revolving through space that seems to be an aesthetic delight to the eyes. Sports journals have noted that winning gymnasts of both sexes are small for their gender – judges are favourably disposed to slender, light frames, which the popularity of little Cathy Rigby, Olga Korbut and Nadia Comaneci bears out.

In his brilliant essays on aesthetics, Friedrich Schiller defined masculine beauty as energetic strength and grandeur, and feminine beauty as gentle harmony and grace. Schiller did not doubt which of the sexes was 'essentially in possession of true grace,' although he railed at the artifice that was thought to enhance it. Perceiving that a woman's gestures were more supple and less percussive, he wrote, 'Woman is a reed which bends under the gentlest breath of passion.' Of course he had no idea that the bending reed might be shot through with oestrogen, or that muscular energy was related to testosterone. Consequently he was quite poetic in his observation: 'The more delicate structure of the woman receives more rapidly each impression and allows it to escape as rapidly. It requires a storm to shake a strong constitution, and when vigorous muscles begin to move we should not find the ease which is one of the conditions of grace.'

The idealization of gender-related movement is romantically expressed in the *pas de deux* of classic ballet, where certain conventions are never broken. A ballerina does not give physical support to her partner: she does not lead him through bends, arches and turns or lift him into the air; and her partner does not strap himself into satin shoes and balance himself on pointe. A male dancer proudly exhibits his upper body strength by lifting, catching and steadying his partner; he exhibits his graceful leg strength through the high jump and the leap. A female dancer uses her arms for balance and expressive motion; and although we know that she must have strong legs, that her calf and thigh muscles have been arduously trained, and her feet are thick and strong and can hold a tough grip, the entire force of her lower body musculature is directed towards an illusion of exquisite, unearthly fragility as she raises herself on her toes.

A ballerina must not be overly tall, or else she might tower over her male partner on pointe. Her breasts and hips cannot be large, for this would spoil the sylphlike illusion. Her feet should not have thin, elegantly pointed toes, however, even though such toes conform to the delicate body preferred for dance. Delicate toes would cause a dancer unbearable pain when compressed and jammed against the hardened, square tip of her toe shoe, and a fine, thin foot is no good for gripping and balance. A thick, stubby hoof is best for a ballerina, not a thin, slender pedestal. Mindful of the feminine contradiction, the great Pavlova insisted that for photographs her feet be pared down to ethereal points by a skilled retoucher. So did Maria Taglioni, Pavlova's idol, who invented the toe shoe in 1831 for her role in *La Sylphide*.

A professional ballerina's body is not typical in any sense. Her knees must be capable of hyper-extension, in order to tuck away the bony kneecap when she is on pointe to create a soft, swanlike curve that extends to the arch of her foot. To execute the classic positions she must have hip sockets that give her extreme natural turnout in the thighs, and a characteristic duck-footed walk when she is not performing. As a rule she should have 'general ligamentous laxity' combined with muscular strength, and she must be a lot thinner than in the days when Degas painted her. If she is a Balanchine dancer she will have long legs and a short torso, in contradiction to the usual female body. 'Ballet is woman,' said Balanchine. Well, sort of.

One doesn't need to have been an Imperial Russian ballerina, or an Imperial Chinese empress, or Greta Garbo in her size nines (the clunker in her feminine perfection) or Susan B. Anthony in her seven and a half (large for her day, as gleefully reported by a hostile press) to have anguished over the natural size and shape of one's feet. The historic role of foot-binding is well understood, but 'emancipated' women still cramp their toes into shoes that give their feet and legs an illusory delicacy and snaky, seductive charm. Like Cinderella's stepsisters, who chopped off a big toe to fool the prince and fit the slipper ('Don't worry, my dears,' said their mother. 'When you are Queen you won't have to walk'), they risk callouses, corns, bunions, the deformity of hammertoes, a twisted ankle, a strained back, shortened tendons and torn ligaments to wear high heels, for the naked foot is seen less frequently than the shod foot anyhow, and physical comfort matters less than the psychological reassurance that comes from surmounting the feminine challenge. 'But I *can* walk in them,' goes the refrain.

Heels and stockings! As the whalebone corset once was a solemn rite of passage, in our time the teenage girl has pined and begged for her first grownup pair of high-heeled shoes. To put them on and try the first few wobbly steps is to enter a new life. The forward pitch of the knees and backward thrust of the buttocks, which startles the young initiate, magically induces a stilted, clickety-click walk, which, she will hear, is deeply provocative and a delight to behold. From this point on, whenever she puts on her heels she will be set apart from the rest of the species, children and men who walk and run and climb with natural ease.

Social critic Bernard Rudofsky has written that a woman is not regarded as seductive or sophisticated unless she surrenders her locomotive freedom to an impractical shoe: 'By depriving her of a secure walk she becomes an irresistible female. The cheeks shake, the breasts shake, the body lumbers and hops. The jutting abdomen, the staccato tripping, it is all delightfully feminine ... Every woman knows that to wear "walking shoes" or "sensible shoes" puts a damper on a man's ardour. The effect of absurdly impractical shoes is as intoxicating as a love potion.'

Devices to weigh down the foot or otherwise hamper the female's natural gait were known in the time of the prophet Isaiah, who heaped scorn on the daughters of Israel for wearing gold ankle chains with tinkling bells, which caused them to walk with mincing steps. Stilted shoes from the Orient became popular in the damp, flooded port of Venice in the sixteenth century, where chopines, as they were called, sometimes reached the staggering height of twenty inches. They persisted into the seventeenth century as the preferred footwear for ladies of leisure. Louis the Fourteenth, a very short king, popularized high-heeled shoes for men in his court, but the custom was short lived, as men felt a greater need for mobility than for artificial elevation. In the 1920s, when women freed their bodies from corsets and dragging long skirts, the high-heeled shoe was reintroduced to fashion, partially to emphasize the newly exposed leg but perhaps unconsciously to offer a new feminine impediment to motion.

An artificial feminine walk seems to gratify many psychological and cultural needs. The female foot and leg are turned into ornamental objects and the impractical shoe, which offers little protection against dust, rain and snow, induces helplessness and dependence. In an interesting double message of the sort that abounds in the exacting but not quite explicit feminine code, the extra wiggle in the hips, exaggerating a slight natural tendency, is seen as sexually flirtatious while the smaller steps and tentative, insecure tread suggests daintiness, modesty and refinement. Finally, the overall hobbling effect with its sadomasochistic tinge is suggestive of the restraining leg irons and ankle chains endured by captive animals, prisoners and slaves who were also festooned with decorative symbols of their bondage.

Those who doubt the subliminal connection between the feminine style of women's footwear and the taming of captives and animals might take a close look at the fancy knee-high leather boots in their closet. Superfluous buckles and straps resemble nothing but reins and stirrups, confusing the wearer with horse and rider. It might also be instructive to take a look at some hardcore pornography, where the honoured place of high heels is secure. One pervasive image is the woman who is bound, gagged and naked except for a pair of spindly black pumps. Another is the dominatrix with whip in hand, who also teeters on six-inch stilettos. So compelling is the imagery of the spiked heel that it serves both ends of the sadomasochistic fantasy, a symbol of immobilized dependence and a weapon that stomps and hurts. (Similarly, long sharp fingernails, which reduce the competence of the hand and preclude the making of a fist, are transmogrified into catlike red claws that scratch and draw blood. Hatpins are another sneaky weapon associated with feminine effects.)

To qualify as passably feminine a shoe does not absolutely require a high heel. All it demands is some ingenious handicap to walking more than a half mile on a country road or on a cobblestone street. A clog, which drags on the foot and offers no support in the heel, might do (very popular with the counter-culture) and so would a platform sole with string ties (big in Miami and other resorts). A paper-thin sole with no supportive cushion (the ballet shoe popularized for street wear) is a perennial favourite of teenage girls, and women of all ages feel chic and fragile in flimsy, strappy, slingback sandals that are perilous on dirty urban pavements.

A high-heeled, backless, open-toed mule, which manages to combine all the important impediments to walking, might at first glance appear to win the race for maximum feminine effect, but few women are willing to go this far. The backless mule is tainted by an unsubtle image of kimono-clad whores who loll about in brothels; it fails the test of refined good taste. What a woman puts on her foot reflects, more than anything else, the historic divisions that separate the lady from the whore. Balancing these contradictory wings of desirable femininity, as men have defined their desires, a woman's shoe walks a crooked line between projections of blatant sexuality and projections of propriety and class. A 'too-high' heel and a too-obvious display of playful hobbling threaten good taste by tipping the balance in favour of the whore. Seen from the other perspective, an over-emphasis on practicality tips the balance in favour of the dowdy. The open-toed, high-heeled ankle strap with its sly imitation of a leg fetter, known in some quarters as the Fuck-me shoe, is another variation on love-slave eroticism that is a trifle too blatant for a lady's good taste. The gold ankle chain ('I'm just a prisoner of love') is dismissed as cheap for similar reasons.

A feminine shoe means different things to women of differing classes, age and occupation, but the unifying factors may be pared down to these: the shoe must make the foot look smaller, it must be light and flimsy in construction, it must incorporate some stylish hindrance that no man in his right mind would put up with. None of this is accidental. A feminine shoe deliberately reverses the functional reason why people initially chose to wear shoes. A feminine shoe is not supposed to serve the foot, leg and hip in the practical work of moving quickly without trouble or pain. A feminine shoe is not designed to enable the wearer to cover ground more easily than if she were barefoot. On the contrary, a feminine shoe insistently drains a certain amount of physical energy by redirecting a woman's movements towards the task of holding her body in balance (and keeping the shoe on her foot) while she avoids the pitfalls of grids on the escalator, cracks in the pavement, and pavement gratings and grilles. A feminine shoe imposes a new problem of grace and self-consciousness on what would otherwise be a simple act of locomotion, and in this artful handicap lies its subjugation and supposed charm.

'Sensible shoes' announce an unfeminine sensibility, a value system that places physical comfort above the critical mission of creating a sex difference where one does not exist in nature. Sensible shoes betray a lack of concern for the aesthetic and sexual feelings of men, or a stubborn unwillingness to compromise graciously in their direction. Sensible shoes aren't fun. They hold no promise of exotic mysteries, they neither hint at incapacitation nor whisper of ineffectual weaponry. Sensible shoes aren't sexy. They betray the unexciting anatomical fact that a woman's foot follows the basic pattern of five toes and a heel, a silhouette essentially no different from the foot of a man. Sensible shoes aren't dressy. They spoil soft, graceful lines, they contradict delicate proportions. Sensible shoes don't glitter and sparkle like bubbly champagne on New Year's Eve. They are crisply efficient, providing a firm, stable anchor, a balanced posture, a sturdy base from which to turn on the heel and quickly move on.

What can a woman do if she doesn't care to wobble? Stand accused of failing to toe the mark? Get out of the obstacle race and settle for the role of little old lady in tennis shoes? Take to wearing sandals summer and winter, like the wily Colette, and paint her toenails bright red, to point up how different from men she really is?

Like Colette, Gertrude Stein had a fondness for sandals, but unlike Colette, who was a mistress of feminine illusion even when she was confined to a wheelchair in her arthritic eighties, it probably never occurred to Stein to enamel her toes. Stein had no truck with feminine artifice. She wasn't concerned with enticing men, except to her evening salon on the Rue de Fleurus. Picasso's arresting portrait reveals a short-cropped, heavy-set woman in a shapeless skirt, seated with her knees spread apart in a most unfeminine manner. Here is an individual, the canvas announces, who does not care a fig about sexual attraction.

I was taught to sit with my knees close together, but I don't remember if I was given a reason. Somewhere along the way I heard that boys like to look up girls' skirts and that it was our job to keep them from seeing our panties, but I didn't put much stock in this vicious slur. 'Put your knes together' seemed to be a rule of good posture like 'Sit up straight,' and nothing more. As with other things that became entrenched in my mind as unquestionably right and feminine, when I thought about it later on I could find an aesthetic reason. The line of a skirt did seem more graceful when the knees weren't poking out in different directions. Slanting them together was the way to avoid looking slovenly in a chair. (Sitting with the legs crossed became an acceptably feminine posture only after skirts were shortened in the 1920s.)

Bending over to pick up a piece of paper was fraught with the danger of indecent exposure during the Sixties mini-skirt era, and like other women who believed the minis looked terrifically dashing when we stepped along the street, I had to think twice, compose myself, and slither down with closed knees if I dropped something. A breed of voyeurs known as staircase watchers made their appearance during this interesting time. Slowly it dawned on me that much of feminine movement, the inhibited gestures, the locked knees, the nervous adjustment of the skirt, was a defensive manoeuvre against an imodest, vulgar display that feminine clothing flirted with in deliberate provocation. My feminine responsibility was to keep both aspects, the provocative and the chaste, in careful balance, even if it meant avoiding the beautifully designed open stairway in a certain Fifth Avenue bookshop.

But why did I think of vulgarity when the focal point at issue – I could no longer deny the obvious – was my very own crotch? And why did I believe that if I switched to trousers, the problem would be magically solved?

Spreading the legs is a biologically crucial, characteristically feminine act. Not only does the female have the anatomical capacity to stretch her legs further apart than the average male because of the shape of her pelvis, but a generous amount of leg spread is necessary to the act of sexual intercourse, to the assertive demand for pleasure, and to the act of giving birth. There may have been a time in history when this female posture was celebrated with pride and joy – I am thinking of the Minoan frescoes on Crete where young women are shown leaping with ease over the horns of a charging bull (the sexual symbolism of the woman and the bull has been remarked upon by others) – but in civilization as we know it, female leg spread is identified with loose, wanton behaviour, pornographic imagery, promiscuity, moral laxity, immodest demeanour and a lack of refinement. In other words, with qualities that the feminine woman must try to avoid, even as she must try to hint that somewhere within her repertoire such possibilities exist.

Capacious female leg spread is fundamental to copulation and sexual pleasure, as routine as the mounting procedure is for the male; in fact, female leg spread must occur first in the natural order of things if sexual activity is going to take place. By contrast there is nothing hidden about the male sexual organ. It is a manifest presence; the legs need not spread to reveal it, not are they usually positioned as wide apart as the female's to accomplish the sexual act. But while copulation and other genital activity require a generous spread of the thighs in order for a woman to achieve her pleasure, in the feminine code of behaviour she is not supposed to take the initiative out of her own desire. Her feminine task is to keep her legs firmly together in the name of modesty and chastity, to guard her 'hidden treasure' while waiting for the one right man (her lawful husband, her persistent lover) to wave the magic wand and perform the ritual of open sesame. His volition and his actions are expected to take precedence over hers.

Initiative is the issue, and the feminine code of movement is designed to inhibit the thought. The ideology of feminine sexual passivity relies upon a pair of closed thighs more intently than it does upon speculative theories of the effects of testosterone on the libido, aggression and the human brain. Open thighs acknowledge female sexuality as a positive, assertive force – a force that is capable of making demands to achieve satisfaction.

Students of Japanese history know that Samurai warriors trained their daughters in the use of weapons to give them the requisite

147

skill to commit hara-kiri when faced with disgrace. As part of the training, girls were taught how to tie their lower limbs securely so they would not embarrass themselves and their family by inadvertently assuming an immodest position in the agony of death. Traditional Japanese etiquette pays close attention to the rules of modest posture for women. In the classic squat position for eating, men are permitted to open their knees a few inches for comfort but women are not. Men may also sit cross legged on the floor but women must kneel with their legs together.

Throughout Asia during the Middle Ages, women either were carried in a litter when they journeyed a long distance or they rode on horseback, straddling the animal and directing its movements like a typical male rider. The ladylike custom of perching sideways, which required a groom to hold the reins and lead the way, and its variation, riding pillion on a cushioned seat behind the male rider, were conventions that arose in medieval Europe. (The demure sideways perch appealed to generations of artists who chose the Flight Into Egypt as a favourite theme. In this popular genre of Holy Family portraits, Mary cradles the infant Jesus in her arms as mother and son are solemnly borne on a donkey led by Joseph.) Exceptional women like Joan of Arc and Diane de Poitiers plainly straddled their mounts with vigour and skill, but conventional ladies restricted their riding to ceremonial occasions and some pleasant outings in the fresh air, and they rode 'aside' with their legs together. For its part, the patient horse could do little more than walk in a measured gait under the precarious burden of its lopsided load.

Catherine de Medici, who is credited with popularizing the corset, is also thought to have devised that ingenuous feminine compromise the side saddle. According to one historian of horsemanship, 'She discovered it was safer than sitting sideways, and more seemly than sitting astride, to hook her right knee round the high pommel of a man's saddle. It was an obvious development to move the pommel a few inches to the left, so as to hold the rider's leg in a secure and comfortable grip.' With variations and refinements, riding side saddle persisted into the twentieth century, when the suffrage movement, trail riding in the American West, and the acceptance of riding breeches eased its decline.

The side saddle was popular for many reasons. Women were not believed to have enough strength in their thighs to straddle a horse and maintain a good grip. Their legs were too short, their backs were too weak, and a sustained bumping on the groin was not only indelicate, it might also be injurious. In the words of Charles Chenevix Trench, the horseman's historian, 'Moreover, the rounded contours of females were considered inelegant when riding astride. Put bluntly, their bottoms were too big.' But with the left leg dangling in a normal stirrup, the right leg crossed over to the left side of the horse, and both legs covered by the drape of a skirt, the view from the rear was asymmetrical and charming. The rider's legs were as close together as they could be, and pleasurable contact between groin and saddle was deftly avoided. It remained for the feminine student of equitation to compensate for the uneven distribution of her weight on the left side of the horse by lifting her left hip and bearing down hard on her right, while she twisted her torso to keep facing front. When mounting or dismounting, two attendants were usually required: a groom to hold the reins and a gentleman cavalier to lift her into and out of the saddle while she modestly arranged her skirts. All of this accomplished, a lady could ride and not look or feel like a man. She could even manage a small jump and a canter. She tired more easily than her male companions because of the uneven stress and strain on her muscles, but ladies were expected to tire and not be as strong as men. The important thing was that she had preserved her femininity on horseback – at the expense of being a one-legged rider.

Prior to the twentieth century the athletic woman was required to accept a multiplicity of handicaps that reduced the efficiency of her natural coordination and made her specially vulnerable to injury from accidental spills and awkward, humiliating falls. Riding side saddle, ice-skating in long skirts, swimming in stockings and bloomers, bicycling in furbelows, playing badminton in corsets, she gamely struggled to keep her balance while preserving a modest deportment. It was not simply that love of sports was somewhat mannish and suspect. She believed her body housed reproductive organs that were morbidly delicate and debilitating by nature. One of her concerns was uterine protection.

In the obsessive Victorian preoccupation with 'the feminine sphere,' partial invalidism and bodily frailty were assumed to be the female's natural state – unless the female was a servant or factory worker. A lady's pregnancy was tantamount to an illness that demanded a lengthy confinement, and menstruation was viewed as a chronic sickness that could best be treated by inactivity and bed rest. In the words of Ehrenreich and English, authors of *For Her Own Good*, 'Medicine had "discovered" that female functions were inherently pathological.' In the doctors' defence, these authors continue, 'Women of a hundred years ago *were*, in some ways, sicker than women of today. Quite apart from tight lacing, arsenic nipping, and fashionable cases of neurasthenia, women faced certain bodily risks which men did not share.' Chief among these was maternal mortality. But beyond the very real risk of death in childbirth, proof of the morbid, sickly state of the uterus was seen in the monthly flow of blood, and there is little evidence that women differed with their doctors in this perception.

The effect of menstruation on mobility has been underrated by those who seek to explain why men evolved as far-ranging hunters while women preferred to gather the fruits and seeds and stay closer to home. Child bearing, nursing and a limited musculature obviously combined to determine the historic direction of gender-related roles, but menstrual blood itself may also have been a significant factor. With lions it is the female who does 90 per cent of the hunting; among cheetahs the female, not the male, ranges far and wide across vast stretches of land. Female rats, as well, are more exploratory and fearless than males and roam over a wider range. There seems to be nothing in femaleness *per se*, nothing in being the sex that bears and cares for the young, that handicaps movement in the lower species. But higher on the evolutionary ladder, the oestrogen-dominated reproductive system grows increasingly complex, and seemingly more burdensome. Some other primates have menstrual cycles, but only the human female is subject to a copious flow of blood that needs to be staunched by external means.

How did they respond to their periods, those Plio-Pleistocene ancestors of ours, those hominid precursors along the track to Homo sapiens? At what point in human evolution, at what stage in the development of what goes under the rubric of Early Man, did Early Woman discover she had a bloody problem at 'those times' of the lunar cycle? In what aeon of pre-history did her menstrual flow increase from an insignificant trickle to an alarming rush down her thigh? Did she grab a handful of leaves and stuff them into her vagina? Were animals attracted to her smell? Did she suffer from cramps? Did she think that something was dreadfully wrong?

Because of frequent impregnation, continuous nursing, nutritional deficiencies and the daily stress of staying alive, the menstrual cycle must have been irregular as a matter of course in the pre-historic age, but irregular or not, with a profuse effluence of blood, it was dramatically immobilizing in comparison to other primate species and especially in comparison to the carefree reproductive system of the human male. Menstruation, gestation, childbirth and nursing the young were a continuum of physiological reasons for avoiding the big hunt among the foraging peoples whose chief sources of food were roots, seeds and fruit. The female's fertility, her awesome periodicity, and the fertility of the land were connected in the earliest Goddess myths; the connection was real.

Primitive menstrual taboos were not necessarily a male invention. Seclusion in a menstrual hut, avoidance of sex and of men in general, and relief from agricultural and cooking labours were pragmatic ways of dealing with cramps and a copious flow. In a practical sense, menstrual taboos meant time off on those days when a woman had reason to feel unclean, unwell, immobilized and cursed.

Depending on what was available in a given climate, a variety of porous fibres were used (and still are used in most countries) to staunch the monthly blood: makeshift paddings of roots and husks, home-made tampons of wadded paper, cotton or wool, and reusable diapers fashioned from folded lengths of heavy cloth, the shameful, bulky menstrual rags of my grandmother's generation that were furtively scrubbed in cold water and left to dry in a secret place. 'The rag' persisted as the routine, cumbersome method of sanitary protection in advanced Western society till the 1920s, when rolls of gauze and cellulose filler developed for bandaging wounds during World War I were cut to standard size and sold commercially in the United States. The marketing of disposable pads with acknowledgment of 'the hygienic handicap' and 'the days a woman used to lose' (these quotes are from a full-page ad for Kotex that appeared in the elegant front section of *Vogue* in 1926) coincided not accidentally with such changes in fashion as the abandonment of the full corset, the shortening and slimming of skirts and a new, eager interest in trousers. Throw-away absorbent tampons with no extraneous belts, loops, safety pins, bulky shape or revealing outline, which truly afforded normal freedom of movement on 'those days,' including swimming, did not reach the market until 1933.

In *Menstruation and Menopause* Paula Weideger has written that the physical reality of menstruation is not considered an attribute of femininity but rather 'a fall from feminine grace.' While a woman with irregular periods may suffer from the belief that she is 'not feminine enough' and while a woman in menopause may associate the end of her child-bearing years with 'a feminine loss,' there is another worrisome concern that occurs thirteen times a year for more than thirty-five years, if one is on an average 28-day cycle. The menstrual flow, despite its testament to female fertility and to gender, runs diametrically counter to the prized feminine virtues of neatness, order and a dainty, sweet and clean appearance.

Put squarely, menstruation is a nasty inconvenience, no matter how positive one's feelings are towards having children. Cut through the menstrual taboos and their primitive origins, and menstruation is still a nasty inconvenience. Brush aside the abhorrence of some men at the thought of a menstruating woman, and menstruation remains a nasty inconvenience, a dripping, bloating, congestive mess. Even the periodicity itself, the inexorable regularity of a cycle that runs like clockwork, is an order of disorder, a disruption of the everyday routine, an imposition of cautious caretaker concerns: secure protection, check against leakage, carry the extra tampon, change the pad, or suffer the mortification of the drip, the gush and the stain. This 'untidy event,' as Simone de Beauvoir called it, forces women to pay minute attention to the inner workings of the body in a way that men find difficult to comprehend. A healthy system must be monitored and managed, and the concentration on details cannot be avoided or put off for another hour, for the consequences will be public embarrassment, a telltale odour and a pile of soiled clothes. It is hardly feminine or polite to stain the back of one's skirt or the bed sheet and mattress, even though the oozing blood is normal and female, indeed is a prime expression of biological femaleness in its reproductive role. Neither is it desirably feminine to be besieged by a monthly eruption of pimples, lank hair, a bloated stomach, painful tenderness in the breasts, dull cramps, irritability and tension. As Beauvoir remarked, 'It is not easy to play the idol, the fairy, the faraway princess, when one feels a bloody cloth between one's legs; and more generally, when one is conscious of the primitive misery of being a body.'

It is not easy, either, to play the jock with a bloody cloth between one's legs, and at the critical moment in adolescence when the young boy revels in his developing musculature, the girl may appear at school with a note that excuses her from gym. To swim or not to swim, to run or not to run, to take the calisthenics class or skip it? To go ahead with plans for the week-long camping trip or to try and switch the date of departure, taking into account the solemn warning of the calendar? Menstruation asserts itself as a negative force to be overcome by the physically active woman. Even for those with an easy period, feeling logy or lethargic is not unusual. The proverbial note to the gym teacher, the female biological exemption, resides in the back of the head as a possible option. Grace Lichtenstein, who wrote a book about professional tennis, acquired enough evidence to report, 'Menstrual cramps were literally the curse of the women's circuit,' and more than one championship player, she noted, has dashed off the court in mid-game for a change of tampon.

The twentieth-century female athlete has placed herself on the cutting edge of some of the most perplexing problems of gender-related biology and the feminine ideal. Although she exercises to build up her body (while other women still exercise to slim down theirs), she may never break the international records set by male athletes in most events because of the genetic limits on her musculature. Her breasts and hips are no asset in running and sprinting; she will move efficiently with a figure that is 'boyish.' Loose, flowing hair, that trusty feminine emblem of such strong, fleet maidens as Atlanta and the Valkyries, must remain in the realm of myth for the real-life track star. Beautiful, free hair would only slow her down and get in her eyes. Even a normal manifestation of strenuous exertion like working up a good sweat runs counter to a feminine image.

How to look feminine while competing is a problem that haunts the psyche of the American female athlete. High-school coaches regularly complain that their best girl runners show up at the track wearing heavy bracelets and dangling earrings, and championship tennis players work to improve their on-court image with mascara, eye shadow and designer dresses. At times the mental conflict spills over into highly defensive verbal expression. An American Olympic swimmer groused bitterly to the press about the unfeminine big shoulders of the East German woman who beat her in the water. A champion runner took to wearing a T-shirt that proclaimed, 'I'm a Lady first, I'm an Athlete second.' The ambivalence of these athletes is rooted in cultural expectations, for while we have come a long way from the time when riding a bicycle was considered dangerous to the female constitution, the track-and-field star knows that her sweaty tank top does not fit the conventional image of glamour, and the swimmer understands that a poolside bathing beauty in a string bikini cuts a sexier figure than the rubber-capped winner of the 400-metre freestyle event.

On a more disturbing level, how can a female athlete not wonder what femaleness means when a male tennis player undergoes surgery, hormone treatments, electrolysis and a change of name and hairstyle and is permitted to play on the women's circuit? How can she not be suspicious of a remarkable new record when some Olympic champions, a beefy Russian shot putter and a couple of Polish sprinters, were found to possess congenital chromosomal abnormalities, an irregular mix of male and female characteristics that gave them a surpassing advantage of strength and speed in competition with true genetic women? What does a young gymnast think when she hears the Romanian national coach put his tiny fourteen-year-old star on a diet of salad, apples and 'brake' drugs in an attempt to retard her bodily changes? How can a runner, a swimmer or ballerina not worry when through hard training, a reduction in body fat and the effects of stress, her menstrual cycle may temporarily cease to function? Biology confronts the woman athlete at every step, for little that is female and nothing that is feminine aids the performance of someone who wants to win, except in those events where style and grace are judged subjectively on points.

Despite anatomical flexibility, women are generally less relaxed than men in their body postures, according to the studies of Albert Mehrabian, who proposes that attitudes of submissiveness are conveyed through postures of tension. In Mehrabian's analysis of body language among high- and low-status males, high-ranking men are more relaxed in their gestures in the presence of subordinates. Not surprisingly, men of all ranks generally assume more relaxed postures and gestures when communicating with women.

Mehrabian's studies correlate with the work of zoologist Thelma Rowell, who studied relationships of dominance and subordination in monkeys and baboons. Rowell postulated that a dominant primate might be defined as 'one who did not think before it acted' in encounters with others. A dominant animal walked down a path or sat on a log where it pleased, without acknowledging a subordinate's presence. Subordinate animals cringed or scattered at the other's approach. 'Thus,' she wrote, 'it was the subordinate animals that cautiously observed and maintained the hierarchy.' Rowell suggested that 'the subordinate's behaviour elicits dominating behaviour rather than the reverse' in many situations. 'Cringing, fleeing and fear-grinning,' she wrote, 'are extremely potent stimuli eliciting attack behaviour in primates, and this has rarely been taken into account in discussing hierarchical relationships.' But perhaps the nervous subordinates had good reason to cringe and grin, having sustained a couple of bad bites on prior occasions.

Women are not supposed to stand up and fight when they hear the bell. Women smile, they retreat into a smaller physical space, and they symbolically 'offer the neck' in appeasement, to use a favourite image of Konrad Lorenz, and from their small, curled space, they look out at the world around them in a state of alert and watchful tension. 'Women's intuition,' that sentimentally valued characteristic, may be nothing more than defensive watchfulness, a picking up and putting together of verbal and non-verbal cues as a strategy of survival, as the subordinate animal is sensitive to the sounds and movements of the dominant animal, which does not need to think before it acts.

Subservience in movement and gesture was the hallmark of feminine modesty in books of deportment that were written for the new bourgeoisie of the Middle Ages. Unseemly mirth, a darting eye, a babbling tongue and a wanton gait were related prohibitions. *The Good Wife* instructed her daughter, 'Go thou not too fast. Brandish not with thy head, nor with thy shoulders cast.' In another volume on manners a husband advises his wife, 'Go with your head turned straight forward, your eyelids low and fixed, and your gaze before you down to the ground ... Turn not your eyes on man or woman, or staring upward, or laughing or stopping to talk to anyone in the streets.' When seated, a maiden kept her hands folded quietly in her lap or busily engaged with needlework.

Inhibition was artfully encouraged by restrictive feminine clothing in the centuries that followed. Unable to stretch freely in the confines of her corset, and weighted down by yards of cloth which hampered her step and usurped the use of a hand to guide and arrange the sweeping grandeur, a woman of the upper and middle classes was schooled in restraint by the social demands of fashion.

For street wear a fanciful hat adorned with ribbons, plumes and veiling served to curtail the motions of her head. Dependence on gentlemen and servants was an understandable consequence of feminine dress.

A sturdy woven mesh of local ordinances and municipal codes dictated some further rules of good conduct. Writes American historian Geoffrey Perrett, 'Before the First World War women were arrested for smoking cigarettes in public, for using profanity, for appearing on beaches without stockings, for driving automobiles without a man beside them, for wearing outlandish attire (for example, shorts, slacks, men's hats), and for not wearing their corsets.' Public-decency regulations received their strongest support from the Sunday sermons in local churches.

Romantically the feminine ideal is often pictured with something pretty and fragile to occupy the hands: a nosegay of violets, the bridal bouquet of white stephanotis and orange blossom, a sheaf of long-stemmed roses presented to the prima ballerina as she takes her curtain call amidst applause. With the passing from the social scene of certain dainty props – a fan, a parasol, a wrist corsage for the prom queen – today's customary restraints on bodily comportment are indicated by fingertips and heels, a handbag on the shoulder, and a schooled inhibition against spreading the knees. In addition, as the French feminist Colette Guillaumin has noted, women are physically burdened by what she calls 'diverse loads,' the habitual signs of chief responsibility for the domestic role – children on the arm, their food and toys in hand, and a bag of groceries or shirts from the dry cleaners hugged to her chest. Rarely does a woman experience the liberty of taking a walk with empty hands and arms swinging free at her sides. So rare is this, in fact, that many women find it physically unnerving when they do. Unaccustomed to the freedom, they are beset by worries that some needed belonging, some familiar presence (a purse, a shopping bag?) has been forgotten.

Small, fluttery gestures that betray nervousness or a practised over-animation are considered girlishly feminine and cute. Toying with a strand of hair, bobbing the head, giggling when introduced, pulling the elbows in close to the body and crossing the legs in a knee-and-ankle double twist are mannerisms that men studiouly avoid. Self-contained and non-aggressive, they might almost be the equivalent of cringing, fleeing and fear-grinning among the lower primates.

Jewellery plays a subtle role in delineating masculine and feminine gestures. To drum one's fingers on the table is an aggressive expression of annoyance and conspicuously unfeminine, but to fidget with a necklace or twist a ring is a non-threatening way of dissipating agitation. Clutching protectively at the throat is not restricted to females, but corresponding masculine gestures are to loosen the collar and adjust the necktie, actions which indicate some modicum of control

Quaint postures that throw the body off balance, such as standing on one leg as if poised for flight, or leading from the hips in a debutante slouch, or that suggest a child's behaviour (the stereotypic sexy secretary taking dictation while perched on the boss's knee), fall within the repertoire of femininity that is alien, awkward and generally unthinkable as a mode of behaviour for men. Reclining odalisque-style, a shocker thirty-five years ago when Truman Capote posed in this manner for a book jacket, is a classic feminine tableau of eroticized passivity with an established tradition in art. Caricatured by Mae West, the standing odalisque – hand on hip, hand on hairdo – invites attention: 'Come up and see me sometime.'

Of course, feminine movement was never intended for solo performance. Vine-clinging, cuddling and birdlike perching require a strong external support. It is in order to appeal to men that the yielded autonomy and contrived manifestations of helplessness become second nature as expressions of good manners and sexual good will. For smooth interaction between the sexes, the prevailing code of masculine action demands a yielding partner to gracefully complete the dance.

Nancy Henley, psychologist and author of *Body Politics*, has written, 'In a way so accepted and so subtle as to be unnoticed even by its practitioners and recipients, males in couples will often literally push a woman everywhere she is to go – the arm from behind, steering around corners, through doorways, into elevators, on to escalators . . . crossing the street. It is not necessarily heavy and pushy or physical in an ugly way; it is light and gentle but firm, in the way of the most confident equestrians with the best-trained horses.'

In this familiar *pas de deux*, a woman must either consent to be led with a gracious display of good manners or else she must buck and bristle at the touch of the reins. Femininity encourages the romance of compliance, a willing exchange of motor autonomy and physical balance for the protocols of masculine protection. Steering and leading are prerogatives of those in command. Observational studies of who touches whom in a given situation show that superiors feel free to lay an intimate, guiding hand on those with inferior status, but not the reverse. 'The politics of touch,' a concept of Henley's, operates instructively in masculine-feminine relations.

Henley was the first psychologist to connect the masculine custom of shepherding an able-bodied woman through situations that do not require physical guidance with other forms of manhandling along a continuum from petty humiliation (the sly pinch, the playful slap on the fanny) to the assaultive abuses of wife beating and rape. This is not to say that the husband who steers his wife to a restaurant table with a paternal shove is no different from the rapist, but rather to suggest that women who customarily expect to have their physical movements directed by others are poorly prepared by their feminine training to resist unwanted interference or violent assault. Fear of being judged impolite has more immediate reality for many women than the terror of physical violation.

The lessons of femininity instruct in polite compliance, and the rules of etiquette demand that the female relinquish her initiative in social encounters. Indeed, the delicate tissue of formalized male-female relations is constructed on artful expressions of feminine dependence. To be helped with one's coat, to let the man do the driving, to sit mute and unmoving while the man does the ordering and picks up the check – such trained behavioural inactivity may be ladylike, gracious, romantic and flirty, and soothing to easily ruffled masculine feathers, but it is ultimately destructive to the sense of the functioning, productive self. The charge that feminists have no manners is true, for the history of manners, unfortunately for those who wish to change the world, is an index of courtly graces addressed towards those of the middle classes who aspire to the refinements of their betters, embodied in the static vision of the cared for, catered-to lady of privilege who existed on a rarefied plane above the mundane reality of strenuous labour. When a feminist insists on opening the door for herself, a simple act of physical autonomy that was never an issue for servants, field and factory workers and women not under the protection of men, her gesture rudely collides with chivalrous expectations, for manly action requires manifest evidence of a helpless lady in order to demonstrate courtly respect. Feminine psychology adjusts to the required denial of routine initiative by claiming that 'feeling ladylike and protected' is a preferred state of being, by incorporating a fair amount of induced passivity into one's behavioural mode, and by denying that self-assertion is an important value.

Animal behaviour studies report exhaustively on the effects of testosterone in fostering aggression. Research into the hormonal influence on human behaviour is notably inconclusive, but too intriguing to dismiss. Aggression is an imprecise concept – as one researcher wrote in good humour, 'Trying to define aggression makes people aggressive' – but the rubric generally covers a cluster of behavioural patterns that are usually more pronounced in the male: expenditure of physical energy, rough-house play, irritability, threatening activity in response to fear, inter- and intra-sex fighting, and the infliction of physical damage. Most students of aggression stretch the definition to embrace territorial defence and the competitive drive for power and dominance within the social hierarchy (the hierarchical order itself is claimed as a product of behavioural aggression) while they shy away from the implications of violence. Few find room in their theories for the phenomenon of maternal aggression, in which a mother utilizes all means at her disposal to protect her young.

Despite the vagueness of the aggression concept, the possibility of a hormonal basis for aggressive behaviour in human conduct undeniably exists, even with the overriding roles played by heredity, environment and learning in mediating the complex circuitry of the human brain. It would be foolhardy to attempt to gauge the precise extent of that hormonal influence, or to claim it as a biological determinant that will continue to affect the destiny of the human race. The testosterone level in human males is ten times higher than in human females, but the male is not ten times as hairy, ten times as muscular or ten times as tall. Within a gender, testosterone levels do not correspond to comparative hairiness, muscularity or height. Yet it is obvious that the endocrine difference between the sexes gave the male a historic advantage in terms of the sheer, brute force of physical aggression that propelled human endeavour to its present place. War, slavery, the earliest known legal concepts and the building of monoliths were products of dimorphic masculine strength more than they were the noble achievements of verbal intelligence, sensitive yearnings or tactical skills. Only in the last century, and only in those parts of the world where industrial development has rendered brute force somewhat irrelevant, if not thoroughly obsolete, can the question of competitive drive be considered without reference to masculinity, and then only partially with some occupational exceptions.

Like all basic behaviour, including eating and parental care, aggression in humans is a learned response and a learned inhibition. affected by childhood training, community values, laws, social customs and religious codes. The psychology of feminine movement, as we know and practise its provocative airs and graces, is based on the premise that direct acts of initiative and self-assertion are a violation of the governance of male-female relations, if not of nature itself. In place of forthright action we are offered a vision so exquisitely romantic and sexually beguiling that few care to question its curious imagery of limitations: a Venus de Milo without arms, a mermaid without legs, a Sleeping Beauty in a state of suspended animation with her face upturned, awaiting a kiss.

Emotion

A 1970 landmark study, known in the field as *Broverman and Broverman*, reported that 'Cries very easily' was rated by a group of professional psychologists as a highly feminine trait. 'Very emotional,' 'Very excitable in a minor crises' and 'Feelings easily hurt' were additional characteristics on the femininity scale. So were 'Very easily influenced,' 'Very subjective,' 'Unable to separate feelings from ideas,' 'Very illogical' and 'Very sneaky.' As might be expected, masculinity was defined by opposing, sturdier values: 'Very direct,' 'Very logical,' 'Can make decisions easily,' 'Never cries.' The importance of *Broverman and Broverman* was not in nailing down a set of popular assumptions and conventional perceptions – masculine-feminine scales were well established in the literature of psychology as a means of ascertaining normality and social adjustment – but in the authors' observation that stereotypic femininity was a grossly negative assessment of the female sex and, furthermore, that many so-called feminine traits ran counter to clinical descriptions of maturity and mental health.

Emotional femininity is a tough nut to crack, impossible to quantify yet hard to ignore. As the task of conforming to a specified physical design is a gender mission that few women care to resist, conforming to a pre-packaged emotional design is another imperative task of gender. To satisfy a societal need for sexual clarification, and to justify second-class status, an emblematic constellation of inner traits, as well as their outward manifestations, has been put forward historically by some of the world's great thinkers as proof of the 'different' feminine nature.

'Woman,' wrote Aristotle, 'is more compassionate than man, more easily moved to tears. At the same time, she is more jealous, more querulous, more apt to scold and to strike. She is, furthermore, more prone to despondency and less hopeful than man, more void of shame or self-respect, more false of speech, more deceptive and of more retentive memory. She is also more wakeful, more shrinking, more difficult to rouse to action, and she requires a smaller amount of nutriment.'

Addressing a suffrage convention in 1855, Ralph Waldo Emerson had kindlier words on the nature of woman, explicating the nineteenth-century view that her difference was one of superior virtue. 'Women,' he extolled, 'are the civilizers of mankind. What is civilization? I answer, the power of good women. . . . The starry crown of woman is in the power of her affection and sentiment, and the infinite enlargements to which they lead.' (In less elevated language, the Emerson view was perhaps what President Reagan had in mind when he cheerfully stated, 'Why, if it wasn't for women, we men would still be walking around in skin suits carrying clubs.')

A clarification is in order. Are women believed to possess a wider or deeper emotional range, a greater sensitivity, say, to the beauties of nature or to the infinite complexities of feeling? Any male poet, artist, actor, marine biologist or backpacker would strenuously object. Rather, it is commonly agreed that women are tossed and buffeted on the high seas of emotion, while men have the tough mental fibre, the intellectual muscle, to stay in control. As for the civilizing influence, surely something more is meant than sophistication, culture and taste, using the correct fork or not belching after dinner. The idealization of emotional femininity, as women prefer to see themselves affirmed, is more exquisitely romantic: a finer temperament in a more fragile vessel, a gentler nature ruled by a twin need to love and to be protected: one who appreciates – without urgency to create – good art, music, literature and other public expressions of the private soul; a flame-bearer of spiritual values by whose shining example the men of the world are inspired to redemption and to accomplish great things.

Two thousand years ago *Dominus flevit*, Jesus wept as he beheld Jerusalem. 'Men ceased weeping,' proposed Simone de Beauvoir, 'when it became unfashionable.' Now it is Mary, *Mater Dolorosa*, who weeps with compassion for mankind. In mystical visions, in the reliquaries of obscure churches and miraculous shrines, the figure of the Virgin, the world's most feminine woman, has been seen to shed tears. There are still extant cultures in which men are positively lachrymose (and kissy-kissy) with no seeming detriment to their masculine image, but the Anglo-Saxon tradition, in particular, requires keeping a stiff upper lip. Weeping, keening women shrouded in black are an established fixture in mourning rites in many nations. Inconsolable grief is a feminine role, at least in its unquiet representations. In what has become a stock photograph in the national news magazines, women weep for the multitudes when national tragedy (a terrorist bombing, an air crash, an assassination) strikes.

The catharsis of tears is encouraged in women – 'There, there, now, let it all out' – while a man nay be told to get a grip on himself, or to gulp down a double Scotch. Having 'a good cry' in order to feel better afterwards is not recommended as a means of raising the spirits of men, for the cathartic relief of succumbing to tears would be tempered by the uncomfortable knowledge that the loss of control was hardly manly. In the 1972 New Hampshire Presidential primary, Senator Edmund Muskie, then the Democratic front-runner, committed political suicide when he publicly cried during a campaign speech. Muskie had been talking about some harsh press comments directed at his wife when the tears filled his eyes. In retrospect it was his watershed moment: Could a man who became tearful when the going got rough in a political campaign be expected to face the Russians? To a nation that had delighted in the hatless, overcoatless macho posturing of John F. Kennedy, the military successes of General Ike and the irascible outbursts of 'Give 'em hell' Harry Truman, the answer was No. Media accounts of Muskie's all-too-human tears were merciless. In the summer of 1983 the obvious and unshakable grief displayed by Israeli prime minister Menachem Begin after the death of his wife was seized upon by the Israeli and American press as evidence that a tough old warrior had lost his grip. Sharing this perception of his own emotional state, perhaps, Begin shortly afterwards resigned.

Expressions of anger and rage are not a disqualifying factor in the masculine disposition. Anger in men is often understood, or excused, as reasonable or just. Anger in men may even be cast in a heroic mould – a righteous response to an insult against honour that will prelude a manly, aggressive act. Because competitive acts of personal assertion, not to mention acts of outright physical aggression, are known to flow from angry feelings, anger becomes the most unfeminine emotion a woman can show.

Anger in a woman isn't 'nice.' A woman who seethes with anger is 'unattractive.' An angry woman is hard, mean and nasty; she is unreliable, unprettily out of control. Her face contorts into unpleasant lines: the jaw juts, the eyes are narrowed, the teeth are bared. Anger is a violent snarl and a hostile threat, a declaration of war. The endless forbearance demanded of women, described as the feminine virtue of patience, prohibits an angry response. Picture a charming old-fasioned scene: The mistress of the house bends low over her needlework, cross-stitching her sampler: 'Patience is a virtue, possess it if you can/Seldom seen in women, never seen in man.' Does the needle jab through the cloth in uncommon fury? Does she prick her thumb in frustration?

Festering without a permissible release, women's undissolved anger has been known to seep out in petty, mean-spirited ways – fits of jealousy, fantasies of retaliation, unholy plots of revenge. Perhaps, after all, it is safer to cry. 'Woman's aptitude for facile tears,' wrote Beauvoir, 'comes largely from the fact that her life is built upon a foundation of impotent revolt.'*

Beauvoir hedged her bet, for her next words were these: 'It is also doubtless true that physiologically she has less nervous control than a man.' Is this 'doubtless true,' or is it more to the point, as Beauvoir continues, that 'her education has taught her to let herself go more readily'?

Infants and children cry out of fear, frustration, discomfort, hunger, anxiety at separation from a parent, and rage. Surveying all available studies of crying newborns and little children, psychologists Eleanor Maccoby and Carol Jacklin found no appreciable sexual difference. If teenage girls and adult women are known to cry more than men – and there is no reason to question the popular wisdom in this regard – should the endocrine changes of adolescence be held to account? What of those weepy 'blue days' of premenstrual tension that genuinely afflict so many women? What about mid-life depression, known in some circles as 'the feminine malady'? Are these conditions, as some men propose, a sign of 'raging hormonal imbalance' that incapacitates the cool, logical functioning of the human brain? Or does feminine depression result, as psychiatrist Willard Gaylin suggests, when confidence in one's coping mechanism is lost?

Belief in a biological basis for the instability of female emotions has a notorious history in the development of medical science. Hippocrates the physician held that hysteria was caused by a

* 'Facile' is the English translator's match for the French *facile*, more correctly rendered as 'easy.' Beauvoir did not mean to ascribe a stereotypic superficiality to women in her remark.

wandering uterus that remained unfulfilled. Discovery in the seventeenth century that the thyroid gland was larger in women inspired the proposition that the thyroid's function was to give added grace to the feminine neck, but other beliefs maintained that the gland served to flush impurities from the blood before it reached the brain. A larger thyroid 'was necessary to guard the female system from the influence of the more numerous causes of irritation and vexation' to which the sex was unfortunately disposed. Nineteenth-century doctors averred that womb-related disorders were the cause of such female complaints as 'nervous prostration.' For those without money to seek out a physician's care, Lydia E. Pinkham's Vegetable Compound and other patent medicines were available to give relief. In the 1940s and '50s, prefrontal lobotomy was briefly and tragically in vogue for a variety of psychiatric disorders, particularly among women, since the surgical procedure had a flattening effect on raging emotions. Nowadays Valium appears to suffice.

Beginning in earnest in the 1960s, one line of research has attempted to isolate premenstrual tension as a contributing cause of accidents, suicide, admittance to mental hospitals and the commission of violent crimes. Mood swings, irritability and minor emotional upsets probably do lead to more 'acting out' by females at a cyclical time in the month, but what does this prove beyond the increasingly accepted fact that the endocrine system has a critical influence on the human emotional threshold? Suicide, violent crime and dangerous psychiatric disorders are statistically four to nine times more prevalent in men. Should we theorize, then, that 'raging hormonal imbalance' is a chronic, year-round condition in males? A disqualifying factor? By any method of calculation and for whatever reason – hormonal effects, the social inhibitions of femininity, the social pleasure of the masculine role, or all of these – the female gender is indisputably less prone to irrational, anti-social behaviour. The price of inhibited anger and a non-violent temperament may well be a bucketful of tears.

Like the emotion of anger, exulting in personal victory is a harshly unfeminine response. Of course, good winners of either sex are supposed to display some degree of sportsmanlike humility, but the merest hint of gloating triumph – 'Me, me, me, I did it!' – is completely at odds with the modesty and deference expected of women and girls. Arm raised in a winner's salute, the ritualized climax of a prize fight, wrestling match or tennis championship, is unladylike, to say the least. The powerful feeling that victory engenders, the satisfaction of climbing to the top of the heap or clinching a deal, remains an inappropriate emotion. More appropriate to femininity are the predictable tears of the new Miss America as she accepts her crown and sceptre. Trembling lip and brimming eyes suggest a Cinderella who has stumbled upon good fortune through unbelievable, undeserved luck. At her moment of victory the winner of America's favourite pageant appears overcome, rather than superior in any way. A Miss America who raised her sceptre high like a trophy would not be in keeping with the feminine ideal.

The maidenly blush, that staple of the nineteenth-century lady's novel, was an excellent indicator of innocent virginal shyness in contrast to the worldliness and sophistication of men. In an age when a variety of remarks, largely sexual, were considered uncouth and not for the ears of virtuous women, the feminine blush was an expected response. On the other side of the ballroom, men never blushed, at least not in romantic fiction, since presumably they were knowledgeable and sexually practised. Lowered eyes, heightened colour, breathlessness and occasional swooning were further proofs of a fragile and innocent feminine nature that required protection in the rough, indelicate masculine world. (In the best-selling Harlequin and Silhouette books devoured by romantic addicts who need the quick fix, the maidenly blush is alive and well.)

In a new age of relative sexual freedom, or permissiveness, at any rate, squeals and moans replace the blush and the downcast eye. Screaming bobbysoxers who fainted in the aisle at the Paramount Theater when a skinny young Frank Sinatra crooned his love ballads during the 1940s (reportedly, the first wave of fainting girls was staged by promoters) presaged the whimpering orgasmic ecstasy at rock concerts in huge arenas today. By contrast, young men in the audience automatically rise to their feet and whistle and shout when the band starts to play, but they seldom appear overcome.

Most emphatically, feminine emotion has become louder. The ribald squeal of the stereotypic serving wench in Elizabethan times, a supposed indicator of loose, easy ways, seems to have lost its lower-class stigma. One by-product of our media-obsessed society, in which privacy is considered a quaint and rather old-fashioned human need, has been the reproduction of the unmistakable sounds of female orgasm on a record (Donna Summer's 'Love to Love You Baby,' among other hits). More than commercialization of sex is operative here. Would the sounds of male orgasm suffice for a recording, and would they be unmistakable? Although I have seen no studies on this interesting sex difference, I believe it can be said that most women do vocalize more loudly and uncontrollably than men in the throes of sexual passion. Is this response physiological, compensatory or merely symptomatic of the feminine mission to display one's feelings (and the corresponding masculine mission to keep their feelings under control)?

Feminine emotion specializes in sentimentality, empathy and admissions of vulnerability – three characteristics that most men try to avoid. Linking these traits to female anatomy became an article of faith in the Freudian school. Erik Erikson, for one, spoke of an 'inner space' (he meant the womb) that yearns for fulfilment through maternal love. Helene Deutsch, the grande dame of Freudian feminine psychology, spoke of psychic acceptance of hurt and pain; menstrual cramps, defloration and the agonies of childbirth called for a masochistic nature she believed was innate.

Love of babies, any baby and all babies, not only one's own, is a celebrated and anticipated feminine emotion, and a woman who fails to ooh and ahh at the snapshot of a baby or cuddle a proffered infant in her arms is instantly suspect. Evidence of a maternal nature, of a certain innate competence when handling a baby or at least some indication of maternal longing, becomes a requirement of gender. Women with no particular feeling for babies are extremely reluctant to admit their private truth, for the entire weight of woman's place in the biological division of labour, not to mention the glorification of motherhood as woman's greatest and only truly satisfactory role, has kept alive the belief that all women yearn to fulfil their biological destiny out of a deep emotional need. That a sizeable number of mothers have no genuine aptitude for the job is verified by the records of hospitals, family courts and social agencies where cases of battery and neglect are duly entered – and perhaps also by the characteristic upper-class custom of leaving the little ones to the care of the nanny. But despite this evidence that day-to-day motherhood is not a suitable or a stimulating occupation for all, the myth persists that a woman who prefers to remain childless must be heartless or selfish or less than complete.

Books have been written on maternal guilt and its exploitation, on the endemic feeling that whatever a mother does, her loving care may be inadequate or wrong, with consequences that can damage a child for life. Trends in child care (bottle feeding, demand feeding, not picking up the crying baby, delaying the toilet training or giving up an outside job to devote one's entire time to the family) illuminate the fear of maternal inadequacy as well as the variability or 'expert' opinion in each generation. Advertising copywriters successfully manipulate this feminine fear when they pitch their clients' products. A certain cereal, one particular brand of packaged white bread, must be bought for the breakfast table or else you have failed to love your child sufficiently and denied him the chance to 'build a strong body twelve ways.' Until the gay liberation movement began to speak for itself, it was a commonplace of psychiatric wisdom that a mother had it within her power to destroy her son's heterosexual adjustment by failing to cut his baby curls, keep him away from dance classes or encourage his interest in sports.

A requirement of femininity is that a woman devote her life to love – to mother love, to romantic love, to religious love, to amorphous, undifferentiated caring. The territory of the heart is admittedly a province that is open to all, but women alone are expected to make an obsessional career of its exploitation, to find whatever adventure, power, fulfilment or tragedy that life has to offer within its bounds. There is no question that a woman is apt to feel most feminine, most confident of her interior gender makeup, when she is reliably within some stage of love – even the girlish crush or the stage of unrequited love or a broken heart. Men have suffered for love, and men have accomplished great feats in the name of love, but what man has ever felt at the top of his masculine form when he is lovesick or suffering from heartache?

Gloria Steinem once observed that the heart is a sex-distinctive symbol of feminine vulnerability in the marketing of fashion. Heart-shaped rings and heart-shaped gold pendants and heart-shaped frames on red plastic sunglasses announce an addiction to love that is beyond the pale of appropriate design for masculine ornamentation. (A man does not wear his heart on his sleeve.) The same observation applies a little less stringently to flowers.

Rare is the famous girl singer, whatever her age, of popular music (blues, country, Top Forty, disco or rock) who is not chiefly identified with some expression of love, usually its down-side. Torchy bittersweet ballads and sad, suffering laments mixed with vows of eternal fidelity to the rotten bastard who done her wrong communicate the feminine message of love at any cost. Almost unique to the female singer, I think, is the poignant anthem of battered survival, from Fanny Brice's 'My Man' to Gloria Gaynor's 'I Will Survive,' that does not quite shut the door on further emotional abuse if her man should return.

But the point is not emotional abuse (except in extreme, aberrant cases); the point is feeling. Women are instructed from childhood to be keepers of the heart, keepers of the sentimental memory. In diaries, packets of old love letters and family albums, in slender books of poetry in which a flower is pressed, a woman's emotional history is preserved. Remembrance of things past – the birthday, the anniversary, the death – is a feminine province. In the social division of labour, the wife is charged with maintaining the emotional connection, even with the husband's side of the family. Her thoughtful task is to make the long-distance call, select the present and write the thank-you note (chores that secretaries are asked to do by their bosses). Men are busy; they move forward. A woman looks back. It is significant that in the Biblical parable it was Lot's wife who looked back for one last precious glimpse of their city, their home, their past (and was turned into a pillar of salt).

Love confirms the feminine psyche. A celebrated difference between men and women (either women's weakness or women's strength, depending on one's values) is the obstinate reluctance, the emotional inability of women to separate sex from love. Understandably. Love makes the world go round, and women are supposed to get dizzy – to rise, to fall, to feel alive in every pore, to be undone. In place of a suitable attachment, an unlikely or inaccessible one may have to do. But more important, sex for a woman, even in an age of accessible contraception, has reproductive consequences that render the act a serious affair. Casual sex can have a most uncasual resolution. If a young girl thinks of love and marriage while a boy thinks of getting laid, her emotional commitment is rooted not only in her different upbringing but in her reproductive biology as well. Love, then, can become an alibi for thoughtless behaviour, as it may also become an identity, or a distraction, à la Emma Bovary or Anna Karenina, from the frustrations of a limited life.*

Christian houses of worship, especially in poor neighbourhoods, are filled disproportionately by women. This phenomenon may not be entirely atttributable to the historic role of the Catholic and Protestant religions in encouraging the public devotions of women (which Judaism and Islam did not), or because women have more time for prayer, or because in the Western world they are believed to be more religious by nature. Another contributing factor may be that the central article of Christian faith, 'Jesus loves you,' has particular appeal for the gender that defines itself through loving emotions.

Women's special interest in the field of compassion is catered to and promoted. Hollywood 'weepies,' otherwise known as four-handkerchief movies, were big-studio productions that were tailored to bring in female box-office receipts. Columns of advice to the lovelorn, such as the redoubtable 'Dear Dorothy Dix' and the current 'Dear Abby,' were by tradition a woman's slot in daily newspapers, along with the coverage of society births and weddings, in the days when females were as rare in a newsroom as they were in a coal mine. In the heyday of the competitive tabloids, sob-sister journalism, that newsroom term for a human-interest story told with heart-wrenching pathos (usually by a tough male reporter who had the formula down pat), was held in contempt by those on the paper who covered the 'hard stuff' of politics, crime and war. (Nathanael West's famous anti-hero laboured under the byline of Miss Lonelyhearts.) Despite its obvious audience appeal, 'soft stuff' was, and is, on the lower rungs of journalism – trivial, weak and unmanly.

In government circles during the Vietnam war, it was considered a sign of emotional softness, of lily-livered liberals and nervous nellies, to suggest that Napalmed babies, fire bombed villages and

* The overwhelming influence of feminine love is frequently offered as a mitigating explanation by women who do unfeminine things. Elizabeth Bentley, the 'Red Spy Queen' of the cold war Fifties, attributed her illegal activities to her passion for the Russian master spy Jacob Golos. Judith Coplon's defence for stealing Government documents was love for another Russian, Valentin Gubichev. More recently, Jean Harris haplessly failed to convince a jury that her love for 'Scarsdale diet' Doctor Herman Tarnower was so great that she could not possibly have intended to kill him.

defoliated crops were reason enough to pull out American forces. The peace movement, went the charge, was composed of cowards and fuzzy thinkers. Suspicion of an unmanly lack of hard practical logic always haunts those men who espouse peace and non-violence, but women, the weaker sex, are permitted a certain amount of emotional leeway. Feminine logic, after all, is reputedly governed by the heart-strings. Compassion and sentiment are the basis for its notorious 'subjectivity' compared to the 'objectivity' of men who use themselves as the objective standard.

As long as the social division of labour ordains that women should bear the chief emotional burden of caring for human life from the cradle to the grave while men may demonstrate their dimorphic difference through competitive acts of physical aggression, emblematic compassion and fear of violence are compelling reasons for an aversion to war and other environmental hazards. When law and custom deny the full range of public expression and economic opportunity that men claim for themselves, a woman must place much of her hopes, her dreams, her feminine identity and her social importance in the private sphere of personal relations, in the connective tissue of marriage, family, friendship and love. In a world out of balance, where men are taught to value toughness and linear vision as masculine traits that enable them to think strategically from conquest to conquest, from campaign to campaign without looking back, without getting side-tracked by vulnerable feelings, there is, and will be, an emotional difference between the sexes, a gender gap that may even appear on a Gallup poll.

If a true shape could emerge from the shadows of historic oppression, would the gender-specific experience of being female still suggest a range of perceptions and values that differ appreciably from those of men? It would be premature to offer an answer. Does a particular emotion ultimately resist separation from its historic deployment in the sexual balance of power? In the way of observation, this much can be said: The entwining of anatomy, history and culture presents such a persuasive emotional argument for a 'different nature' that even the best aspects of femininity collaborate in its perpetuation.

Ambition

If prettiness and grace were the extent of it, femininity would not be a puzzle, nor would excellence in feminine values be so completely at odds with other forms of ambition. In a sense this entire inquiry has been haunted by the question of ambition, for every adjustment a woman makes to prove her feminine difference adds another fine stitch to the pattern: an inhibition on speech and behaviour, a usurpation of time, and a preoccupation with appearance that deflects the mind and depletes the storehouse of energy and purpose. If time and energy are not a problem, if purpose is not a concern, if the underlying submissiveness is not examined too closely, then the feminine aesthetic may not be a handicap at all. On the contrary, high among its known satisfactions, femininity offers a welcome retreat from the demands of ambition, just as its strategic use is often good camouflage for those wishing to hide their ambition from public view. But there is no getting around the fact that ambition is not a feminine trait. More strongly expressed, a lack of ambition – or professed lack of ambition, or a sacrificial willingness to set personal ambition aside – is virtuous proof of the nurturant feminine nature which, if absent, strikes at the guilty heart of femaleness itself.

When applied to women, nurturance embraces a love of children, a desire to bear them and rear them, and a disposition that leans towards a set of traits that are not gender-specific: warmth, tenderness, compassion, sustained emotional involvement in the welfare of others, and a weak or non-existent competitive drive. Nurturant labour includes child care, spouse care, cooking and feeding, soothing and patching, straightening out disorder and cleaning up dirt, little considerations like sewing a button on a grown man's raincoat, major considerations like nursing relationships and mending rifts, putting the demands of family and others before one's own, and dropping one's work to minister to the sick, the troubled and the lonely in their time of need.

When nurturance is given out of love, disposition or a sense of responsible duty, the assumption exists that whatever form it takes

– changing a nappy or baking a tray of raisin-nut cookies – the behaviour expresses a woman's biological nature. When nurturing acts are performed by men, they are interpreted as extraordinary or possibly suspect. When nurturance is provided by maids, house-keepers, kindergarten teachers or practical nurses, its value in the market place is low.

Are women the nurturing sex by anatomical design? In the original sense of nurture, what the body can do to support new life, of course the answer is yes. Femaleness in humans and other mammals is defined by the manner of reproduction: gestation and nourishment inside the womb followed by nursing the dependent young upon birth. Few would deny that the nurturant responsibili-ties of motherhood begin as a biological process, and that suckling connects the labour of birth to the social obligation of continuing care. Or so the rhythms of nature undisturbed by human civilization suggest.

In the depths of the forest or on the grassy plains of the savanna, wherever groupings of mammals exist in the wild, milk is the crucial lifeline from mother to infant. Cleaning, carrying and protecting from danger are closely related acts, although the indiffer-ent mother is not unknown. Active maternal nurturance is the stable core of the social order for animals that live in groups, marked by strong bonds of kinship and positions of high rank and power (for some) that frequently pass to the next generation. Behaviour that appears more pronounced in the male of some species – fighting, displays of dominance, defence against predators, grabbing the best and largest portion – does not compare in social cohesion to the bond of maternal relation. In hunting and gathering bands, the earliest form of human society that was once universal, the dual purpose of female work was central to group survival. Responsible for bearing and rearing the next generation, as well as for collecting and preparing the basic foods for everyday needs, woman the mother and gatherer matched the productive labour and communal importance, at least, of man the hunter, as she does today in the Kalahari desert where remnant foraging groups, the !Kung San, continue their traditional ways.

It was no fault of women or men, or even of their ambitious yearnings, that as civilization advanced, the unchanging nature of biologically determined work became increasingly tangential to societal progress. To gain dominion over nature and bend it to

173

human will, the restless intelligence of the Homo sapiens brain required a carefree reproductive system and physical strength, attributes that were characteristically male. With the cultivation of land and permanent towns, with the unleashing of competitive drives and personal ambitions that led to the accumulation of property and the rise of stratified classes, the necessary tasks of reproduction and nurture were no longer at the vital centre of human endeavour. Inexorably and conclusively, the logic of femaleness with its inherent capacity for two kinds of purposeful labour, reproductive and 'other,' became a less powerful force in the social order than the single-minded capabilities of males.

Examining the social contribution of women's work in four preindustrial economies (foraging, slash-and-burn horticulture, animal herding and intensive farming), the anthropologist Sharon Tiffany suggests that the perception of motherhood as woman's sole valuable function goes hand in hand with severe prohibitions on other opportunities for work, and with a devaluation of womanhood in general, in economic systems where men unquestionably dominate the means of production and the balance of power. When motherhood, child tending and housekeeping chores become a socioeconomic and cultural ideal that excludes the performance of income-producing work, female sexuality in turn becomes a male concern that reflects male interests. The right to free sexual expression, the right to control fertility and to choose whether or not to be a mother, and the right to value a girl child and her promise as much as a boy and his are determined by considerations that are male-defined.

Thousands of years ago in the pantheistic religions of the Eastern and Western worlds, worship of the Mother Goddess (Asarte, Isis and many others) was a reverent acknowledgment of the life-giving powers of woman and nature. Reflective of patriarchal domination over woman and land, monotheistic belief turned away from the concept of primordial birth and superimposed the divine will of a male deity on the act of procreation. Motherhood plays no part in the Genesis myth of creation. Adam is not born of woman; he is fashioned directly by the hand of God. Eve, his helpmate, is fashioned in turn from man's proverbial rib. With this unusual reordering of biological birth, the submission of woman was given a firm theological basis. The historic terms under which motherhood was sanctioned (only in marriage, to ensure inherited wealth) further eroded maternal power and placed upon pregnancy elements of coercion, punishment and shame. As Christianity spread and suppressed the pagan religions, gestation in the womb was reduced to a caretaker function; and the pain and peril of childbirth, ironically a consequence of the large human head and its capacity for knowledge, came to be seen as the wages of original sin.

As the means of survival shifted perceptibly from agricultural systems to industrial economies, the traditional scope of women's work suffered new forms of attrition. The hearth, the broom, the spinning wheel and the cradle had been honoured symbols of the female share in the household partnership of productive family labour, but the home itself as a central place of work was diminished in importance when spinning and weaving, among other skills, were gradually supplanted by mass production. Developing technology, mechanized power, specialization of labour and a system of wages increased the mobility and status of men in the economy at large, but the isolated performance of women's domestic work remained 'free,' except when performed by servants. Even milk from the breast suffered a drastic loss in status when a wet nurse of the peasant class or milk from a cow or goat (and later a powdered formula) were found to suffice, and moreover to improve the chance for infant survival when maternal breast feeding was unavailable, insufficient or discouraged by social custom.

While the power of law and religion combined to prohibit a woman from seeking out income-producing work that was stamped as male, an appeal to her feminine nature was duly employed to assuage her ambitions and keep her content. In a poignant example of feminine sentiment used as a wedge against female ambition, childbirth itself was placed under male supervision when the skills of midwifery were surpassed by medical study from which women were barred as unfit by their delicate nature. Armed with the newest antiseptic and surgical knowledge, a doctor in the nineteenth century did have more to offer than a midwife limited to traditional skills, a sorry fact that did much to destroy a historic bond of sisterhood at the urgent moment of new life. Yet a woman doctor, or a woman who wished to become a doctor, was typically caricatured as unwholesomely mannish or likely to faint at the sight of blood – fated to fail one way or another in her foolish attempt to transgress the limits of her sex. Only the soft, unchallenging aspects of human behaviour remained in the female province – a sweet disposition, the habits of neatness, a gentle desire to care for others – and these were enshrined as the superior values of unspoiled femininity as a moral ideal: the dutiful daughter, the good little wife and the virtuous mother who were grateful to live within the protected enclosure of their shrinking domestic sphere.

Refinement of one's feminine nature by staying at home in love and devotion was not meant for women of the working poor who laboured side by side with their men on the land, or those who came to the city with their families to put in twelve hours a day at the mills. Neither did women at the upper levels of society need instruction in the feminine impropriety of labour. Born to a fashion-able life of aesthetic indulgence and a continual round of social engagements, they showed the usual eagerness of their privileged station to hand over all practical work, including the rearing of children, to the care of servants. It took the scrambling ambitions of a powerful new middle class – hardworking, ingenious, acquisitive and insecure – to impose the ideal of the aristocratic, leisured lady on women of its own kind as a hall-mark of upward direction. It took a bourgeois value system propelled by industrious struggle and material gain to pridefully create a woman of total economic dependency in a home in which she now ranked as an ornamental possession, and to see her as a reward of free enterprise, a tribute to the virile success of men.

Marxist theoreticians of the nineteenth century might analyze reproduction as the means by which the exploited masses provided their oppressors with cannon fodder and factory hands, but they could find no place within their strict definitions of work and class for motherhood and nurturance as genuine forms of productive labour. Viewing the new rich in a kinder light, Social Darwinians attempting to explain the human struggle developed the concept of survival of the fittest as an exclusive matter of male-against-male competition. In the first half of the twentieth century it fell to the Freudians to puzzle over the unhappiness of middle-class women with their suppressed ambitions, and to offer the solution of marriage and motherhood as full-time work. The goal of a healthy, mature and adjusted woman was to rid herself of mannish, competi-tive drives, as she was to transcend her immature, mannish clitoral pleasure. Complete fulfilment and sexual satisfaction could reside only in her vagina, her uterus and her feminine role.

Two centuries before the Christian era, the moral goodness of motherhood was extolled by the Romans in the story of the widow Cornelia, mother of the noble Gracchi, who sacrificed the chance of remarriage and wealth to devote her life to raising her sons, whom she proudly called her 'jewels.' Cornelia's example soon was surpassed, however, by another mother whose impact on the feminine ideal has been felt for nearly two thousand years. Created by the Catholic Church on a few scant references in the Gospels, not always favourable at that, the story of Mary, mother of Jesus, is a moral exhortation to the high purpose of motherhood as the pinnacle of feminine ambition that excludes the reality of sex.

As Marina Warner reminds us in her brilliant treatise, *Alone of All Her Sex*, the Virgin is not tainted by worldly desires, She never gets angry or seeks to impose her will. She prayerfully intercedes with the difficult Father, but she does not interfere with His commands or wishes, nor with the commands or wishes of His Son. The Madonna's perfection resides in her simplicity, her chastity, her gentle devotion, her merciful compassion, her modest humility and her dutiful submission, and her luck in having been chosen as the Holy Womb and Comforting Breast for the Son of God. For these humble qualities she is ultimately rewarded as a Queen in Heaven. Alone among women, she has pleased the Lord. (The suckling goddess was an important fixture in religious iconography as far back as discovered civilization. In Roman legend the Milky Way was created when Juno, who was nursing Hercules, squirted her milk across the night sky. Warner records that the one female biological function permitted the Virgin in Christian faith was the act of nursing, yet by the sixteenth century contemporary prudishness and the upper-class custom of employing a wet nurse led to the virtual disappearance from art of the suckling Madonna.)

Collected and told by the brothers Grimm, German folklore in the eighteenth century put forward another vision of motherhood that was also a moral lesson. In *Hansel and Gretel*, *Cinderella* and the tale of *Snow White*, the story turns on a mother who is not really a mother at all. She is, instead, an uncaring stepmother, a stock figure of selfishness, overweening pride and personal ambition. Unmindful of her nurturant duties or actively plotting to get rid of her children (her husband is either too busy, too weak or too blinded by love to notice), the Wicked Stepmother is a cautionary example of maternal negligence and rejection who always gets her comeuppance in the end.

By the mid-twentieth century another negative parable of mother-hood had assumed the proportions of popular myth. Stereotyped in modern American folklore as the nagging Jewish Mother, although hardly restricted to one ethnic type, she was a melodramatic matriarch past her child-bearing years who could not accept that her job was over and done. A caricature of over-bearing nurture, this mother belittled and bossed her husband, scrubbed the floor on her hands and knees when the maid had finished, overcooked the food in her efforts to provide a nourishing meal, and made her son feel guilty for not calling home. In psychoanalytic thinking, the 'domineering' or 'suffocating' or 'over-protective' mother was held responsible for humankind's problems (homosexuality and criminal behaviour, including rape, among them) as much as the 'rejecting' mother who refused to accept her feminine role.

The point is this: While the sentiments of motherhood are designed to collect the ambitions a woman might hold in her heart and direct them towards the goal of nurture, even the nurturing woman can be too ambitious and powerful for the public good. Aggressive nurturance looms as yet another unfeminine fault, or perhaps as a contradiction in terms. Although managerial direction of the career of a husband or child has produced some important reputations in art, music and literature, the Stage Mother who encourages her offspring's talent and the Professional Widow who works tirelessly to keep her husband's work in the public eye are still perceived as unpleasantly pushy.

When it comes to her own success, it has never been becoming for a woman to try hard. Sweat under the arms, a clenched jaw, an unlady-like grunt – these are, after all, the unavoidable signs of straining effort. A man may keep his nose to the grindstone, but a woman had better stop now and again to powder hers. Appearance, we are told, is more feminine than result. Unremarkably, the tiny handful of ambitious careers with certified feminine allure remain those glamorous big dreams with a slim chance for realization (actress, singer, model, interviewer on television) in which looking attractive is a part of performance, so the desire to be noticed can be partly excused.

But not totally excused. Not long ago a lady was someone whose name appeared in the papers only at birth, marriage and death, and a castrating bitch was a woman whose competence equalled a man's. Despite the celebrity mania of the last few decades, unreserved approval of an outstanding woman is still debatable in the public mind, and when asked, she is expected to profess as an article of faith that her husband and children come first, or would come first were she lucky enough to have them. Talent, ability and intellectual promise integrate uneasily with a feminine ideal romantically connected to the superior accomplishments of husband and lover. A lust for power, status, money or immortal fame stands outside the framework of womanly values on the grounds of brash immodesty and selfish indulgence, if not high romance.

Metaphoric reminders of the feminine ideal are doubly instructive when they cast the ambitions of women in a monstrous light. Think of the glamorous facade on a chilling Faye Dunaway in *Network*, the sugary frosting on a poisonous Anne Baxter in *All About Eve*. As a frightening image of femininity abandoned, the ugly witch with her crooked nose and hairy chin is all the more satanic when she rides her broomstick at midnight, subverting the trusty symbol of loyal housewifery, the moral goodness of sweeping clean, to nefarious ends. In *A Tale of Two Cities* Madame Defarge makes sinister use of a nurturant task, her knitting, to implement her vengeance. Childless and driven, she embodies the terrifying excesses of the French Revolution. Lady Macbeth and Hedda Gabler, possibly the two most ambitious and destructive females in theatrical history, are childless women; a third, Medea, destroys her children in an act of revenge. Well into the Sixties, before the new feminist movement, it was conventional in books, movies, plays and psychoanalytic writing to ascribe success, achievement and, especially, destruction, in women to motherhood denied and nurturance thwarted.

By contrast, as we are forever reminded, the ambitions of men, their manly striving and competitive struggles, find inspiring metaphors in the acts of erection, copulation, ejaculation, in seminal fluid itself, and in a fairy-tale picture of the physiology of conception in which eager, aggressive, adventurous sperm are imagined to elbow each other out of the way in their dash to reach an impassive egg. (As it happens, the swimming motions of sperm are random, not directed. They are actively transported upwards through the female tract by oestrogen-induced secretions, cervical filaments and muscular contractions along the passage. Sperm of unusual size and shape are shunted aside, destroyed and discarded. Scientific information, however, is slow to catch up with popular myth, particularly when it contradicts a cherished bias.)

Motherhood and ambition have been seen as opposing forces for thousands of years. Largely because of the new feminist movement, the internalized conflict as well as the external reality recently have become a subject of renewed attention. For many women, perhaps most, motherhood versus personal ambition represents the heart of the feminine dilemma. In the work of psychologist Carol Gilligan, ambivalence in making and sticking to some hard decisions (abortion, career choice), long considered a feminine weakness, has been shown to stem from the ethics and responsibilities of motherhood – the importance of 'caring relationships' – as women perceive their role.

But if ambition and motherhood have been in conflict, femininity and motherhood have not had a happy conjunction either. The swollen belly, oedema in legs and feet, the heaving flood tide of birth, the breast as a lactating organ, and the fatiguing chores of child care are not glamorous, sexy, delicate, romantic, refined or passive, as these words are usually defined.

The desire to be a mother can be a powerful ambition, too, especially when the opportunity is slow in coming. Responsive to the ticking of the biological clock, the motivation to produce and raise a child of one's own (for whatever reason, and the reasons are legion) and the gratifications that a child may bring are spurred by an urgency that is as unique to femaleness as motherhood itself. On the other hand, motherhood is so universally perceived as the ultimate proof of the feminine nature and the intended purpose of female existence that few women have the courage to admit that they do not have the gift for it, or that given a choice, they would rather marshal their energies, their sensitivities and their gratifications in other directions.

Duality of purpose is built into female biology in ways that are hard to resist (and without the freedom of contraceptive choice, in ways that are hard to avoid). The single-mindedness with which a man may pursue his non-reproductive goals is foreign not only to the female procreational ability, it is alien to the feminine values and emotional traits that women are expected to show. The human sentiments of motherhood (goodness, self-sacrifice and a speciality in taking care of the wants of others) are without question desirable characteristics for the raising of children, but I would argue strenuously that women do not possess these traits to a greater degree by biological tendency than men.

Without a radical restructuring of a social order that works well enough in its present form for those extremely ambitious, competitive men whose prototypical ancestors arranged it, and who have little objective reason, just yet, to change the rules, what hope is there for a real accommodation of dual-purpose ambition? The corporate hierarchy has no compelling motivation to modify what it demands of its career employees, and the prizes at the top of the heap go to those who pursue them with single-minded devotion. Pursuit of achievement in literature, science and the arts is a single-minded ambition that will never be restructured, for the competition, understandably, is fierce. Whatever form it takes, satisfying work that earns a decent income is always in short supply, and men are right when they say that the required expenditure of time and effort leaves little room for life's other rewards. Yet a man, if he wishes, may acquire a woman, or a succession of women, to provide him with the rewards of emotional support, practical nurturance, a home and a family. A woman responding to the same needs and desires must split in two and become the traditional reward herself, at least that part which is firmly rooted in biological fact.

Is it unfair for a woman to expect that her desire to be a full-time mother should be accommodated for an unspecified number of years? Should another woman avoid motherhood entirely in order to secure the full chance that any man might have for economic autonomy and satisfying work? Does a society that understands the need for successive generations have a moral obligation to ease the way for a third woman intent on fulfilling both aspects of her dual-purpose ambition? Should one set of expectations be viewed as a predictable retreat into a feminine tradition of dependence, another as a singular expression of unfeminine aspirations, and the third as an admirable solution possible only for the extremely ambitious, extremely energetic few, or for those who are lucky to live with more mildly ambitious, nurturing partners?

There are no easy answers to these questions.

Epilogue

My aim is not to propose a new definition of femininity, one that better suits the coming decade or one that lays claim to moral (or physical) superiority as some sort of intrinsic female province, but to invite examination of a compelling aesthetic that evolved over thousands of years – to explore its origins and the reasons for its perseverance, in the effort to illuminate the restrictions on free choice.

Historically, as I have attempted to show, the fear of not being feminine enough, in style or in spirit, has been used as a sledge hammer against the collective and individual aspirations of women since failure in femininity carries the charge of mannish or neutered, making biological gender subject to ongoing proof. The great paradox of femininity, as I see it, is that a judicious concession here and there has been known to work wonders as protective coloration in a man's world and as a means of survival, but total surrender has stopped women point blank from major forms of achievement. However femininity is used – and if one fact should be clear, it is that femininity *is used* – all approaches towards what men have defined as proper masculine pursuits are set up with road blocks and detours that say, 'For Femininity, Turn Here,' or 'For Femininity, Turn Back,' and the lonesome traveller who wishes to ignore the signs still proceeds at her own risk.

During femininity's own cautious movement through centuries of social upheaval, at least three nostalgic objectives – woman as symbolic aristocrat, woman as humble servant, and woman as glamorous plaything – became melded into a prettified composite that understandably shows its strains. In whatever terms the divisions are cast – the lady and the whore; the provocative and the chaste; noble, altruistic nurturance and childlike dependency – the embedded contradictions leave every woman uncertain: Has she correctly followed all the instructions? Additionally, the conflicts that are rife in ladylike refinement, a submissive demeanour and dazzling allure guarantee that women will be divided among themselves, suspicious of other women as they seek to master an impossible formula to win the approval of men.

There is no denying that femininity's dependence on established traditions, be they styles of dress or codes of behaviour, offers a psychological grip on one's sexual identity, particularly for those whose dimorphic characteristics fall within the statistical overlap that is biologically normal, yet far from the cultural ideal. (This holds true for masculinity as well. An androgynous appearance may be fine for a person of androgynous persuasion; it is not so fine – and can be devastating – when androgyny is not the intention.) What happens next is that certain arbitrary cues and symbols – a hair style, an inflection, an attitude towards work – become the social determinants of gender, and they in turn act as conservators of outworn social values and as levers against social change. In the great cultural need to differentiate one sex from the other with absolute clarity, there are burdens of proof on each side of the aisle, but while the extremes of masculinity can harm others (rape, wife beating, street crime, warfare and a related inability to concede or admit defeat), the extremes of femininity are harmful only – only! – to women themselves in the form of a self-imposed masochism (restraint, inhibition, self-denial, a wasteful use of thought and time) that is deliberately mistaken for 'true nature.'

Most hurtfully, perhaps, femininity is not something that improves with age, for girlishness, with its innocent modesty, its unthreatening impudence and its promise of ripe sexuality in the rosy future, typifies the feminine principle at its ephemeral best. Women who rely on a feminine strategy as their chief means of survival can do little to stop the roaring tide of maturity as they watch their advantage slip by. No doubt a sociobiologist would argue that this female misfortune is, after all, the way things are supposed to be, for the cultural clock merely reflects the biological clock and ticks off the years of reproductive readiness that are finite in number.

This will not do. Gender does ultimately rest on how the species reproduces, but while femaleness will continue to be defined by the XX chromosomal count and its reproductive potential, many women have ceased to define themselves by their reproductive role. (Men were never constrained, anatomically or philosophically, to see themselves primarily as fathers, for reproductive biology is not demanding of the time and energies, and consequently the commitment, of males.) Earning a living, however much the neo-Darwinians would like to frame it as male-against-male competition and survival of the fittest, has become something other than that. Increasingly it is a necessity for both of the sexes, with parenthood fitted in optionally as a gratifying interest, not as service to the species or moral duty (or perpetuation of one's genes). The post-reproductive years grow longer and longer, putting into perspective an emerging truth: the problem is not that some women are feminine failures, but that femininity fails as a reliable goal.

So much for theory. Women still remain emotionally and financially needy, and understandably they will grasp at strategies that seem to have worked in the past and that appear to be working for some right now. Even as they reintroduce themselves to the higher heel, the shorter skirt, the thinner brow, the longer lash, and step back with that inimitable, feminine self-conscious absorption to admire the effect and scrutinize for imperfection, they are thankful they need not put up with the full armature of deceits and handicaps of earlier generations. For things do improve, and progress is made, and they are, in their freedom to choose, a little closer to being themselves.

A Note on Sources

For each chapter I have cited some general reference works, if I used them, followed by specific citations in the order that they appear in my text.

BODY

Carmine D. Clemente, *Anatomy: A Regional Atlas of the Human Body*, Baltimore and Munich: Urban & Schwarzenberg, 1981.

Madge Garland, *The Changing Face of Beauty*, New York: M. Barrows, 1957.

Kenneth Clark's theories of the perfect body are in Kenneth Clark, *The Nude: A Study in Ideal Form*, New York: Pantheon, 1956.

Quote from Byron is from *Don Juan* (1819–24).

The story of Mary Richardson and the Rokeby Venus is in Midge Mackenzie, ed., *Shoulder to Shoulder*, New York: Knopf, 1975.

Miss America demonstration statement of 1968 is in Robin Morgan, ed., *Sisterhood Is Powerful*, New York: Vintage, 1970.

Léa is the heroine in Colette, *The Last of Chéri* (Paris, 1926).

Description of adolescent maturation is from Herant Katchadourian, *The Biology of Adolescence*, San Francisco: W. H. Freeman, 1977.

Oestrogenic properties in Constance R. Martin, *Textbook of Endocrine Physiology*, Baltimore: Williams & Wilkins, 1976.

Growth and sexual maturation in J. M. Tanner, *Growth at Adolescence*, Oxford: Blackwell Scientific Publications, 1973; J. M. Tanner, 'Growing Up,' *Scientific American*, Sept. 1973. Tanner observes that sexual maturation puts a fast brake on growth in the female. He does not propose that the resulting dimorphism in size has a survival advantage for the reproducing mother and her offspring. A female-reproductive theory of growth and size may be found in Lila Leibowitz, 'Perspectives on the Evolution of Sex Differences' in Rayna R. Reiter, ed., *Toward an Anthropology of Women*, New York: Monthly Review Press, 1975.

Infertility at the start of menstruation is reported in Ashley

Montagu, *Sex, Men and Society*, New York: Tower Publications, 1969.

Comparative height statistics for American males and females, and percentile groupings, from National Center for Health Statistics, 1976.

World's Tallest Woman: *New York Times*, Aug. 7, 1978, D–9.

Lady Di postage stamp: *New York Times*, July 26, 1981, Arts & Leisure.

Comparative international height statistics: Howard V. Meredith, 'Worldwide Somatic Comparisons Among Contemporary Human Groups of Adult Females,' *American Journal of Physical Anthropology* (Vol. 34, No. 1), Jan. 1971; Phyllis B. Eveleth and J. M. Tanner, *Worldwide Variations in Human Growth*, Cambridge: Cambridge University Press, 1976.

Sexual maturation of baboons: Cynthia Moss, *Portraits in the Wild: Behavior Studies of East African Mammals*, Boston: Houghton Mifflin, 1975; of gorillas: George Schaller, *The Year of the Gorilla*, Chicago: University of Chicago Press, 1964; of gibbons: J. R. Napier and P. H. Napier, *A Handbook of Living Primates*, London and New York: Academic Press, 1967.

Dimorphism and monogamy: Sarah Blaffer Hrdy, *The Woman That Never Evolved*, Cambridge: Harvard University Press, 1981; Robert D. Martin and Robert M. May, 'Outward Signs of Breeding,' *Nature* (Vol. 293), Sept. 1981.

Hyenas: Moss *op. cit.* Walpole's comment on Mary Wollstonecraft: Eleanor Flexner, *Mary Wollstonecraft*, New York: Coward, McCann & Geoghegan, 1972.

Species with larger females: Katherine Ralls, 'Mammals in Which Females Are Larger then Males,' *Quarterly Review of Biology* (Vol. 51, No. 2), June 1976; Lorus J. and Margery J. Milne, *The Mating Instinct*, Boston: Little, Brown, 1954; Dean Amadon, 'The Significance of Sexual Differences in Size Among Birds,' *Proceedings of the American Philosophical Society* (Vol. 103, No. 4), Aug. 1959; Caroline M. Earhart and Ned K. Johnson, 'Size Dimorphism and Food Habits of North American Owls,' *The Condor* (Vol. 72, No. 3), July 1970; Karl E. Lagler, John E. Bardach and Robert R. Miller, *Ichthyology*, New York: John Wiley, 1962; James A. Oliver, *The Natural History of North American Amphibians and Reptiles*, Princeton: Van Nostrand, 1955.

Hrdy on bullying in Hrdy, *op. cit.*

Ring-tailed lemurs: Alison Jolly, *Lemur Behaviour, A Madagascar Field Study*, Chicago: University of Chicago Press, 1966.

Female body fat content and ovulation, pregnancy and milk production: Jack H. Wilmore, 'The Female Athlete,' *Journal of School Health*, April 1977; Rose E. Frisch, Roger Revelle and Sole Cook, 'Components of Weight at Menarche and the Initiation of the Adolescent Growth Spurt in Girls: Estimated Total Water, Lean Body Weight and Fat,' *Human Biology* (Vol. 45, No. 3), Sept. 1973; Rose E. Frisch and Janet W. McArthur, 'Menstrual Cycles: Fatness as a Determinant of Minimum Weight for Height Necessary for Their Maintenance or Onset,' *Science* (Vol. 185, No. 4155), Sept. 13, 1974.

Rudofsky's theory and Chinese footbinding: Bernard Rudofsky, *The Kimono Mind*, New York: Doubleday, 1965; Bernard Rudofsky, *Are Clothes Modern?*, Chicago: Paul Theobald, 1947. For an extensive discussion of footbinding see Andrea Dworkin, *Woman Hating*, New York: Dutton, 1974.

Corsets: Helene E. Roberts, 'The Exquisite Slave: The Role of Clothes in the Making of the Victorian Woman,' *Signs: Journal of Women in Culture and Society* (Vol. 2, No. 3), 1977; Cecil Willett Cunnington and Phillis Cunnington, *Handbook of English Costume in the Sixteenth Century*, London: Faber and Faber, 1970;——, *The History of Underclothes*, London: M. Joseph, 1951; Norah Waugh, *Corsets and Crinolines*, London: Batsford, 1954; William Barry Lord, *The Corset and the Crinoline*, London: Ward, Lock, and Tyler, 1868; M. D. C. Crawford and Elizabeth A. Guernsey, *The History of Corsets in Pictures*, New York: Fairchild Publications, 1951.

Anne Hollander's observations may be found in Anne Hollander, *Seeing Through Clothes*, New York: Viking Press, 1978.

For the feminist-hygienic approach to dress reform in the late nineteenth century see Abba Louisa Goold Woolson, ed., *Dress Reform: a series of lectures delivered in Boston on dress as it affects the health of women*, Boston: Roberts Brothers, 1874; Mary E. Tillotson, *Progress vs Fashion, an essay on the sanitary & social influences of woman's dress*, Vineland, N. J., 1873; and Mary A. Livermore, *What Shall We Do with Our Daughters?*, Boston: Lee & Shepard, 1883. An extensive discussion of the physical-culture and aesthetic dance cults of the late nineteenth century, and their relationship to corsetry and dress reform, may be found in Elizabeth Kendall, *Where She Danced*, New York: Knopf, 1979.

The War Industries Board announcement, preserved by Rudofsky, may be found in L. M. Vincent, *Competing with the Sylph*, Kansas City and New York: Andrews and McMeel, Inc., 1979.

For lingerie of the Twenties and Thirties see Stella Blum, ed., *Everyday Fashions of the Twenties as Pictured in Sears and Other Catalogs*, New York: Dover Publications, 1981; Christina Probert, ed., *Lingerie in Vogue Since 1910*, New York: Abbeville Press, 1981; and Crawford and Guernsey, *op. cit.*

'She has no thighs' is a frequent comment in Emile Zola, *Nana* (Paris, 1880).

For a photographic essay detailing the variety in women's breasts see Daphna Ayalah and Isaac J. Weinstock, *Breasts: Women Speak About Their Breasts and Their Lives*, New York: Summit Books, 1979.

For an essay on the evolutionary origins of bipedalism see C. Owen Lovejoy, 'The Origin of Man,' *Science* (Vol. 211, No. 4480), Jan. 23, 1981.

Medical evidence that large breasts present a strain to the spine, chest and back: Christine E. Haycock, M.D., Gail Shierman, Ph. D., and Joan Gillette, C.A.T., 'The Female Athlete – Does Her Anatomy Pose Problems?,' presented at the 19th AMA Conference on the Medical Aspects of Sports, June 1977, published in the proceedings of the conference; Christine E. Haycock, M.D., 'Breast Problems–Jogging and Other Sports,' *Nautilus Magazine* (Vol. 3, No. 4), Aug.–Sept. 1981; Christine E. Haycock, 'Breast Support and Protection in the Female Athlete,' American Association of Health, Physical Education, Recreation and Dance, Symposium Papers, Vol. I, Book 2, 1978; Gena Vandestienne, 'Breast Reduction–When Less Is More,' *Ms.*, Feb. 1982; Author's Interview with Ronald S. Levandusky, M.D., Jan. 11, 1982; Author's Interview with Peter I. Pressman, M.D., Jan. 12, 1982; Author's Interview with Richard M. Bachrach, D.O. Jan. 13, 1982.

Trends in plastic surgery for breasts from the Levandusky interview.

Desmond Morris's speculation on the evolution of the full breast may be found in Desmond Morris, *The Naked Ape*, McGraw-Hill, 1967.

Florenz Ziegfeld's feminine ideal, with measurements, is in Marjorie Farnsworth, *The Ziegfeld Follies*, New York: Bonanza Books, 1956.

Measurements of Lillian Russell and Anna Held, and newspaper interviews with them regarding tight-lacing, from the Robinson Locke Collection, Vol. 264, New York Public Library at Lincoln Center. A discussion of the rumours regarding Held's ribs, and a denial, may be found in Charles Higham, *Ziegfeld*, Chicago: Regnery, 1972.

An analysis of the competitive pressures on ballerinas to keep thin, and a short history of the anorectic ideal, including Twiggy, may be found in L. M. Vincent, *Competing With the Sylph, op. cit.*

Differences in basal metabolism of males and females, and in caloric consumption, is reported in M. P. Vessey, 'Gender Differences in the Epidemiology of Non-neurological Disease' in Ounsted and Taylor, eds., *Gender Differences: Their Ontogeny and Significance*, Baltimore: Williams and Wilkins, 1972.

A discussion of anorexia and striving for perfection may be found in Steven Levenkron, *Treating and Overcoming Anorexia Nervosa*, New York: Scribner's, 1982. A feminist perspective on the ideal body may be found in Kim Chernin, *The Obsession: Reflections On the Tyranny of Slenderness*, New York: Harper & Row, 1981.

HAIR

Wendy Cooper: *Hair: Sex, Society, Symbolism*, New York: Stein and Day, 1971.

Smithsonian Institution, *Hair*, an illustrated catalogue published in conjunction with an exhibit at the Cooper-Hewitt Museum, New York City, June 10 to Aug. 17, 1980.

Genetics of baldness: Curt Stern, *Principles of Human Genetics*, San Francisco: W. H. Freeman, 1973; James B. Hamilton, 'Age, Sex, and Genetic Factors in the Regulation of Hair Growth in Man: A Comparison of Caucasian and Japanese Populations,' in Montagna and Ellis, eds., *The Biology of Hair Growth*, New York: Academic Press, 1958; Owen Edwards and Arthur Rook, 'Androgen-dependent Cutaneous Syndromes' in Arthur Rook and John Slavin, eds., *Recent Advances in Dermatology*, No. 5, Edinburgh, London, New York: Churchill Livingston, 1980. Baldness is troubling to neo-Darwinians: see Ernst Caspari, 'Sexual Selection in Human Evolution,' in Bernard Campbell, ed., *Sexual Selection and the Descent of Man*, Chicago: Aldine, 1972.

Samson's long hair: Judges 16; Absalom's long hair: II Samuel 14, 18.

Long-haired Greeks: Homer, *Iliad*, Book II.

Short-haired Romans: Suetonius, *The Lives of the Twelve Caesars*, Julius Caesar, XLV.

Saint Paul on hair: I Corinthians 11.

Saint Chrysostom on hair: *Homilies on First Corinthians*, Homily 26.

Philip Stubbes on hair: Philip Stubbes, *Anatomy of Abuses*, Part II (London, 1583).

William Prynne on hair: William Prynne, *Histrio-Mastix* (London, 1633).

Milton on hair: John Milton, *Paradise Lost*, Book IV (1667).

Bruno Bettelheim's interpretation of the Rapunzel story may be found in Bruno Bettelheim, *The Uses of Enchantment: The Meaning and Importance of Fairy Tales*, New York: Knopf, 1976.

Liane de Pougy's observations are in Liane de Pougy, *My Blue Notebooks*, New York: Harper & Row, 1979.

Irene Castle on short hair: Irene Castle Treman, 'I Bobbed My Hair and Then—,' *Ladies' Home Journal*, Oct. 1921.

Charlotte Perkins Gilman's talk to the working women was reported in *The New York Times*, March 15, 1916, 22:7. The *Times* ran its satire the following day: *The New York Times*, March 16, 1916, 13:3. The story of Marshall Field firing an employee for short hair appeared in *The New York Times*, Aug. 10, 1921, 13:1; the *Times* editorial appeared three days later: *The New York Times*, Aug. 13, 1921, 8:4. *The Nation*'s editorial comment was published in the issue of Aug. 24, 1921.

Mary Garden and Mary Pickford on hair length: *Pictorial Review*, April 1927. Further information on Pickford from Robert Windeler, *Sweetheart, The Story of Mary Pickford*, New York: Praeger, 1974.

Marjorie Rosen's observations on Hollywood blondes may be found in Marjorie Rosens, *Popcorn Venus*, New York: Coward, McCann & Geoghegan, 1973.

Life magazine's five pictorial features on Veronica Lake ran in the issues of March 3, 1941; April 14, 1941; Nov. 24, 1941 (the statistics celebrating her hair); March 8, 1943 (Veronica puts up her hair as a wartime safety measure); and May 17, 1943. Further information on Lake from Veronica Lake with Donald Bain, *Veronica*, New York: Bantam Books, 1972.

Scene between Hagar, Reba and Pilate from Toni Morrison, *Song of Solomon*, New York: Knopf, 1977.

'today i'ma be a white girl' is from the play *Spell No 7*, by Ntozake Shange, 1979.

Roman hairdressing customs from Jerome Carcopino, *Daily Life in Ancient Rome*, New Haven: Yale University Press, 1940.

Edith Wharton's observation on women and hair is from Edith Wharton, 'The Touchstone' (1900), *Madame de Treymes and Others*, New York: Scribner's 1970.

CLOTHES

Bernard Rudofsky, *Are Clothes Modern?*, Chicago: Paul Theobald, 1947.

Cecil Willett Cunnington and Phillis Cunnington, *Handbook of English Costume in the Sixteenth Century*, London: Faber and Faber, 1970; ——, *Handbook of English Costume in the Seventeenth Century*, London: Faber and Faber, 1966; ——, *Handbook of English Costume in the Eighteenth Century*, London: Faber and Faber, 1957; ——, *Handbook of English Costume in the Nineteenth Century*, London: Faber and Faber, 1959.

Quentin Bell, *On Human Finery*, New York: Schocken Books, 1976.

Ernestine Carter, *20th Century Fashion*, London: Eyre Methuen, 1975.

Jane Dorner, *Fashion in the Twenties and Thirties*, London: Ian Allan, 1973.

Thorstein Veblen, *The Theory of the Leisure Class* (1899), New York: Random House Modern Library edition, 1934.

Jane Trahey, ed., *Harper's Bazaar: 100 Years of the American Female*, New York: Random House, 1967.

James Laver, *The Concise History of Costume and Fashion*, New York: Abrams, 1969.

Biblical injunction concerning sex-distinctive garments: Deuteronomy 22:5.

A documentary history of Sumptuary Laws may be found in Frances Elizabeth Baldwin, *Sumptuary Legislation and Personal Regulation in England*, Baltimore: Johns Hopkins, 1926.

To tell the history of the suffragists and the Bloomer costume, I relied on the following sources: Ida Husted Harper, *The Life and Work of Susan B. Anthony* (3 vols.), Indianapolis: The Hollenbeck Press, 1899, Vol. 1, pp. 112–117; Theodore Stanton and Harriet Stanton Blatch, eds., *Elizabeth Cady Stanton, As Revealed in Her Letters,*

Diary and Reminiscences (2 vols.), New York: Harper, 1922, Vol. 1, pp. 200–204; Vol. 2, pp. 32–50, 339; Elizabeth Cady Stanton, Susan B. Anthony, Matilda Joslyn Gage, eds., *History of Woman Suffrage*, Rochester: Susan B. Anthony, publisher, 1881, Vol. 1, pp. 470–1, 836–844; Amelia Bloomer, ed., *The Lily*, a journal published during the 1850s in Seneca Falls, New York. Much of this documentary material may be found in Aileen S. Kraditor, ed., *Up from the Pedestal*, New York: Quadrangle, 1968.

For a short account of the later fortunes of the rational dress, written in the 'improved' spelling, see Mary E. Tillotson, *History ov the First Thirty-Five Years ov the Science Costume Movement in the United States ov America*, Vineland, N.J., 1885.

The story of the colliery workers of Lancashire and Wigan, with pictures, is told in Michael Hiley, *Victorian Working Women*, Boston: David R. Godine, 1979.

For my reflections on women who have worn men's clothes, the following books were helpful: Andrew Lang, *The Maid of France*, London: Longmans, Green, 1908 (Joan of Arc); Joseph Barry, *Infamous Woman: The Life of George Sand*, New York: Doubleday, 1977; Theodore Stanton ed., *Reminiscences of Rosa Bonheur*, New York: Hacker Art Books, 1976; Jane Cannary Hickok, *Calamity Jane's Letters to Her Daughter* (1877–1902), Berkeley: Shameless Hussy Press, 1976; Frances Anne Kemble, *Records of a Later Life*, New York: H. Holt, 1884; Robert Phelps, *Belles Saisons, a Colette Scrapbook*, New York: Farrar, Straus and Giroux, 1978; Nigel Nicolson, *Portrait of a Marriage*, London: Weidenfeld and Nicolson, 1973 (V. Sackville-West); Meryle Secrest, *Between Me and Life*, New York: Doubleday, 1974 (Romaine Brooks, Natalie Barney *et al.*); Elizabeth Evans, *Weathering the Storm*, New York: Scribner's, 1975 (Deborah Sampson Gannett).

Virginia Woolf's autobiographical comments on dressing: 'A Sketch of the Past' in Virginia Woolf, *Moments of Being*, ed., by Jeanne Schulkind, New York and London: Harcourt Brace Jovanovich, 1976.

Denunciations of women for indulging in fashion as a sign of pride, ambition and whoredom may be found in Isaiah 3 and in Tertullian, *On the Apparel of Women* (A.D. 202).

VOICE

Voice changes in puberty: Herant Katchadourian, *The Biology of Adolescence*, San Francisco: W. H. Freeman, 1977; James M. Tanner,

M.D., 'Growth and Endocrinology of the Adolescent,' in Lytt I. Gardner, ed., *Endocrine and Genetic Diseases of Childhood*, Philadelphia & London: W. B. Saunders, 1969.

Transsexual voice changes: Richard Green and John Money, eds., *Transsexual and Sex Reassignment*, Baltimore: Johns Hopkins, 1969, 1975.

Pitch and range: Dennis Fry, *Homo Loquens: Man as a Talking Animal*, Cambridge: Cambridge University Press, 1977; ———, *The Physics of Speech*, Cambridge: Cambridge University Press, 1979; Dorothy Uris, *A Woman's Voice*, New York: Stein and Day, 1975.

The sexually dimorphic brain: Literature in this field is proliferating. One helpful review article is Jerre Levy, 'Sex and the Brain,' *The Sciences*, March 1981. The comprehensive text is Robert W. Goy and Bruce S. McEwen, *Sexual Differentiation of the Brain*, The MIT Press, 1980. The most extensive compilation of sex differences in performance, which the authors do not claim are innate, remains Eleanor Emmons Maccoby and Carol Nagy Jacklin, *The Psychology of Sex Differences*, Stanford University Press, 1974.

Shakespeare's line is from *King Lear*.

Rousseau's theories of feminine education may be found in Jean Jacques Rousseau, *Emilius; or, A Treatise of Education* (1726), translated from the French, Edinburgh: A Donalson, 1768 (3 vols.), Vol. 3. Wollstonecraft's attack on Rousseau appears in Mary Wollstonecraft, *A Vindication of the Rights of Woman* (1792), New York: W. W. Norton, 1967. Kant's definition of the feminine characteristics and his theories on education are in Immanuel Kant, *Observations on the Feeling of the Beautiful and the Sublime* (1763), translated from the German by John T. Goldthwait, Berkeley: University of California Press, 1960, Section III.

Dorothy Parker said, 'Men seldom make passes/At girls who wear glasses,' 'News Item,' *Enough Rope*, New York: Boni and Liveright, 1926.

Victorian consternation over education's effect on the uterus is documented in John S. Haller, Jr. and Robin M. Haller, *The Physician and Sexuality in Victorian America*, Urbana: University of Illinois Press, 1974.

Milton's saying and his biographer's defence are in William Riley Parker, *Milton*, Oxford: Clarendon Pess, 1968, Vol 1.

An essay on the exemption of Orthodox Jewish women from synagogue prayer was written by Cynthia Ozick, *Lilith* No. 6, 1979.

Paul's command to silence in church is in *Corinthians* I, 14:34.

A discussion of the active role of women in the early Christian church may be found in Rosemary Radford Reuther, ed., *Religion and Sexism*, New York: Simon and Schuster, 1974; and in Rosemary Reuther and Eleanor McLaughlin, eds., *Women of Spirit*, New York: Simon and Schuster, 1979. Tyndale's fight with Thomas More and *The Book of the Knight of La Tour-Landry* are reported in G. G. Coulton, *Medieval Panorama*, New York: Macmillan, 1946.

The common scold is defined in *Blackstone's Commentaries on the Laws of England*, Book 4, Chap 13.

Ducking stools and branks: Alice Morse Earle, *Curious Punishments of Bygone Days*, Chicago: Herbert A. Stone, 1896 ——, *Colonial Dames and Good Wives*, Boston: Houghton Mifflin, 1895; Carl Holliday, *Woman's Life in Colonial Days*, Boston: Cornhill, 1922.

Grammatical gender: William J. Entwhistle, *Aspects of Language*, London: Faber and Faber, 1953; Otto Jespersen, *The Philosophy of Grammar*, London: Allen and Unwin, 1924; William Graff, *Language and Languages*, New York: Russell and Russell, 1964; Herman Paul, *Principles of the History of Language*, trans. from the German, College Park, Md.: McGrath, 1970.

Maxine Hong Kingston's invention of an American-feminine speaking personality is from Maxine Hong Kingston, *The Woman Warrior*, New York: Knopf, 1976.

Speaking in feminine: Barrie Thorne and Nancy Henley, eds., *Language and Sex: Difference and Dominance*, Rowley, Mass.: Newbury House, 1975 (contains the key articles by Thorne, Henley, Cheris Kramerae, Ruth M. Brend and Jacqueline Sachs); Nancy M. Henley, *Body Politics: Power, Sex and Nonverbal Communication*, Englewood Cliffs, N.J.: Prentice-Hall, 1977; Mary Ritchie Key, *Male/Female Language*, Metuchen, N.J.: The Scarecrow Press, 1975; Robin Lakoff, *Language and Woman's Place*, New York: Harper Colophon, 1975; Sally McConnell-Ginet, 'Intonation in a Man's World,' *Signs*, Spring 1978; Pamela M. Fishman, 'Interaction: The Work Women Do,' *Social Problems*, April 1978; George Steiner, *After Babel*, London & New York: Oxford University Press, 1975.

Colourblindness: Curt Stern, *Principles of Human Genetics*, San Francisco: W. H. Freeman, 1973.

Barbara Howar's advice to Luci Baines Johnson may be found in Barbara Howar, *Laughing All the Way*, New York: Stein and Day, 1973.

194

The Great Call of the gibbon: Joe T. Marshall, Jr. and Elsie R. Marshall, 'Gibbons and Their Territorial Songs,' *Science* (Vol. 193, No. 4249), July 16, 1976.

Expletives: Lee Ann Bailey and Lenora A. Timm, 'More on Women's–and Men's Expletives,' *Anthropological Linguistics* (Vol. 18, No. 9), Dec. 1976.

Criticism of Margaret Thatcher's voice appeared in *Newsweek*, May 14, 1979, and in *The New York Times*, March 6, 1981 (Op Ed piece).

The use of *kana* by Lady Murasaki and Sei Shonagon is discussed in Ivan Morris, *The World of the Shining Prince*, New York: Knopf, 1964.

Writing in Yiddish for women and unlearned men is discussed in Mark Zborowski and Elizabeth Herzog, *Life Is with People: The Culture of the Shtetl*, New York: Schocken, 1962.

Virginia Woolf on feminine writing: Virginia Woolf, *A Room of One's Own* (1929), and 'A Sketch of the Past' in Virginia Woolf, *Moments of Being*, ed. by Jeanne Schulkind, New York and London: Harcourt Brace Jovanovich, 1976.

Rachel Brownstein's comment on Jane Austen is in Rachel M. Brownstein, *Becoming a Heroine*, New York: The Viking Press, 1982.

The university study gauging reader response to a piece of writing is reported in Mary Ritchie Key, *Male/Female Language, op. cit.*

Study of one hundred contemporary authors: Mary Hiatt, *The Way Women Write*, New York: Teachers College Press, 1977.

Southey's letter to Charlotte Bronte is quoted in Margot Peters, *Unquiet Soul: A Biography of Charlotte Bronte*, New York: Doubleday, 1975.

SKIN

Thomas B. Fitzpatrick, M.D. *et al.*, *Dermatology in General Medicine*, New York: McGraw-Hill, 1979.

Fenja Gunn, *The Artificial Face: A History of Cosmetics*, London: David & Charles, 1973.

Neville Williams, *Powder and Paint*, London: Longmans, Green, 1957.

Wendy Cooper, *Hair: Sex, Society, Symbolism*, New York: Stein and Day, 1971.

Richard Corson, *Fashions in Makeup*, New York: Universe, 1972.

Report on four-year study of skin disease in the United States: Marie-Louise Johnson, M.D. and Robert S. Stern, M.D., 'Prevalence and Ecology of Skin Disorders' in Fitzpatrick, *Dermatology, op. cit.*

Japanese ideal of the white powdered face: Ivan Morris, *The World of the Shining Prince*, New York: Knopf, 1964.

Michele Wallace's observations are in Michele Wallace, *Black Macho and the Myth of the Superwoman*, New York: Dial Press, 1979.

Elizabeth Bennet's summer tan is a subject of discussion in Jane Austen, *Pride and Prejudice* (London, 1813).

Acne, its greater prevalence in men, and the calming effects of oestrogen: John S. Strauss, M.D., 'Sebaceous Glands' in Fitzpatrick, *Dermatology, op. cit.*

Effects of pregnancy: Robert B. Scoggins, M.D., 'Skin Changes and Diseases in Pregnancy' in Fitzpatrick, *Dermatology, op. cit.*

Her mental anguish at Oxford and her fear of growing a beard is recorded by Vera Brittain, *Testament of Youth* (London, 1933), USA.: Wideview Books, 1980.

Beard and body hair, follicles, comparative growth by race and sex: James B. Hamilton, 'Age, Sex, and Genetic Factors in the Regulation of Hair Growth in Man: A Comparison of Caucasian and Japanese Populations,' in Montagna and Ellis, eds., *The Biology of Hair Growth*, New York: Academic Press, 1958; Edith McKnight, 'The Prevalence of "Hirsutism" in Young Women,' *The Lancet*, Feb. 22, 1964 (University of Wales study); P. K. Thomas and D. G. Ferriman, 'Variation in Facial and Pubic Hair Growth in White Women,' *American Journal of Physical Anthropology* (Vol. 15, No. 2), June 1957; John A. Ewing and Beatrice A. Rouse, 'Hirsutism, Race and Testosterone Levels: Comparison of East Asians and Euroamericans,' *Human Biology* (Vol. 50, No. 2), May 1978; Owen Edwards and Arthur Rook, 'Androgen-dependent Cutaneous Syndromes' in Arthur Rook and John Slavin, eds., *Recent Advances in Dermatology*, No. 5, Edinburgh, London, New York: Churchill Livingston, 1980.

Anthropological obsession with beards: See John Hurrell Crook, 'Sexual Selection, Dimorphism, and Social Organization in the Primates' in Bernard Campbell, ed., *Sexual Selection and the Descent of Man*, Chicago: Aldine, 1972.

Schaller on lions: George B. Schaller, 'Life With the King of the

Beasts,' *National Geographic*, April 1969; ———, *The Serengeti Lion: A Study of Predator-Prey Relations*, Chicago: University of Chicago Press, 1972.

Tanner's theory of sexual hair as a handy clutch for an infant: James M. Tanner, M.D., 'Growth and Endocrinology of the Adolescent' in Lytt I. Gardner, ed., *Endocrine and Genetic Diseases of Childhood*, Philadelphia and London: W. B. Saunders, 1969.

Darwin's views on hairlessness and sexual selection are discussed in Crook, *op. cit.* The modern elaboration of this theory is in Desmond Morris, *The Naked Ape*, New York: McGraw-Hill, 1967.

Ovid's 'rude goat' image is from *Ars Amatoria*.

Lombroso's theories: Cesare Lombroso and William Ferrero, *The Female Offender*, trans. from the Italian, New York: D. Appleton, 1897. For a discussion of Lombroso, see Ann Jones, *Women Who Kill*, New York: Holt, Rinehart and Winston, 1980.

Evolution of the swimsuit: Claudia B. Kidwell, *Women's Bathing and Swimming Costume in the United States* (United States National Museum Bulletin 250), Washington, D.C.: Smithsonian Institution Press, 1968; Christina Probert, *Swimwear in Vogue Since 1910*, New York: Abbeville Press, 1981.

Popularity of chorus-girl movies in the Twenties: Marjorie Rosen, *Popcorn Venus*, New York: Coward, McCann & Geoghegan, 1973.

Evolution of stockings from opaque to sheer: Milton N. Grass, *History of Hosiery*, New York: Fairchild Publications, 1955; Ira J. Haskell, *Hosiery Thru the Years*, Lynn, Mass. (mimeo), 1956, at the New York Public Library.

Ads for Zip and Neet appeared in the back pages of *The Delineator* during 1923 and 1924.

Shelley Winters tells her strapless-gown story in Shelley Winters, *Shelley, Also Known as Shirley*, New York: Morrow, 1980.

Eccrine and apocrine sweat glands: R. H. Champion, 'Sweat Glands' in Champion *et al.*, *An Introduction to the Biology of the Skin*, Philadelphia: F. A. Davis, 1970; Harry J. Hurley, Jr., M.D., 'Apocrine Glands' in Fitzpatrick, *Dermatology, op. cit.*; Dorothy V. Harris, 'Conditioning for Stress in Sports' in Dorothy V. Harris, ed., *DGWS Research Reports: Women in Sports*, Vol. II, Washington, D.C.: American Association for Health, Physical Education and Recreation, 1973.

Anne Hollander's observations on pubic hair in art may be found in Anne Hollander, *Seeing Through Clothes*, New York: Viking Press, 1978.

Compilation of euphemisms for pubic hair is from Wendy Cooper, *Hair, op. cit.* (Venus plats can be found in a translation of *Lysistrata*; sweet bottom-grass is in *Venus and Adonis*).

Among the Christian exhortations against cosmetics are Tertullian, *On the Apparel of Women* (A.D. 202); Philip Stubbes, *Anatomy of Abuses* (1583); and William Prynne, *Histrio-Mastix* (1633).

Speer's comments on cosmetics production in Nazi Germany and his observations on Goering are in Albert Speer, *Inside the Third Reich*, New York: Macmillan, 1970.

Effect of oestrogen on thinning of the skin during the aging process: A. Jarrett, *The Physiology and Pathophysiology of the Skin*, Vol. I, London and New York: Academic Press, 1973; Author's interview with Norman Orentreich, M.D., March 1981.

MOVEMENT

The story of Athene and her flute is in Robert Graves, *The Greek Myths*, Vol. 1, Harmondsworth, England: Penguin Books, 1960, and in H. J. Rose, *A Handbook of Greek Mythology*, New York: Dutton, 1959.

Huck dresses as a woman in Chapters 10 and 11 of Mark Twain, *The Adventures of Huckleberry Finn* (1884).

Tricks of female impersonation: Esther Newton, *Mother Camp: Female Impersonators in America*, Englewood Cliffs, N.J.: Prentice-Hall, 1972; Peter Underwood, *Life's a Drag!*, London: Leslie Frewin, 1974.

Surgical and cosmetic changes: Richard Green and John Money, eds., *Transsexualism and Sex Reassignment*, Baltimore: Johns Hopkins University Press, 1975. Observations of James Morris are in Jan Morris, *Conundrum*, London: Faber and Faber, 1974.

Anatomical differences affecting strength and movement: Jack Wilmore, 'The Female Athlete,' *Journal of School Health*, April 1977; Jack H. Wilmore, 'Alterations in Strength, Body Composition and Anthropometric Measurements Consequent to a 10-Week Weight Training Program,' *Medicine and Science in Sports* (Vol. 6, No. 2) Summer 1974; ——, 'Body Composition and Strength Development,' *Journal of Physical Education and Recreation*, Jan. 1975; James

McIlwain, 'Physiological Considerations for Training Female Track and Field Athletes,' *Athletic Journal* (Vol. 58, No. 7) March 1978.

Uterine musculature, differences in pelvic shape, angle of the sockets: J. M. Tanner, *Growth at Adolescence*, Oxford: Blackwell, 1973; Author's interview with William G. Hamilton, M.D., Feb 9, 1981.

Limberness and flexibility: Janice Kaplan, *Women and Sports*, New York: Viking, 1979; H. Harrison Clarke, ed., 'Joint and Body Range of Movement,' *Physical Fitness Research Digest* (Series 5, No. 4), Oct. 1975, published by The President's Council on Physical Fitness and Sports; H. Harrison Clarke, ed., 'Physical and Motor Sex Differences,' *Physical Fitness Research Digest* (Series 9, No. 4), Oct. 1979, published by The President's Council on Physical Fitness and Sports; John L. Marshall *et al.*, 'Joint Looseness: A Function of the Person and the Joint,' *Medicine and Science in Sports and Exercise* (Vol. 12, No. 3), 1980.

Finger dexterity reported in Eleanor Emmons Maccoby and Carol Nagy Jacklin, *The Psychology of Sex Differences*, Stanford University Press, 1974.

Theory of erotic appeal in long fingernails is in David Kunzle, *Fashion and Fetishism*, Totowa, N. J.: Rowman and Littlefield, 1982.

Personal accounts of nail-growing appear in Shirley MacLaine, *You Can Get There From Here*, New York: Norton, 1975; Helen Gurley Brown, *Having It All*, New York: Linden/Simon and Schuster, 1982.

Suzy Parker and Revlon: Andrew Tobias, *Fire and Ice*, New York: Morrow, 1976.

Tripp's explanation of swish: C. A. Tripp, *The Homosexual Matrix*, New York: McGraw-Hill, 1975.

Small, light frames of winning gymnasts: Patricia C. Morris and Carol S. Underwood, 'The Woman Athlete: Structurally Speaking' in Dorothy V. Harris, ed., *DGWS Research Reports: Women in Sports*, Vol. II, Washington, D.C.: American Association for Health, Physical Education and Recreation; Harold B. Falls and L. Dennis Humphrey, 'Body Type and Composition Differences between Placers and Non-placers in an AIAW Gymnastics Meet,' *Research Quarterly* (Vol. 49, No. 1), March 1978.

Schiller's definition of masculine and feminine beauty may be found in Friedrich Schiller, *Essays Aesthetical and Philosophical*, translated from the German, London: George Bell & Sons, 1875. See especially 'On Grace and Beauty.'

Ballet conventions: Jennifer Dunning, 'Partnering as an Art,' *The New York Times*, Feb. 6, 1981; Lee Edward Stern, 'Feet–the Fragile Pedestal of Ballet,' *The New York Times*, July 20, 1980; John and Roberta Lazzarini, *Pavlova*, New York: Schirmer, 1981; Author's interview with William G. Hamilton, M.D., Feb. 9, 1981.

Susan B. Anthony's shoe size and the newspaper comments are reported in Ida Husted Harper, *The Life and Work of Susan B. Anthony*, Indianapolis: The Hollenbeck Press, 1899.

Medical problems of high heels: Jane Brody, 'Personal Health,' *The New York Times*, Feb. 14, 1979.

Rudofsky on the impractical shoe: Bernard Rudofsky, *The Kimono Mind*, New York: Doubleday, 1965; see also Bernard Rudofsky, *Are Clothes Modern?*, Chicago: Paul Theobald, 1947.

Isiah on footgear: Isaiah 3.

Colette's sandals and toenail polish: Robert Phelps, *Belles Saisons*, New York: Farrar, Straus and Giroux, 1978.

Samurai history and Japanese etiquette from Rudofsky, *The Kimono Mind, op. cit.* See also Ruth Benedict, *The Chrysanthemum and the Sword* (1946), New York: New American Library, 1974.

Side saddle: Charles Chenevix Trench, *A History of Horsemanship*, New York: Doubleday, 1970; Lida Fleitmann Bloodgood, *The Saddle of Queens*, New York: J. A. Allen, 1959.

The pathological uterus: Barbara Ehrenreich and Deirdre English, *For Her Own Good: 150 Years of the Experts' Advice to Women*, New York: Anchor Press/Doubleday, 1978.

Range of cheetahs: George W. and Lory Herbison Frame, 'Cheetahs: In a Race for Survival,' *National Geographic*, May 1980.

Open-field behaviour of rats: Jeffrey A. Gray *et al.*, 'Gonadal Hormone Injections in Infancy and Adult Emotional Behaviour,' *Animal Behaviour*, Vol. 13, No. 1, Jan. 1965.

Menstruation: Janice Delaney, Mary Jane Lupton and Emily Toth, *The Curse: A Cultural History of Menstruation*, New York: Dutton, 1976; Paula Weideger, *Menstruation and Menopause*, New York: Knopf, 1976. Beauvoir's observations are in Simone de Beauvoir, *The Second Sex* (1949), trans. from the French by H. M. Parshley, New York: Knopf, 1953. Cramps on the tennis circuit: Grace Lichtenstein, *A Long Way, Baby: Behind the Scenes in Women's Pro Tennis*, New York: Morrow, 1974.

Sports and the feminine ideal: Sue Tyler, 'Adolescent Crisis: Sport Participation for the Female' in Dorothy V. Harris, ed.,

DGWS Research Reports: Women in Sports, Vol. II, American Association for Health, Physical Education and Recreation, 1973; Jack H. Wilmore and C. Harmon Brown, 'Physiological Profiles of Women Distance Runners,' *Medicine and Science in Sports* (Vol. 6, No. 3), Fall 1974; Dorothy V. Harris, 'Research Studies on the Female Athlete: Psychosocial Considerations,' *Journal of Physical Education and Recreation*, Jan. 1975; P. S. Wood, 'Sex Differences in Sports,' *The New York Times Magazine*, May 18, 1980; Nadine Brozan, 'Training linked to Disruption of Female Reproductive Cycle,' *The New York Times*, April 17, 1978; Neil Amdur, 'Seven Women Athletes Banned for Drugs,' *The New York Times*, October 26, 1979; ——, 'The Drug Game Threatens International Amateur Sport,' *The New York Times*, Nov. 4, 1979; ——, 'Women Facing More Than an Athletic Struggle,' *The New York Times*, Dec. 21, 1980; Dick Lacey, 'Women Athletes Help to Educate a Male Coach,' *The New York Times*, Dec. 18, 1977.

Mehrabian's studies are reported in Nancy M. Henley, *Body Politics: Power, Sex, and Nonverbal Communication*, Englewood Cliffs, N.J.: Prentice-Hall, 1977.

Rowell on primate dominance: Thelma E. Rowell, 'The Concept of Social Dominance,' *Behavioral Biology;* II, 1974.

Deportment in the Middle Ages: G. G. Coulton, *Medieval Panorama*, New York: Macmillan, 1946.

American public decency regulations before World War I: Geoffrey Perrett, *America in the Twenties*, New York: Simon and Schuster, 1982.

Guillaumin's theory: Colette Guillaumin, 'The Question of Difference,' *Feminist Issues* (Vol. 2, No. 1), Spring 1982. See also Colette Guillaumin, 'The Appropriation of Women,' *Feminist Issues* (Vol. 1, No. 2), Winter 1981.

Nancy Henley's analysis of masculine and feminine movement in *Body Politics, op. cit.,* is the classic in the field.

Testosterone and aggression: K. E. Moyer, 'A Preliminary Physiological Model of Aggressive Behavior' and F. H. Bronson and C. Desjardins, 'Steroid Hormones and Aggressive Behavior in Mammals' in Eleftheriou and Scott, eds., *The Physiology of Aggression and Defeat*, New York: Plenum Press, 1971; Arthur Kling, M.D., 'Testosterone and Aggressive Behavior in Man and Non-Human Primates' in Eleftheriou and Sprott, eds., *Hormonal Correlates of Behavior*, Vol. 1, New York: Plenum Press, 1975; Rod Plonik, 'Brain Stimulation and Aggression: Monkeys, Apes, and Humans' in Ralph L. Holloway, ed.,

Primate Aggression, Territoriality, and Xenophobia, New York: Academic Press, 1974 (Plotnik is the researcher I quote); Robert M. Rose *et al.,* 'Androgens and Aggression: A Review and Recent Findings in Primates' in Holloway, *Primate Aggression, op. cit.;* David M. Hamburg, 'Psychobiological Studies of Aggressive Behaviour,' *Nature,* Vol. 230, March 5, 1971; Laurel Holliday, *The Violent Sex,* Guerneville, Cal.: Bluestocking Books, 1978.

Comparative testosterone levels in males and females: Figures vary from study to study, as do the testosterone levels themselves, especially in males. Metabolic conversions from one hormone to another also take place. The average difference of ten to one for males and females is reported in W. R. Butt *et al., Hormone Chemistry,* Vol. 2, New York: John Wiley, 1976. This correlates with the production rates cited in Goodman and Gilman, *The Pharmacological Basis of Therapeutics,* New York: Macmillan, 1975.

EMOTION

Broverman and Broverman: Inge K. Broverman, Donald M. Broverman *et al.,* 'Sex-Role Stereotypes and Clinical Judgments of Mental Health,' *Journal of Consulting and Clinical Psychology* (Vol. 34, No. 1), 1970. See also Jacob Orlofsky, 'Relationship Between Sex Role Attitudes and Personality Traits and the Sex Role Behavior Scale–1: A New Measure of Masculine and Feminine Role Behaviors and Interests,' *Journal of Personality and Social Psychology* (Vol. 40, No. 5), 1981.

Selections from Aristotle and Ralph Waldo Emerson appear in Rosemary Agonito, ed., *History of Ideas on Woman: A Source Book,* New York: Putnam, 1977.

President Reagan's remark: *Time,* Sept. 12, 1983.

Jesus wept: Luke 19:41.

Mary as *Mater Dolorosa*: Marina Warner, *Alone of All Her Sex: The Myth and the Cult of the Virgin Mary,* New York: Knopf, 1976.

Muskie's tears: 'Campaign Teardrops,' *Time,* March 13, 1972.

Begin's grief: 'Begin's Deep Depression,' *Newsweek,* Sept. 26, 1983; 'Begin's Clouds of Gloom,' *Newsweek,* Aug. 1, 1983.

Beauvoir on crying: Simone de Beauvoir, *The Second Sex* (1949), trans. from the French by H. M. Parshley, New York: Knopf, 1953.

Studies on crying newborns and little children: Eleanor Maccoby and Carol Jacklin, *The Psychology of Sex Differences*, Stanford University Press, 1974.

Raging hormonal imbalance: Edgar Berman, *The Compleat Chauvinist: A Guide for the Bedeviled Male*, New York: Macmillan, 1981.

Depression: Willard Gaylin, *Feelings*, New York: Harper and Row, 1979; Pauline Bart, 'Depression in Middle-Aged Women,' in Gornick and Moran, eds., *Woman in Sexist Society*, New York: Basic Books, 1971.

Hippocrates and the wandering uterus: Joanna B. Rohrbaugh, *Women: Psychology's Puzzle*, New York: Basic Books, 1979.

Thyroid gland theories: Louis S. Goodman and Alfred Gilman, *The Pharmacological Basis of Therapeutics*, New York: Macmillan, 1975.

Nervous prostration: Sarah Stage, *Female Complaints: Lydia Pinkham and the Business of Women's Medicine*, New York: Norton, 1979.

Premenstrual tension: the pioneer in this field is Katharina Dalton, *The Menstrual Cycle*, New York: Pantheon, 1969.

Inner space: Erik Erikson, *Identity, Youth and Crisis*, New York: Norton, 1968.

Female masochism: Helene Deutsch, *The Psychology of Women* (2 vols.) New York: Grune and Stratton, 1944, 1945.

Maternal guilt is discussed in Shirley Radl, *Mother's Day Is Over*, New York: Charterhouse, 1973; Angela Barron McBride, *The Growth and Development of Mothers*, New York: Harper and Row, 1973; Adrienne Rich, *Of Woman Born*, New York: Norton, 1976; Jane Lazarre, *The Mother Knot*, New York: McGraw-Hill, 1976.

Feminine emotions in popular music: Aida Pavletich, *Rock-a-Bye, Baby*, New York: Doubleday, 1980.

Gender gap in Gallup poll: *Newsweek*, Sept. 19, 1983.

AMBITION

Nurturance: According to Eleanor Maccoby and Carol Jacklin (*The Psychology of Sex Differences*, 1974), the term 'nurturance' was coined by H. A. Murray (*Explorations in Personality*, Oxford University Press, 1938) to describe the giving of aid and comfort to others. Since then, 'nurturance' has been used freely by psychologists, feminists and popular writers as a shorthand word for supportive behaviour that goes beyond the dictionary definition of 'nurture.'

For descriptions of maternal nurturance in the animal world, and the relationship of maternal rank to the future rank of offspring, see Thelma Rowell, *The Social Behaviour of Monkeys*, London: Penguin Books, 1972; Cynthia Moss, *Portraits in the Wild: Behavior Studies of East African Mammals*, Boston: Houghton Mifflin, 1975; and Sarah Blaffer Hrdy, *The Woman That Never Evolved*, Harvard University Press, 1981.

For a description of the mother-gatherer in the !Kung San, see Richard Borshay Lee, *The !Kung San: Men, Women, and Work in a Foraging Society*, Cambridge University Press, 1979.

Sharon Tiffany's analysis of motherhood in pre-industrial economies may be found in Sharon Tiffany, *Women, Work, and Motherhood*, Englewood Cliffs, N. J.: Prentice-Hall, 1982.

Pre-monotheistic worship of the Mother Goddess is detailed with attention to sources in Merlin Stone, *When God Was a Woman*, New York: Harcourt Brace Jovanovich, 1976.

Status in breastfeeding is discussed in Lawrence Stone, *The Family, Sex and Marriage in England* 1500–1800, London: Weidenfeld and Nicolson, 1977.

The elimination of midwives in nineteenth and early twentieth century America by the medical establishment is discussed, with documentation, in Barbara Ehrenreich and Deirdre English, *For Her Own Good: 150 Years of the Experts' Advice to Women*, New York: Anchor Press/Doubleday, 1978.

One satirical portrait of a woman doctor may be found in Henry James, *The Bostonians* (1886).

For a comprehensive view of femininity from the Freudian perspective, see Helene Deutsch, *The Psychology of Women* (2 vols), New York: Grune & Stratton, 1944, 1945.

The evolution of Mary is examined in Marina Warner, *Alone of All Her Sex: The Myth and the Cult of the Virgin Mary*, New York: Knopf, 1976.

The popular classic in the field of blame-the-mother is Philip Wylie, *Generation of Vipers*, New York: Holt, Rinehart and Winston, 1942, which put the term 'momism' into the vernacular. For a full discussion of mother-baiting in the Forties and Fifties, see Chapter 7, 'Motherhood as Pathology,' in Ehrenreich and English, *op. cit*. For a discussion of the attempts of Freudian psychologists and criminologists to blame mothers for their sons' acts of rape, see Chapter 6, 'The Police-Blotter Rapist,' in Susan Brownmiller,

Against Our Will: Men, Women and Rape, New York: Simon and Schuster, 1975.

The passage of sperm into the uterus is described in Constance R. Martin, *Textbook of Endocrine Physiology*, Baltimore: Williams and Wilkins, 1976.

Women's decision-making is discussed in Carol Gilligan, *In a Different Voice: Psychological Theory of Women's Development*, Harvard University Press, 1982.

Acknowledgements

Collecting research material for this project in its early stages took a special intelligence and a pioneer spirit; I would like to thank Barbara Mehrhof for tracking through the scientific journals and for her keen professional interest in primate studies. Those who volunteered to read drafts of chapters – Myra Terry, Diana Russell, Jane Alpert, Susan Jacoby, Marilyn Kaskell, Barbara Milbauer and Ann Jones – will see that their insights and observations are reflected in the final copy. I am grateful to Sharon Frost, who took on the role of chief adviser in matters of art and asthetics, and to Leslie Leinwand, who offered a crash course in genetics and molecular biology.

Dori O'Donnell, Dianne Burden, Helen Payne, Marta Vivas, Lillian Lent, Jo Whitlow, Minda Bikman, Andrea Dworkin, Alice Straus, Lilia Melani, Ruby Rohrlich, Andrea Eagen, Mary Cantwell, Charles Mee and Eden Lipson passed along books and articles and suggested fresh avenues of inquiry. Discussions with Holly Forsman, Lynne Shapiro, Merle Rubine, Arthur Rubine, Maggie Smith, Florence Rush, Ros Fleigel, Alison Owings, David Gurin, Dan Stewart, Susan Braudy, Nancy Milford, Lois Gould, Paula Weideger, Wendy Weil, Claudio Ugalde, Don Conte, Lynn Campbell, Dorchen Leidholdt, Rosetta Reitz and Carol Rinzler turned into paragraphs which I know they will recognize. The in-house editing of Paul Johnson, who never said that he minded when I interrupted his own writing labours, smoothed many a sentence and clarified many ideas.

Once again I am indebted to the New York Public Library for the privilege of stashing my typewriter in the Frederick Lewis Allen Room while I roamed its divisions. The Mid-Manhattan branch of the New York Public Library, the New York Academy of Medicine Library, and the Fashion Institute of Technology Library, with its open shelves and knowledgeable personnel, were indispensable storehouses of enlightenment and information.

The formal interviews I conducted were exceedingly valuable. I would like to thank William G. Hamilton, M.D. (orthopaedics and dance), Richard M. Bachrach, D.O. (osteopathy and movement), Ronald G. Levandusky, M.D. (plastic surgery), Peter M. Pressman, M.D. (oncology and breast surgery), Norman Orentreich, M.D. (dermatology), Marcia Storch, M.D., and Shelley Kolton, M.D. (gynaecology), and Ronni Kolotkin (electrolysis) for their cooperation, their expertise and their candour.

For the second time I have had the good fortune to work with that energizing corporate entity known as Simon and Schuster. Marjorie Williams of the Linden Press applied her elegant sensibility to the manuscript pages. Gerry Sachs, Carol Wilson and Fran Ross made some graceful catches. Joni Evans, as editor, was a sustaining force from inception to publication. Her unflagging determination produced a better book.

Index

posture:
    effects of corset wearing on, 19–21
    upright, origins of, 26
powder, powder puffs, 126
power relationship, speaking style and, 84–5, 93
pregnancy, 114, 149
    skin changes during, 103
premenstrual tension, 165
Pride and Prejudice (Austen), 102
'Princess and the Pea, The' (Andersen), 97
prostitution, 48, 69, 109
    cosmetics and, 125–6
    footwear and, 144
Prynne, William, 39
psychology, 176
    effects of dress on, 57, 71
    feminine emotion and, 167
puberty, 12, 115
    hair changes in, 105, 107, 108
    voice changes in, 76
pubic hair, 107, 108, 118–19
punishment, 84
    of scolds, 83
Puritan heritage, 27, 30, 38, 126
Pygmalion (Shaw), 79

rape, 29, 68, 158, 178
Rational Dress Society, 65
Reagan, Nancy, 31
Reagan, Ronald, 162
Récamier, Madame, 23
religion:
    activity of women in, 83–4
    clothing and, 56, 66, 69–70, 72
    pantheistic vs. monotheistic, 174
    in subjugation of women, 5, 38–9, 70, 82, 84, 174, 175
    see also Christianity; Islam; Jews
Renaissance, 39, 48, 99, 126
    feminine ideal in, 8, 29
Richardson, Mary (Polly Dick), 9
Rigby, Cathy, 140
Rokeby Venus (Velásquez), 9
Rome, ancient:
    clothing in, 58
    hair in, 38, 48, 52
Room of One's Own, A (Woolf), 94
Rosen, Marjorie, 46, 111

Roth, Philip, 27
Rousseau, Jean-Jacques, 79, 80, 81
Rowell, Thelma, 154
Rudofsky, Bernard, 17, 142
Russell, Jane, 10, 22
Russell, Lillian, 29

Sacher-Masoch, Leopold von, 73
Sachs, Jacqueline, 85
Sackville-West, Vita, 66, 67
sadomasochism, 143
Sand, George, 65, 94
Savitch, Jessica, 86
Schaller, George, 106
Schiller, Friedrich, 140–1
scolds, women as, 81, 83
Scotland, clothing in, 57
Seeing Through Clothes (Hollander), 21
sex:
    emotion and, 166–7, 169
    male excitement and, 17, 21
    violence and, 6, 17, 28, 68, 82, 158, 178
    see also homosexuality; pornography; prostitution
sex differences:
    body and, 11–17, 31–2, 135–6
    hair and, 36, 106–7
    orgasm and, 167
    skin and, 99
    weight and, 31–2
sexual morality, clothing and, 56, 58, 70, 73
Shakespeare, William, 78, 104, 120
Shange, Ntozake, 51
Shaw, George Bernard, 79
Sheppard, Eugenia, 55
Shields, Brooke, 107
Shikibu, Murasaki (Lady Murasaki), 93–4
shoes, 54, 56, 74, 142–5
    high-heeled, 142–3, 144
    sensible, 142–3, 145
Shonagon, Sei, 93
shopping, 55, 72, 87
sidesaddles, 149
sitting, position of legs and, 146
skin, 96–130
    dark, 47, 97, 99
    diseases of, 96